AQA History

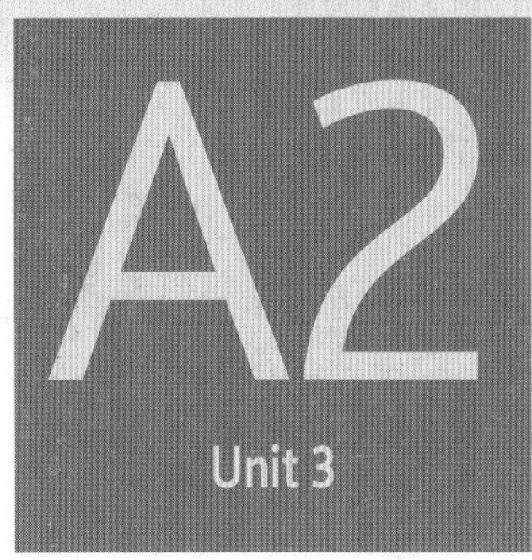

Aspects of International Relations, 1945–2004

Exclusively endorsed by AQA

John Aldred
Series editor
Sally Waller

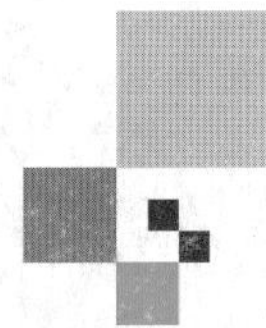

Nelson Thornes

Published in 2010 by:
Nelson Thornes Ltd
Delta Place
27 Bath Road
CHELTENHAM
GL53 7TH
United Kingdom

11 12 13 14 / 10 9 8 7 6 5 4 3

A catalogue record for this book is available from the British Library

ISBN 978 0 7487 9950 3

Cover photograph courtesy of Corbis/Image Source

Illustrations by David Russell Illustration

Page make-up by Thomson Digital

Printed in China by 1010 Printing International Ltd

Author acknowledgements:

The author and publisher would like to thank the following for permission to reproduce material:

Source texts:
p19 Short extract from a speech by Winston Churchill at Fulton, Missouri, 6 March 1946. Reprinted with permission of Curtis Brown; p40 Short extract from *Modern America: the USA, 1865 to the Present* by Joanne de Pennington, Hodder Murray 2005. Reprinted with permission of John Murray (Publishers) Ltd; p117 Short extract from *Memoirs* by Mikhail Gorbachev, published by Doubleday. Reprinted with permission of The Random House Group Limited and Random House, Inc USA; p122 Short extract from *My Six Years with Gorbachev* by Anatol Chernyaev, Penn State Press. Reprinted with permission; p153 Short extract from *No New Diving Lines* by Hans van den Broek, Financial Times, Personal View, 22 September 1997. © Hans van den Broek 1997. Reprinted with kind permission of the author.

Photographs courtesy of:
Ann Ronan Picture Library 18, 53, 64, 68, 106, 110; Edimedia Archive 35, 43 (bottom), 45, 61, 63, 70, 84, 121, 130, 140, 144, 163; Germania Collection 33, 48; International Court of Justice 169; Photos12 7, 10, 16, 22, 29, 46, 50, 58, 73, 75, 76, 90, 96, 129, 131, 179; Topfoto 11, 27, 43 (top), 55, 77, 80, 94, 97, 101, 105, 109, 113, 116, 117, 125, 135, 137, 149, 159, 161, 174, 176; United Nations – Agência Brasil 165; World History Archive 14, 25, 38, 142, 145, 148, 180.

Photo research by Tara Roberts, Jason Newman and Alexander Goldberg of www.uniquedimension.com

Every effort has been made to trace the copyright holders but if any have been inadvertently overlooked the publishers will be pleased to make the necessary arrangements at the first opportunity.

Contents

AQA Introduction

Nelson Thornes and AQA

Nelson Thornes has worked in collaboration with AQA to ensure that this book offers you the best support for your AS or A Level course and helps you to prepare for your exams. The partnership means that you can be confident that the range of learning, teaching and assessment practice materials has been checked by the senior examining team at AQA before formal approval, and is closely matched to the requirements of your specification.

How to use this book

This book covers the specification for your course and is arranged in a sequence approved by AQA.

The features in this book include:

Timeline

Key events are outlined at the beginning of the book. The events are colour-coded so you can clearly see the categories of change.

Learning objectives

At the beginning of each section you will find a list of learning objectives that contain targets linked to the requirements of the specification.

Key chronology

A short list of dates usually with a focus on a specific event or legislation.

Key profile

The profile of a key person you should be aware of to fully understand the period in question.

Key terms

A term that you will need to be able to define and understand.

Did you know?

Interesting information to bring the subject under discussion to life.

Exploring the detail

Information to put further context around the subject under discussion.

A closer look

An in-depth look at a theme, person or event to deepen your understanding. Activities around the extra information may be included.

Sources

Sources to reinforce topics or themes and may provide fact or opinion. They may be quotations from historical works, contemporaries of the period or photographs.

Cross-reference

Links to related content within the book which may offer more detail on the subject in question.

Activity

Various activity types to provide you with different challenges and opportunities to demonstrate both the content and skills you are learning. Some can be worked on individually, some as part of group work and some are designed to specifically 'stretch and challenge'.

Question

Questions to prompt further discussion on the topic under consideration and are an aid to revision.

Summary questions

Summary questions at the end of each chapter to test your knowledge and allow you to demonstrate your understanding.

AQA Examiner's tip

Hints from AQA examiners to help you with your study and to prepare for your exam.

AQA Examination-style questions

Questions at the end of each section in the style that you can expect in your exam.

Learning outcomes

Learning outcomes at the end of each section remind you what you should know having completed the chapters in that section.

Web links in the book

Because Nelson Thornes is not responsible for third party content online, there may be some changes to this material that are beyond our control. In order for us to ensure that the links referred to in the book are as up-to-date and stable as possible, the web sites provided are usually homepages with supporting instructions on how to reach the relevant pages if necessary.

Please let us know at **webadmin@nelsonthornes.com** if you find a link that doesn't work and we will do our best to correct this at reprint, or to list an alternative site.

Introduction to the History series

When Bruce Bogtrotter in Roald Dahl's *Matilda* was challenged to eat a huge chocolate cake, he just opened his mouth and ploughed in, taking bite after bite and lump after lump until the cake was gone and he was feeling decidedly sick. The picture is not dissimilar to that of some A-level History students. They are attracted to history because of its inherent appeal but, when faced with a bulging file and a forthcoming examination, their enjoyment evaporates. They try desperately to cram their brains with an assortment of random facts and subsequently prove unable to control the outpouring of their ill-digested material in the examination.

The books in this series are designed to help students and teachers avoid this feeling of overload and examination panic by breaking down the AQA History specification in such a way that it is easily absorbed. Above all, they are designed to retain and promote students' enthusiasm for history by avoiding a dreary rehash of dates and events. Each book is divided into sections, closely matched to those given in the specification, and the content is further broken down into chapters that present the historical material in a lively and attractive form, offering guidance on the key terms, events and issues, and blending thought-provoking activities and questions in a way designed to advance students' understanding. By encouraging students to think for themselves and to share their ideas with others, as well as helping them to develop the knowledge and skills they will need to pass their examination, this book should ensure that students' learning remains a pleasure rather than an endurance test.

To make the most of what this book provides, students will need to develop efficient study skills from the start and it is worth spending some time considering what these involve:

- Good organisation of material in a subject-specific file. Organised notes help develop an organised brain and sensible filing ensures time is not wasted hunting for misplaced material. This book uses cross-references to indicate where material in one chapter has relevance to material in another. Students are advised to adopt the same technique.
- A sensible approach to note-making. Students are often too ready to copy large chunks of material from printed books or to download sheaves of printouts from the internet. This series is designed to encourage students to think about the notes they collect and to undertake research with a particular purpose in mind. The activities encourage students to pick out information that is relevant to the issue being addressed and to avoid making notes on material that is not properly understood.
- Taking time to think, which is by far the most important component of study. By encouraging students to think before they write or speak, be it for a written answer, presentation or class debate, students should learn to form opinions and make judgements based on the accumulation of evidence. These are the skills that the examiner will be looking for in the final examination. The beauty of history is that there is rarely a right or wrong answer so, with sufficient evidence, one student's view will count for as much as the next.

Unit 3

The topics chosen for study in Unit 3 are all concerned with the changing relationship between state and people over a period of around 50 years. These topics enable students to build on the skills acquired at AS level, combining breadth, by looking at change and continuity over a period of time, with depth, in analysing specific events and developments. The chosen topics offer plentiful opportunities for an understanding of historical processes enabling students to realise that history moves forward through the interaction of many different factors, some of which may change in importance over a period of time. Significant individuals, societies, events, developments and issues are explored in an historical context and developments affecting different groups within the societies studied from a range of historical perspectives. Study at Unit 3 will therefore develop full synoptic awareness and enable students to understand the way a professional historian goes about the task of developing a full historical understanding.

Unit 3 is assessed by a 1 hour 30 minute paper containing three essay questions from which students need to select two. Details relating to the style of questions, with additional hints, are given in the accompanying table and helpful tips to enable students to meet the examination demands are given throughout this book. Students should familiarise themselves with both the question demands and the marking criteria which follow before attempting any of the practice examination questions at the end of each section of this book.

Answers will be marked according to a scheme based on 'levels of response'. This means that an essay will be assessed according to which level best matches the

Unit 3 (three essay questions in total)	Question types	Marks	Question stems	Hints for students
Two essay questions	Standard essay questions addressing a part of the specification content and seeking a judgement based on debate and evaluation	45	These are not prescriptive but likely stems include: To what extent... How far... A quotation followed by 'How valid is this assessment/view?'	All answers should convey an argument. Plan before beginning to write and make the argument clear at the outset. The essay should show an awareness of how factors interlink and students should make some judgement between them (synoptic links). All comments should be supported by secure and precise evidence.
One essay question	Standard essay question covering the whole period of the unit or a large part of that period and seeking a judgement based on debate and evaluation	45	As above	Evidence will need to be carefully selected from across the full period to support the argument. It might prove useful to emphasise the situation at the beginning and end of the period, identify key turning points and assess factors promoting change and continuity.

historical skills it displays, taking both knowledge and understanding into account. All students should keep a copy of the marking criteria in their files and need to use them wisely.

Marking criteria

Level 1 Answers will display a limited understanding of the demands of the question. They may either contain some descriptive material which is only loosely linked to the focus of the question or they may address only a part of the question. Alternatively, they may contain some explicit comment but will make few, if any, synoptic links and will have limited accurate and relevant historical support. There will be little, if any, awareness of differing historical interpretations. The response will be limited in development and skills of written communication will be weak. *(0–6 marks)*

Level 2 Answers will show some understanding of the demands of the question. They will either be primarily descriptive with few explicit links to the question or they may contain explicit comment but show limited relevant factual support. They will display limited understanding of differing historical interpretations. Historical debate may be described rather than used to illustrate an argument and any synoptic links will be undeveloped. Answers will be coherent but weakly expressed and/or poorly structured. *(7–15 marks)*

Level 3 Answers will show a good understanding of the demands of the question. They will provide some assessment, backed by relevant and appropriately selected evidence, which may, however, lack depth. There will be some synoptic links made between the ideas, arguments and information included although these may not be highly developed. There will be some understanding of varying historical interpretations. Answers will be clearly expressed and show reasonable organisation in the presentation of material. *(16–25 marks)*

Level 4 Answers will show a very good understanding of the demands of the question. There will be synoptic links made between the ideas, arguments and information included showing an overall historical understanding. There will be good understanding and use of differing historical interpretations and debate and the answer will show judgement through sustained argument backed by a carefully selected range of precise evidence. Answers will be well-organised and display good skills of written communication. *(26–37 marks)*

Level 5 Answers will show a full understanding of the demands of the question. The ideas, arguments and information included will be wide-ranging, carefully chosen and closely interwoven to produce a sustained and convincing answer with a high level of synopticity. Conceptual depth, independent judgement and a mature historical understanding, informed by a well-developed understanding of historical interpretations and debate, will be displayed. Answers will be well-structured and fluently written. *(38–45 marks)*

Introduction to this book

Key terms

Great Powers: those states in Europe which controlled the exercise of international power and influence.

Euro-centric: international power was centred among European states rather than states from other continents.

Balance of power: the idea that no single state should become dominant. This protects the security of all states.

Status quo: this Latin term refers to the existing state of affairs in any situation, but is particularly applied to politics as meaning the desire to keep matters as they are.

Nationalism: the idea that people who shared common cultural and linguistic foundations should be free to form their own nation states.

By 1945 a new era of international relations had begun. Changes that had been in process since the start of the 20th century, if not before, brought about a move away from the domination of Europe over the rest of the world, towards a new age of the global superpower.

In 1900 international power had been dominated by five major European states, the **Great Powers**: Great Britain, France, Germany, Russia and Austria–Hungary. Power, in international relations, was **Euro-centric**. One in four of the world's population lived in Europe and approximately 500 million others lived under European colonial rule, particularly within the British and French Empires. The resources of the Great Powers had not been drained through the effects of conflict. There had been no major war between them since 1815 and a **balance of power** had been preserved. However, this stability, and the continuity of dominance in international relations that it facilitated, was more apparent than real. The years 1900 to 1945 brought a systematic collapse of the Euro-centric order in international relations.

The beginning of the end, 1900–14

The growing uncertainty for the continuance of a Euro-centric basis for international relations into the 20th century was apparent in the condition of Great Britain's economy and the growing challenge to Britain's economic global dominance from Japan, Germany and particularly America. In manufacturing, Britain depended on a narrow range of staple industries such as coal, iron, steel and textiles. A lack of modernisation and investment in these industries meant that Britain's manufacturing industry began to lose out to its competitors. By 1914 Britain was in danger of being economically outpaced by the USA. Britain produced 14 per cent of the world's manufactured goods while the USA produced 35 per cent and Germany had reached 16 per cent.

Great Power status and the global dominance it commanded depended on economic and military power, but most importantly it depended on stability among the Great Powers. There had to be an acceptance of, and a commitment to, the preservation of the **status quo**. There had to be continued economic growth, particularly in the face of new European economic rivals. Global empires had to be stable and fulfil their roles as strategic and economic supports for their imperial masters. For Great Britain, the rise of **nationalism** was becoming a threat, by posing increasing challenges to its imperial security. With this had come a potential threat to its global mastery, as Britain's international power was derived principally from its vast empire, whose territories included India, Canada, Australia and many parts of Africa. Imperialism depended on stable and loyal colonies to promote its power and economic growth. Nationalism, by contrast, meant that the colonised peoples looked to take possession of their own resources and political processes. By doing so, they threatened to deprive imperial powers of their foreign territories and thus weaken the colonising nation.

A fundamental change in international relations came through Germany's bid for world power status. Although only unified in 1871, by the turn of the 20th century Germany was the dominant state of central Europe. Its population was only second in size to the Russian Empire. Rapid industrialisation and the economic power that came with it formed the basis of Germany's ability to enhance its global influence.

From approximately 1890 Germany pursued a policy of **Weltpolitik**. This translated into Germany seeking to enhance its global influence and particularly its imperial and military strength. The balance of power in Europe was under threat and this motivated other European states to form alliances to prevent Germany from exploiting its economic power and **geo-strategic location** in central Europe. Germany also had its own ally in Austria–Hungary. The culmination of this process was the First World War.

Key terms

Weltpolitik: German policy at the start of the 20th century aimed at strengthening Germany's international influence.

Geo-strategic location: the physical location of a state in relation to other states and the strategic significance of this.

The impact of the Great War

Fig. 1 *Map of Europe, c. 1920*

The war led to the reshaping of Europe. Economic hardships, military defeats and political unrest caused by war led to many empires losing their colonies, which in turn reshaped the political map of the world. The disappearance of the old order accelerated. The Austro-Hungarian Empire was dismembered and a series of new and smaller states were created in central and eastern Europe. Germany was reduced in size; it lost 13 per cent of its land and nearly 7 million of its population. Its empire was seized and its military power emasculated. Germany was also faced with a crushing reparation debt justified through the War Guilt clause in the peace settlement. The Treaty of Versailles had, in part, been designed to contain any future German resurgence. Poland and Czechoslovakia had been created to act as guardians in the east to maintain a degree of deterrence to ward off any German revenge against the allies in the future and to maintain stability in central Europe. This allied commitment to the Treaty of Versailles was to be the cornerstone of global influence remaining in Europe. In the event, both Britain and France failed to enforce the Treaty and this proved to be a fundamental factor in the outbreak of a second, and more devastating, conflict in 1939.

A closer look

World War I

World War I was a critical event in the political and social history of the world. The conflict began in 1914 and ran for the next four years. Its initial cause was a clash between Austria and Serbia, following the assassination of the Austrian Archduke Franz Ferdinand in Sarajevo, Serbia. The consequent political fallout resulted in various European alliances forming the two sides of a major international conflict. Britain, France, Russia and (from 1917) the United States formed the principal allies, and fought against Germany and Austria–Hungary (although many other nations were involved).

In western Europe, the initial German offensive in 1914 was stopped, and the war devolved into trench warfare that cost both sides millions of men. In the east, the war between Russia and Germany was fought against the backdrop of revolutionary unrest in Russia. In 1917, the Russian Revolution saw the communists take power and Russia drop out of the world war the following year. Also in 1917 the United States entered the conflict. Its industrial might was enough to finally overwhelm a war-weary Germany, and it surrendered in November 1918.

A more subtle problem faced the continuity of European dominance in global politics. From the beginning of the century the USA had assumed a pivotal position in the global economy. The First World War underlined the USA's economic dominance and the fact that European powers were now secondary in importance compared to the economic power of the USA. European states had become debtors in receipt of American credit.

Table 1 *Wartime and post-war loans provided by the USA (millions of $)*

Debtor state	Pre-1918	Post-1918	Total debt
Great Britain	3,696	581	4,277
France	1,970	1,434	3,404
Italy	1,031	617	1,648

This not only illustrated the economic vulnerability of European powers but also reinforced another fundamental shift in the forces which drove international relations. By 1929 America generated 42 per cent of the world's industrial output. In 1910 Norman Angell announced that the international order was integrated to a hitherto unheard-of level. The 'economically civilised world' was inextricably united by 'credit and commercial contract'. Europe could no longer function outside this global economic system and the dominant member of this system was the USA.

National economics, and therefore the power and global influence that they underpinned, were enmeshed in a global economic system. The significance of this became apparent from 1929. The Wall Street Crash saw the collapse of the US stock market and the beginning of a global economic depression. Above all the Depression starkly illustrated the dependency the rest of the world had on the state of America's economy. This revealed America's status as a world power and America's untapped political influence in international relations to this point. Since the end of the First World War, America had pursued an **isolationist** foreign policy; its main international concerns were focused on disarmament and security within the Pacific. Even during the Manchurian Crisis of 1931, when Japan invaded the Chinese territory of Manchuria, America took no direct action against Japanese aggression even though it perceived Japan as the greatest single threat to America's Pacific security. Throughout the years 1920 to 1941 America's influence internationally lay in the area of economics rather than diplomacy.

Key terms

Isolationist: a policy in which a state focuses primarily on its domestic interests and places little focus on the wider world.

In the 1920s, economic events were not the only driving forces in international relations. In February 1917, a revolution in Russia saw the old monarchical regime of Tsar Nicholas II overthrown and replaced by a Provisional Government. The changes brought by rapid industrialisation in Russia coupled with Soviet defeats during the First World War against Germany brought disillusionment with the Tsarist autocracy and stirred up revolutionary sentiments. The Provisional Government was in turn overthrown by Marxist Bolshevik revolutionaries led by Vladmir Lenin and Leon Trotsky in October 1917. A civil war followed (1918–21), from which the Bolsheviks emerged victorious and established a Bolshevik dictatorship over what became known as the Soviet Union.

The Russian Revolution would have profound effects on international relations for the rest of the 20th century. What was emerging was the fundamental struggle between communist and capitalist ideas. Communism advocated the common (i.e. state) ownership of the means of production (such as industry and farming) and property, the end of social classes and the redistribution of wealth among the people. Capitalism, by contrast, promoted societies based on private businesses run for profit, with each person attempting to increase their wealth independently. The Bolshevik philosophy pitted the workers and the poor against big business and the rich, and attacked the idea of private property. These ideas were obviously a threat to imperial and capitalist powers and hence there grew an intense suspicion and often outright hostility between the generally capitalist West and the communist Soviet Union. Such friction intensified when the Soviet Union came under the leadership of Joseph Stalin, the Soviet General Secretary from 1922 until his death in 1953. Stalin became known for his utterly ruthless leadership which, combined with high levels of paranoia, meant that he was profoundly opposed to any Western influences that might threaten the communist regime.

The final chapter, 1939–45

On 3 September 1939 Great Britain and France once again declared war on Germany. This heralded the demise of what remained of the remnants of European global power.

Key terms

Appeasement: a policy designed to avoid war and conflict by reaching agreement with the potential aggressors.

British and French responses to the aggressive nationalism of the 1930s, amply illustrated through their attempt to distance themselves from Hitler's pre-war foreign policy, the Japanese invasion of Manchuria in 1931 and Italy's invasion of Abyssinia in 1935, were based on **appeasement**. This clearly showed that the leading states of Europe were no longer capable of moulding world affairs. This, and American isolationism, had permitted the outbreak of the Second World War and brought about an important change in international relations.

The Japanese attack on the US naval base at Pearl Harbour on 7 December 1941 marked the end of American isolationism. Roosevelt had already intimated that the USA could not remain isolationist as early as June 1940 in his Charlottesville Address.

> Some indeed still hold to the now somewhat obvious delusion that we of the United States can safely permit the United States to become a lone island in a world dominated by the philosophy of force. Such an island may be the dream of those who still talk and vote as isolationists. Such an island represented to me and to the overwhelming majority of Americans today as a helpless nightmare, a helpless nightmare of people without freedom.

Key dates

The decline of the Great Powers

- **1902** The Triple Alliance between Germany, Austria and Italy
- **1904** The Entente Cordiale between Britain and France
- **1906** British naval expansion
- **1908** German naval expansion
- **1914** The outbreak of the First World War
- **1917** The Russian Revolution and the rise of the Communist movement
- **1918** The armistice and the end of the First World War
- **1919** The post-war settlement and the Treaty of Versailles
- **1920** The formation of the Nazi Party
- **1929** The Wall Street Crash
- **1933** Hitler becomes leader of Germany
- **1939** The outbreak of the Second World War
- **1941** Germany invades the USSR
Japan's attack at Pearl Harbour
Germany declares war on the USA
- **1945** Germany finally surrenders in May
The Second World War finally ends in August with the use of US nuclear weapons against Japan

In March 1941 Roosevelt had already established the Lend-Lease Act which allowed the USA to provide aid to any state whose defence was in the interests of the defence of America. Britain was able to receive arms and supplies from the USA and pay for them when the war ended. In the relatively early stages of the war it was clear that Britain's economy could not bear the burden of a lengthy conflict. Britain's financial indebtedness to the USA was rising and with it the inevitable political dependency that was to characterise the US–GB relationship after 1945. By the end of the war Britain had received $11.3 billion. The war revitalised the US economy. The Depression was effectively brought to an end. Mass production of weapons of all kinds began. In 1940, for example, the USA had produced 6,000 war planes. By 1945 this had risen to an annual production of 96,000. The war enabled the US economy to grow and economic might was the foundation of international power. Not only did the war offer the USA economic recovery; it also stimulated technological advances. The most significant of these was the development of the atom bomb. By 1945 the USA possessed a destructive technology that no other nation had at that time.

The other major change brought about by the war affected the Soviet Union. The Soviet Union had initially made a pact with Germany at the beginning of the war, sharing Poland between them, but Germany's invasion of the Soviet Union in June 1941 brought the Soviets into the war as an allied nation. Britain and the USA had an uneasy relationship with the Soviets throughout the war. Stalin felt that the Soviet Union was doing the lion's share of the fighting – 25 million Soviets would die during the war, as opposed to around 400,000 Americans and a similar number of British soldiers and civilians, and he was suspicious of the western allies' seeming reluctance to open up a second front against the Nazis through an invasion of France. As the war turned against Germany, the West suspected that Stalin's main goal was to take over as much territory in eastern Europe as possible. Western suspicions proved well founded, although Stalin would argue that the Red Army's occupation of eastern Europe was in self-defence, and in the last year of the war the United States and the Soviet Union ensured that their own political colours were put on the countries they liberated from the Germans.

Just as the war awakened new superpowers, it also destroyed the capacity of the old European powers to resume their roles as key players in international relations. The war devastated the economies of European powers and it left a **power vacuum**. France, for example, had been one of the world's great powers, but four years of German occupation had crippled both its finances and its international standing. The result was that France, like Britain, would steadily lose many of its overseas colonies in Africa and South-East Asia over the next 30 years, in a process often called 'decolonisation'.

Key terms

Power vacuum: the idea that those states which influenced affairs are no longer able to do so but there is no replacement of that essential influence.

Fig. 2 *A US Army unit in France, 1944, during the allied operation to free Europe from German occupation*

The USA was left with the stark choice of leaving post-war Europe to its own fate or filling the power void in Europe that the war had created. The question facing US policy makers in 1945 was whether the USA should revert to its 1920 position on international relations and America's place within world affairs or whether it should embrace a more proactive and interventionist stance. One thing was certain by the end of the Second World War: the notion of Euro-centric global dominance was finally laid to rest and the emergence of the global superpower had arrived.

Timeline

The colours represent different types of events as follows: Political, Economic, Social and International

1945	1946	1947	1948	1949	1950	1951
(Feb) Yalta Conference held. Britain, USA and USSR plan for post-war Europe (May) Germany surrenders (July–Aug) Potsdam Conference held	(March) Churchill's 'Iron Curtain' speech Kennan's 'Long Telegram'	(Jan) Bizonia created by USA and GB (March) Truman Doctrine announced (June) Marshall Plan announced	(Feb) Final communist regime established in eastern Europe once Czechoslovakia is forced to accept communism (June) Berlin blockade begins	(Jan) Comecon set up (April) NATO set up (May) Berlin blockade lifted (Sept) West Germany established (Oct) East Germany set up	(Jan) Truman announces plan to build hydrogen bomb (June) Korean War begins	(April) Beginnings of the European Union with the formation of the European Coal and Steel Community Treaty

1960	1961	1962	1963	1964	1965	1966	1967
(May) USA U-2 spy plane shot down over USSR (June) Relations between China and the USSR begin to collapse	(June) Kennedy and Khrushchev meet in Vienna. Khrushchev demands the demilitarisation of Berlin (August) Berlin Wall started	(Oct–Nov) Cuban Missile Crisis	(Aug) Test Ban Treaty signed	(Oct) Khrushchev removed from office	(Feb) US attacks on North Vietnam start	(March) USSR increases its military spending	(Oct) USA, USSR and GB agreement on the peaceful use of space

1975	1976	1977	1978	1979	1980	1981	1982
(July) Joint USA–Soviet space mission (Aug) The Helsinki Final Act is signed (Oct) US–Soviet Trade Agreement	(May) The USSR and USA agree to limit size of underground nuclear tests	(Oct) New Soviet constitution adopted	(July) Imprisonment of dissidents in the Soviet Union	(June) SALT II signed in Vienna (Dec) The USSR invades Afghanistan	(Jan) US trade embargo imposed on the USSR Ratification of SALT II suspended (Sept) Solidarity movement begins in Poland	(April) US trade embargo lifted (Nov) Reagan proposes the removal of INF weapons	(June) US–USSR begin START in Geneva (Nov) Brezhnev dies and is replaced by Yuri Andropov

1990	1991	1992	1993	1994	1995	1996	1997
(March) Free elections in Hungary (April) Elections in Yugoslavia's Republics (Aug) Iraq invades Kuwait (Oct) Germany is reunited	(Jan) International intervention in Kuwait (March) The Warsaw Pact is dissolved (June) Slovenia and Croatia declare independence and fighting breaks out (Dec) The USSR is formally dissolved	(Jan) UNPROFOR is created (April) USA recognises Bosnia-Herzegovina, Slovenia and Croatia	(Jan) Vance–Owen Peace Plan	(Feb) Civilians slaughtered in Sarajevo (April) Genocide in Rwanda ends	(Jan) Sweden, Finland and Austria join EU (July) Large numbers of Muslim males massacred in Srebrenica (Nov) Dayton Agreement	(Dec) Stabilisation Force (SRFOR) replaces IFOR in Yugoslavia	(Dec) Kosovo Albanians begin to organise resistance against Serbs

1952	1953	1954	1955	1956	1957	1958	1959
(March) Stalin proposes a neutral, united Germany. The West ignores it (May) European Defence Community established	(March) Stalin dies (July) Korean War ends (Aug) USSR explodes hydrogen bomb	(Jan–Feb) Austrian State Treaty (Sept–Oct) Khrushchev visits China	(May) Warsaw Pact created	(Feb) Khrushchev criticises Stalin at the 20th Party Congress (Oct–Nov) Revolution in Hungary brutally suppressed by the USSR	(March) Treaty of Rome sets up the EEC	(Nov) Khrushchev demands the allies leave Berlin	(Sept) Khrushchev visits USA and withdraws Berlin demands

1968	1969	1970	1971	1972	1973	1974
(July) Nuclear Non-Proliferation Treaty signed (Aug) Warsaw Pact states, led by USSR, invade Czechoslovakia	(Sept) Willy Brandt takes office (Nov–Dec) SALT begins	(Aug) Beginning of Ostpolitik through Soviet–West German Treaty	(Sept) Four Power Treaty on Berlin (Dec) Hotline set up between the Kremlin and the White House	(May) SALT Treaty signed and détente begins (Oct) Anti-Ballistic Missile (ABM) Treaty signed (Nov) Helsinki talks on European security and cooperation begin	(May) Ten-year agreement on economic cooperation between West Germany and the USSR (Oct) International conference on the peaceful use of atomic energy	(June) Nixon visits USSR for talks on limiting strategic arms

1983	1984	1985	1986	1987	1988	1989
(March) Reagan refers to the USSR as the 'evil empire' Reagan announces SDI	(Dec) Gorbachev visits Britain and Thatcher says he is 'a man one can do business with'.	(March) Mikhail Gorbachev becomes General Secretary of the Communist Party and leader of the Soviet Union (Nov) Summit meeting between Gorbachev and Reagan	(Feb) Gorbachev talks of 'years of stagnation' under Brezhnev and calls for economic reforms (Oct) Reykjavik summit begins (Nov) Withdrawal of Soviet troops in Afghanistan begins	(Dec) Gorbachev visits USA and agrees to a ban on INF missiles	(Dec) Gorbachev announces reduction in Soviet armed forces	(Nov) Berlin Wall comes down

1998	1999	2000	2001	2002	2003	2004
Fighting erupts in Kosovo	(March) Operation Allied Force begins	(Oct) Milosevic retires from office	(June) Milosevic handed over to war crimes tribunal in The Hague (Sept) Terrorist attacks strike the USA (Oct) Operation Enduring Freedom launched against Afghanistan by the USA	(Feb) Milosevic's trial begins (March) Operation Anaconda begins in Afghanistan	(March) US and British forces invade Iraq (Dec) Saddam Hussein captured	(May) Many eastern European states become EU members US forces remain in Afghanistan at this point

1 The Emergence of the Superpowers, 1945–62

1 The Beginning of the Cold War

In this chapter you will learn about:

- the wartime alliance system between the Western powers and the Soviet Union
- the breakdown of the alliance and the early stages of the Cold War
- the significance of Germany on early post-war East–West relations
- East–West objectives for post-war Europe
- the development of Soviet-influenced communist regimes in eastern Europe.

On 27 April 1945, Soviet and American soldiers met in Germany on the River Elbe. The Soviet soldiers had been advancing against the Germans from the east, and the Americans from the west and the meet-up signalled that the end of the war was in sight. Film cameras captured scenes of warm handshakes while the British Prime Minister, Winston Churchill, said, "We meet in true and victorious comradeship and with inflexible resolve to fulfil our purpose and our duty. Let all march forward upon the foe." Yet although the warmth between soldiers was genuine, the reality of East–West political relations was very different.

Fig. 1 *American and Soviet troops meet on the River Elbe, 25 April 1945*

Yalta, Potsdam and the collapse of the Grand Alliance

By 30 April 1945 Hitler had committed suicide and a week later the Second World War had come to an end. The British and Americans had been fighting their way across Europe since the D-Day landings of June 1944 in France. Soviet forces had systematically liberated most of eastern Europe as they pushed in from the east towards Germany. Before he died, Hitler made what was to become a prophetic statement about the nature of international relations in the post-war world. He predicted the end of the wartime alliance and the start of the Cold War.

> After the collapse of the German Reich, and until there is a rise in nationalism in Asia, Africa or Latin America, there will only be two powers in the world: The United States and Soviet Russia. Through the laws of history and geographical position these giants are destined to struggle with each other either through war, or through rivalry in economics and political ideas.

1 *Hitler's Political Testament, April 1945*

Historical perspectives

There is a view that the collapse of the Grand Alliance and the subsequent development of the Cold War as the basis of post-war international relations was inevitable. An early school of historical interpretation is known as the Orthodox group (see 'A closer look' on the next page). Essentially this interpretation placed the blame for the development of the Cold War squarely on the shoulders of the Soviet Union. American policy was interpreted as a legitimate response to Soviet provocation. The Soviet Union was seen as an aggressive expansionist state shielded under the disguise of benign self-protection. The Soviet Union had no interest in preserving the Grand Alliance because its existence was contrary to Soviet expansionist aims.

Cross-reference

To find out more about the Grand Alliance, see page 12.

An alternative interpretation known as Revisionism later developed. This view saw Soviet actions from 1945 as a legitimate response to American economic and strategic imperialism in Europe and ultimately beyond. This is simply the Orthodox interpretation in reverse. Both views are predicated by the certainty that the **unilateral** actions of one side determined the outcome of international relations for the next 45 years.

Key terms

Unilateral: action by one side only, as opposed to all parties involved.

Revisionist historians argued that the primary reason why the Americans rejected communist regimes in eastern Europe was not because they saw this as part of aggressive expansionism by the Soviet Union, but because they deprived America of access to economic opportunities there. Revisionists regarded America's primary foreign policy aim as that of expanding capitalism under the guise of protecting freedom and democracy. The Soviet Union had no choice other than to expand its own influence in eastern Europe in order to protect itself from aggressive American economic expansionism.

Orthodox historians present the Soviet Union as calculating in its determination to establish a power base in eastern Europe. The peoples of eastern Europe were merely a means to an end for Stalin. America is presented as a sleeping giant that finally awakes to the Soviet threat. During the 1980s both these views were reworked into the so-called Post-Revisionist interpretation which, in basic terms, was an amalgam of the Orthodox and Revisionist interpretations.

Fig. 2 *'The European hotch-potch'*, Punch *magazine*

Activity

Thinking point

Why has there been so much historical controversy over the outbreak of the Cold War? Write six reasons and number them in what you consider their order of importance. Compare lists within the class.

A closer look

Cold War historiography

John L. Gaddis classified Cold War historiography as 'Orthodox', 'Revisionist' and 'Post-Revisionist' in his work *The Emerging Post-Revisionist Synthesis on the Origins of the Cold War* (1983). Gaddis himself had produced an Orthodox interpretation in his work *The United States and the Origins of the Cold War, 1941–1947* (1972). The Orthodox interpretation was still being supported as late as 1979 through the work of Vojtech Mastny. In 1959 a revised interpretation of the causes of the Cold War was offered by William Appleman Williams in *The Tragedy of American Diplomacy*. The Revisionists not only challenged the benign view of US foreign policy as presented by the Orthodox interpretation, but they also doubted the notion that Soviet communism was expansionist. Historians such as Joyce Kolko and Gabriel Kolko, *The Limits of Power: The World and the United States Foreign Policy, 1945–1954* (1972) placed the blame for the development of the Cold War firmly at the feet of the USA. Stephen Ambrose's *Rise to Globalism: American Foreign Policy Since 1938* (1971) also promoted a strong Revisionist stance that had developed through the 1960s among many American historians. The Revisionist position continued to challenge orthodoxy and, in 1994, the work of R. N. Lebow and J. G. Stein presented a reassessment of the role of nuclear deterrence in *We All Lost the Cold War*.

The Grand Alliance

In June 1941 Germany invaded the USSR. In December 1941, after Japan's attack on the US naval base at Pearl Harbour, Germany declared war on the USA. Thus, by the end of 1941 the so-called 'Grand Alliance' was in place. The principal allies had little in common before the war. They were ideological opposites. The war united them because they faced a common enemy, Germany. Ideologically communism was the polar opposite of Nazism but Russia and Germany had formed a non-aggression pact in August 1939. In international relations **ideology** was secondary to pragmatism and it was not inconceivable that this realism would continue when the war ended. Communism and capitalism could co-exist if the political leaders saw some advantage in it. The Grand Alliance did collapse but was this the result of a purely ideological split that was inevitably revived once Nazism had been defeated and normality had been restored?

Key terms

Ideology: a set of ideas and assumptions about how society should be organised. This can extend beyond individual states and consider global organisation. Ideologies may have long-term aims and may drive foreign-policy decisions. Often conflict may occur because there is an ideological determination not to compromise or dilute any beliefs and aims.

In August 1941 Roosevelt and Churchill had signed the Atlantic Charter and thereby committed the Western powers to a post-war world based on self-determination, peace, prosperity and democracy. In January 1942 these principles were reinforced through the Declaration of the United Nations. The new world order was to be based on freedom, justice and peace and the USSR was one of the signatories. It appeared as if the Grand Alliance would survive the war and the profound ideological differences which could divide its members would continue into the new era of peace. The first test to the unity of the Grand Alliance came in February 1945 when the Alliance members met at Yalta.

Key profiles

Franklin D. Roosevelt, 1882–1945

Roosevelt was born into a wealthy American family. He was President of the USA from 1933 until his death in 1945, having been elected three times. He was an immensely popular leader with ordinary Americans. In 1933 he introduced his plan to restore America's economy and reduce the mass unemployment brought about by the Wall Street Crash and the subsequent Depression. This plan was called the 'New Deal'. At the outbreak of World War II in Europe in 1939, Roosevelt was sympathetic to Britain but remained an isolationist. Only when Japan attacked the USA did Roosevelt enter the wider world war. Having steered the USA through the war Roosevelt died a few weeks before the final victory was achieved.

Winston Churchill, 1874–1965

Churchill came from an aristocratic English family although his mother was an American. He entered politics and held a number of senior jobs. During the First World War he was First Lord of the Admiralty and in charge of the British Navy. During the 1930s he experienced a period of political isolation and he was out of favour with his Conservative Party colleagues. His political revival came with the outbreak of the Second World War. In May 1940 he replaced Neville Chamberlain as Prime Minister and he went on to lead Britain through the war. In the summer of 1945 he was defeated in the General Election and although he had represented Britain at Yalta and all previous conferences he was unable to carry on.

Table 1 *World War II – Principal Allied Powers and Axis Powers*

Allied Powers	Axis Powers
Great Britain	Germany
United States	Austria
France	Soviet Union (1939–40)
Soviet Union (from 1941)	Japan
Belgium	Italy
The Netherlands	Romania
Denmark	Hungary
Norway	
Italy (from 1943)	
Yugoslavia	
China	
India	

Fig. 3 *Allied leaders at the Yalta Conference. Seated left to right: Churchill, Roosevelt and Stalin*

The Yalta Conference, 4–11 February 1945

The so-called 'Big Three' were Stalin, Roosevelt and Churchill. This conference represented the highpoint of inter-allied cooperation and its outcomes appeared to reaffirm the belief that the Grand Alliance was still alive and well and that its members were committed to a lasting consensus in international relations in the post-war order.

Key profile

Joseph Stalin, 1879–1953

Stalin's real name was Joseph Djugashvili and he was born into a poor family from southern Russia. He later adopted the name Stalin because it meant 'Steel'. He became General Secretary of the Soviet Communist Party in 1922 and, by 1927, he had used his political skills and ruthlessness to succeed in his struggle to replace Lenin (d.1924) as the new Party leader. He quickly established himself as a dictator and removed anyone whom he remotely suspected of opposing him. All opposition, real or imagined, was eliminated during the purges and show trials of the 1930s. He was paranoid about protecting his own power. He formed a cynical alliance with Nazi Germany in August 1939 although when Hitler invaded Russia he allied with the Western powers. He ensured that after the war eastern European states had communist regimes in place that were clones of the Soviet model and compliant to him and the USSR.

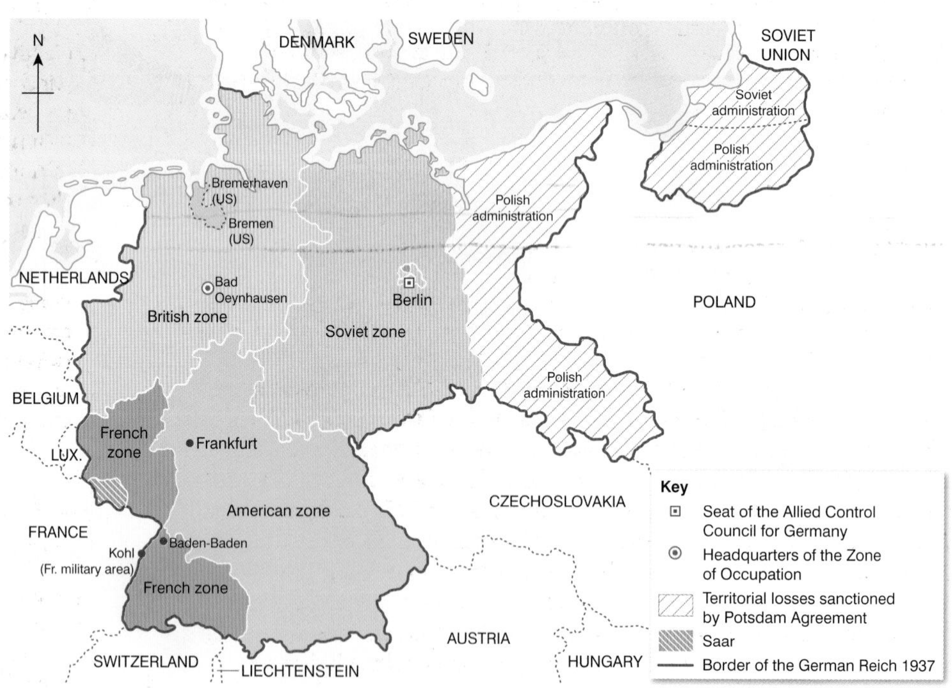

Fig. 4 *Germany 1945 – Zones of Occupation*

Decisions made at Yalta:

- Germany would be divided into four zones, each administered by an allied power
- Berlin would be similarly divided

- The United Nations organisation was formally ratified
- The USSR gained land from Poland. Poland expanded to the west and north
- The Declaration on Liberated Europe was agreed. This committed Britain, the USA and the Soviet Union to:

> ... jointly assist the people in any European liberated state ... to form interim governmental authorities broadly representative of all democratic elements in the population and pledged to the earliest possible establishment through free elections of governments responsive to the will of the people and to facilitate ... the holding of such elections.

← Sham

2

The Yalta talks appeared to deliver cause for great optimism for successful peaceful reconstruction but underlying them were fundamental differences between Stalin's and Roosevelt's vision for the post-war international order.

Table 2 *US (Roosevelt) and Soviet (Stalin) objectives at Yalta*

Roosevelt	Stalin
Collective security founded on the UN	The USSR to be in control of its own destiny
Cooperation with the USSR	Cooperation with the Anglo-Americans
The right to national self-determination and no **spheres of influence**	The USSR's security guaranteed through Soviet spheres of influence in Europe
Germany's reconstruction and re-education as a democratic nation	Germany to remain weak for the indefinite future
World economic reconstruction through the creation of the IMF and the World Bank	Economic reconstruction for the USSR – mainly at Germany's expense

After Yalta there were early signs that the truce, and the Grand Alliance, would not last long. The war had devastated the Soviet Union. A conservative estimate suggested 25 million Russian dead along with the mass destruction of Soviet towns, agriculture and industry. Stalin's absolute priority was the long-term security of the USSR and this was founded upon his commitment to a Soviet sphere of influence and particularly upon the certainty that Germany could never represent a future threat to the USSR. The Grand Alliance was founded upon international cooperation. Its existence implied that there was no longer any relevance in international relations being driven by a balance of power maintained through spheres of influence. States would simply work together to preserve peace and there would be no need or desire for international dominance or aggressive strategies necessary to guarantee national security in a hostile international environment. The Declaration on Liberated Europe appeared to place little significance on the relevancy of spheres of influence in post-war Europe. It meant little to Stalin. He simply agreed to it because it was expedient to do so.

Did you know?

The United Nations organisation replaced the League of Nations (an international peacekeeping and diplomatic entity formed after World War I). Like the League of Nations, the UN was to act as a peacekeeping organisation and work towards settling international disputes before they developed into armed conflict and war.

Key terms

Collective security: this was the principle whereby states would cooperate with each other as a means of reducing insecurity and minimising the need for defensive alliances.

Spheres of influence: an area or region where one power, or a group of powers, has significant control over apparently independent states. This can be achieved through levels of military, political and economic dominance.

Activity

Group activity

Split into two groups, one group taking the position of Roosevelt, the other that of Stalin. Jointly prepare a short speech defending the objectives listed in the table. Allow about 15 minutes for preparation, then appoint a spokesperson for each group, and allow him/her five minutes to present your arguments. Follow this up with questioning from each side.

Exploring the detail

The IMF

The IMF was the International Monetary Fund. It was established in 1944. Its purpose was to be one of the central institutions managing post-war economic relations. It was to manage a system of exchange rates. It was also to lend money to member states facing problems with their balance of payments. The US dollar exchange rate was the foundation of the IMF system and this emphasised the importance of the US economy in international economics.

Activity

Group activity

Produce a spider diagram showing the factors which undermined the unity of the Grand Alliance between Yalta and Potsdam in 1945. As a group, add numbers in order to prioritise the factors in terms of their relative importance.

Stalin was also wary of the USA's economic thinking for the post-war world. He was convinced that the USA's economic power would dominate the proposed new financial system based on the IMF and the World Bank. He saw these as an American strategy designed to establish the USA as a world power and against the economic interests of the USSR. Again, these policies developed by the USA seemed to challenge Stalin's priority for Soviet security. To add to these ominous cracks in the Grand Alliance there came a devastating blow for the post-war leaders. On 12 April 1945 Roosevelt died and his Vice President, Harry S. Truman assumed the Presidency.

Key profile

Harry S. Truman, 1884–1972

Truman was born into a Missouri farming background. He became a member of the US Senate in 1935 and in 1944 he was appointed Roosevelt's Vice President. He had little knowledge of international affairs but became President upon Roosevelt's untimely death. It was Truman who ordered that nuclear weapons should be used against Japan in August 1945. He was elected for a further term in office and remained as President until 1952.

The Potsdam Conference, 17 July–1 August 1945

The day before the Big Three met at Potsdam, the first successful detonation of the atomic bomb had taken place. Truman hoped that this would provide him with the diplomatic leverage he needed to ensure Stalin stayed loyal to his agreements at Yalta. Potsdam was characterised by Truman's abrasive diplomacy and the determination of Stalin and and his Foreign Minister, Vyacheslav Molotov, not to be intimidated by the USA's monopoly of nuclear technology. The Potsdam Conference resulted in some agreement but, significantly, there was no medium- or long-term blueprint laid out for either the future of Germany or the parameters of international relations in the new world order. However, it was agreed that:

- Germany was to be completely disarmed and demilitarised
- de-Nazification was to be carried out. War crimes would be judged and all former Nazi Party members were to be removed from public office. The educational system was to be purged of all Nazi influences
- decentralisation of the political system was to be undertaken and local responsibility developed
- freedom of speech and a free press were to be restored as was religious tolerance
- Germany was to become a single economic unit with common policies on industry and finance
- the USSR was to receive reparations from its own zone and an additional 25 per cent from the western zones.

Fig. 5 *The opening of the Potsdam Conference, 17 July 1945*

Key profile

Vyacheslav Mikhailovich Molotov, 1890–1986

Molotov joined the Bolshevik movement in 1906 and eventually became a committed and loyal supporter of Stalin. He served as the Soviet Foreign Minister from 1939 to 1949 and then from 1953 to 1957. He was the leading Soviet representative at Yalta and Potsdam and many regarded his attitudes as making a major contribution to the collapse of East–West relations soon after the end of the war. He was finally expelled from the Communist Party in 1964.

The Potsdam Conference did nothing to reinforce the apparent unity achieved at Yalta. It failed to define a consensus between East and West. It failed to establish clarity on the scale of Soviet reparation claims. It contributed to the growing suspicion and uncertainty that had developed between the USA and the Soviet Union. The unity of the Grand Alliance was further challenged by a range of crises of which the inadequacies of both Yalta and Potsdam were merely a part.

The German problem, 1945–7

The most immediate practical issue that faced East–West relations was the question of reparations to be exacted from Germany by the Soviet Union. Potsdam enabled the USSR to take 15 per cent of industrial capital equipment from metallurgic, chemical and manufacturing industries from the western zones in exchange for a range of materials in the Soviet zone, such as food, coal and timber. They could also take a further 10 per cent without any exchange. Within this arrangement lay two problems. Firstly the Soviet reparations were dependent upon the vague proviso that only those resources that were 'unnecessary for the German peace recovery' could be taken. Secondly the agreement necessitated day-to-day cooperation between East and West. Stalin's agenda for the future of Germany became a fundamental issue for the USA. Soviet demands for coal from the western zones raised the issue of not merely Russia's desire for revenge, but also the spectre of a Soviet plan to systematically weaken Germany in order to undermine its ability to recover economically and politically.

In April 1946 Truman ordered that 25 million tonnes of coal from the western zones be made available for export to western European states. In May General Clay, the Military Governor of the American zone, announced that reparation payments from that zone would end until an overall plan for the German economy had been implemented. The Russians saw these moves as an American strategy not only to strengthen western European economies in order to neutralise the growing popularity of communism but also to restore a united and reconstructed German economy based on an international capitalist system. It also served to heighten growing suspicions between the USSR and the USA. The lack of precision in the reparation details arrived at Potsdam became a breeding ground for international tension.

The future of Germany became the focus for political divisions between East and West. The collapse of Nazi Germany meant that there was no single political power structure existing in post-war Germany from May 1945. Stalin was determined that the Soviet-controlled zone would act as a springboard to extend communism throughout the new Germany. His strategy was to manipulate the unification of the German Communist Party (KPD) and the Social

Democratic Party (SPD). This led to the creation of the communist-controlled Socialist Unity Party (SED). The SED was not popular and Stalin did not achieve his real objective of complete communist domination. A useful insight into Soviet aims in Germany may be gleaned from a report on the condition of the SED by September 1946, produced by a Soviet adviser, Colonel Sergei Tiul'panov:

> Deviations from Marxist positions pose a substantial danger for the party. Still, neither the Communists nor the Social Democrats understand the new forms shaping the struggle for power, the movement towards socialism. They do not speak about the dictatorship of the proletariat, but about democracy and they have no understanding of the nature of the struggle after World War II. They argued that they did not have to orient themselves on the Soviet Union. They said that Russian workers live badly and that they, the Germans, should only think about the German working class.

3 *J. Hanhimaki and O. A. Westad,* ***The Cold War*** *(2003)*

Britain and the USA rapidly became interested in minimising the punitive elements of their occupation in favour of reconstruction that might ultimately lead to Germany becoming part of an integrated Europe. The Americans saw the economic recovery of Germany as a fundamental prerequisite for Germany's political stability. Linked to this was America's perception of the vital importance of European post-war economic recovery. America wanted the full political unification of Germany but it also wanted to weaken Soviet influence throughout eastern Europe as a whole. A report from General Clay presented in November 1946 on the idea of uniting the British and American occupation zones reveals America's aims for post-war Europe and the resulting division of power in international relations.

Divisions between East and West widened by July 1946 as the USA refused to increase Soviet reparation payments while such a move would delay Germany's economic recovery. Britain agreed to the USA's proposal to unify their zones. The economic cost of maintaining its zone had become excessive for Britain and such a unification was an escape route from these costs. In January 1947 the British and American zones were merged economically to form Bizonia. This did nothing to reinforce the unity of the Grand Alliance.

Key terms

Atomic diplomacy: this is based on the idea that America's monopoly of nuclear technology would be used to put additional diplomatic pressure on other states.

Fig. 6 *The mushroom cloud from the US nuclear attack on Nagasaki, Japan, 9 August 1945. Nuclear weapons would overshadow international relations for the next 50 years*

The USA's atomic monopoly

The Americans regarded the atomic bomb primarily as a diplomatic tool in East–West relations. The USA wanted to make the USSR more compliant in Europe, and particularly in Germany. America's strategy was based on '**atomic diplomacy**'. If the bomb was a diplomatic tool then its role was a failure. There is no tangible evidence to suggest that Soviet actions were driven towards more cooperation with the USA because of the existence of nuclear technology. The Soviet response, given its obsession with security, was to develop its own nuclear weapons by 1949.

The Polish question

Although they had agreed to the Declaration on Liberated Europe at Yalta, the Russians failed to conduct free elections in Poland. Poland was the route Russia's enemies had always taken in their attacks. For Stalin the idea that Poland would not fall under Soviet influence was inconceivable. A simple sphere of influence was not enough to guarantee Russia's long-term security. A pro-Moscow communist regime had to be in place. This was also essential in terms of Russia's relationship with the rest of eastern Europe. If democracy was allowed to flourish in Poland then that would set a Soviet policy preference that would not go unrecognised by the western allies or Soviet liberated eastern European states. The dispute over Poland simply raised an atmosphere of mistrust within the Grand Alliance. America was convinced that what had happened in Poland would be replicated in other eastern European states and the USSR was convinced that the USA had no regard for legitimate Soviet security interests. This was quickly transformed into a Soviet certainty that the USA wanted to create its own sphere of diplomatic, strategic and economic influence across Europe.

Activity

Group discussion

Was the USSR's desire for extensive reparations from Germany justified? Prepare a short speech either supporting or arguing against the USSR's attitude. Having heard some of these speeches, take a class vote. You are not allowed to 'sit on the fence'!

Soviet expansionism in eastern Europe, 1945–9

On 6 March 1946 Churchill made a highly influential speech at Fulton, Missouri. President Truman was a member of the audience.

> From Stettin in the Baltic to Triest in the Adriatic, an iron curtain has descended across the continent. Behind that line lie all the capitals of the ancient states of central and eastern Europe. The populations around them lie in what I must call the Soviet sphere, and all are subject in one form or another, not only to Soviet influence but to a very high measure of control from Moscow. I do not believe that Soviet Russia desires war. What they desire is the fruits of war and the indefinite expansion of their powers and doctrines.

4

Stalin made an almost immediate response to Churchill's 'Iron Curtain' speech.

> Mr Churchill now stands as a firebrand of war. He has friends not only in England but also in the United States of America. It may be that some quarters are trying to push into oblivion the sacrifices of the Soviet people which ensured the liberation of Europe from the Hitlerite yoke. But the Soviet Union cannot forget them. One can ask therefore, what can be surprising in the fact that the Soviet Union, in a desire to ensure its security for the future, tries to achieve that these countries should have governments whose relations with the Soviet Union are loyal? How can one qualify these peaceful aspirations of the Soviet Union as 'expansionist tendencies' of our Government?'

5

Fig. 7 *Soviet expansion, 1938–48*

Activity

Source analysis

Why did Churchill make the speech given in Source 4 and what was its significance in terms of the collapse of the Grand Alliance? What does Stalin's reaction to it in Source 5 suggest about the Soviet position?

Stalin's response presented a benign Soviet Union peacefully seeking eastern European allies to reinforce Russia's security. This was the traditional Soviet explanation for its policies towards eastern Europe. By September 1947 the Soviet Union had a much more developed and robust analysis of the state of international relations which acted as a justification for Soviet policy. Essentially the Americans were seen as imperialists who had all the characteristic imperialist policies based on strategic aggression, ideological control and economic exploitation. Russia accused the USA of becoming a strategic threat by developing military bases in countries far away from the American continent and therefore of little direct strategic use other than to intimidate the USSR. Bases existed in Alaska, Japan, Italy, South Korea, Egypt, Turkey, Greece, western Germany and Afghanistan. American economic imperialism was also presented as a justification for a Soviet sphere of influence in eastern Europe. The USA was looking for opportunities to expand its economic control by investing in Europe and thereby finding markets for its own export goods. A communist bloc in eastern Europe would prevent this subtle form of economic imperialism and prevent Europe being sucked into the bondage of American capital. Finally America was accused of violating national sovereignty by promoting the idea of 'world government'. America was presented as a protector of universal laws. America promoted the idea of a new world order based on the assumption that America was the champion of world order, world peace and democratic ideology. The Soviet Union saw itself as the defender of Europe against the imperialistic ambitions of the USA.

Above all, Stalin's actions in eastern Europe were motivated by a determination to do whatever was necessary to safeguard Soviet international interests and Soviet territory. Stalin's methods of imposing communist regimes on eastern European states also reveal something of his motives. Communist regimes were not simply imposed forcibly across eastern Europe. There was a clear element of gradualism and a focus on the specific and individual circumstances relevant to each state. Communists had figured prominently in anti-fascist wartime resistance groups and emerged as committed patriots. In post-war Czechoslovakia the Communist Party emerged as the largest single party and won 38 per cent of the vote in the relatively free elections held in May 1946. There was a compliance towards communism in eastern Europe. The impact of the war had been to leave these states with mass unemployment and insecurity. There was a lack of confidence among the industrial workers in the old ruling elites. Communism promised a better world. It promised employment and massive upward social mobility. However, this view was not shared by all sectors of eastern-European society. The rural peasants looked to the agrarian parties to deliver land redistribution and to be responsive to the particular needs of the very large numbers of rural peasants.

Activity

Group activity

Divide into three groups. One group adopts the Orthodox interpretation, one the Revisionist interpretation and the third the Post-Revisionist position on the origins of the Cold War. Each group then prepares a presentation explaining the collapse of the Grand Alliance in terms of their historiographical perspective.

Stalin was committed to power rather than ideology. His willingness to tolerate other political parties, albeit temporarily, was purely pragmatic (based on practical considerations). The communist regimes that were established could not be independent of Soviet influence. Loyalty to Moscow was a prerequisite of their survival. The purity of the communist ideology operating in eastern-European states was not an issue for Stalin. The leaders of these states had to function as Stalinist puppets. This level of commitment and loyalty gave Stalin, and the Soviet Union, power and power gave security.

The Warsaw Pact

Poland

The case of Poland reveals some significant forward planning by Stalin. During the war, the 'Government of the Republic of Poland in Exile' was established in Britain by Polish political figures who had fled the Nazis. Known as the 'London Poles', they stood as a figurehead of Polish rule during the war and theoretically continued to exist until 1990. Yet communism was imposed on Poland via a Soviet-controlled government. The Polish Committee for National Liberation (the Lublin Government) was Stalin's instrument of political control. By agreeing to free elections at Yalta, Stalin was able to preserve the role of the pro-Moscow Lublin government. The Provisional Government of National Unity was formed in June 1945 and it contained parties from both ends of the political spectrum. This became typical of Stalin's pluralist approach. To some extent Poland became a testing ground for Stalin's methodology but it by no means established a model that Stalin would not deviate from. Poland had a Peasant Party and it was led by Stanislaw Mikolajczyk. The Communists weakened this group by strengthening their own links with the Polish socialists. In January 1947 these two groups merged and the Communists were the dominant group within this merger. Some Polish Communists were not totally pro-Moscow. The Deputy Prime Minister Wladslaw Gomulka was one such. He declared in 1945:

> Our party has been tempered by the hard struggle against German occupation, our blood and our lives are the foundation stone of reborn Poland. We pioneered her liberation. Blood and combat have given us the right to determine her future and character.

6

Gomulka opposed Soviet policies which he felt were irrelevant to Poland. He was accused of 'nationalist deviation' and replaced by a compliant pro-Stalinist, Boleslaw Bierut. Poland was safely under Soviet influence.

Romania, Bulgaria and Hungary

With the Soviet army of liberation still in Romania, the King was forced to appoint a communist-led government. The communists were popular because they offered an alternative to the pre-war regime. The establishment of communism in Romania was relatively easy for Stalin. Opposition was minimal and easy to deal with.

Gradualism, manipulated elections and the forced removal of opponents characterised the process in Bulgaria. The strongest political opponent facing the communists was the Agrarian Party, led by Nikola Petkov. Despite winning over 20 per cent of the popular vote in the October 1946 elections, Petkov was faced with trumped-up charges and executed. His party was forcibly absorbed into the Bulgarian communist movement. By April 1947 all other political parties had been banned.

In Hungary the communists used the tactic of allying with other political groups in order to challenge the power of their greatest opponent, the Smallholders Party. As in Poland and elsewhere, political opponents were arrested and elections were rigged. As in Poland, Hungarian

Key dates

1945	The Provisional Government of National Unity is formed
1946 June	The communist-led Democratic Bloc win elections in Poland
October	The Communists win 75 per cent of the popular vote in Bulgaria
November	The Communists in Romania win 80 per cent of the votes in national elections and Romania is, from this point, under unchallenged Soviet influence
1947	Persecution of opposition parties begins in Poland
	In Hungary, Communists and Socialists win 45 per cent of the votes and control 15 government posts
	All opposition political parties are banned in Bulgaria
1948	The hard-line pro-Moscow leader, Boleslaw Bierut, takes over in Poland
February	Czech communists carry out a political coup and seize control of Czechoslovakia
1949	Single party communist rule is finally established in Hungary
	The new communist state of East Germany comes into existence
	Every central and eastern European state is now within the direct Soviet sphere of influence – except Yugoslavia
1955	The Warsaw Pact is established

communists did not display the degree of loyalty to Moscow that Stalin wanted. They formed close links with Yugoslavia, where a non-Soviet communist regime was in place under the partisan leader Marshal Tito. In 1949 the Hungarian communist leader, Laszlo Rajk, was executed for 'anti-Socialist' activities. By 1949 all political opposition to the Moscow-backed Hungarian communists had disappeared.

Czechoslovakia

Unlike much of the rest of eastern Europe, Czechoslovakia was industrialised and it had a large, unionised urban working class. Czech communists were popular with the rural peasants because they had given them land at the end of the war. The Czech Communist Party's leader, Klement Gottwald, became Prime Minister. His fatal error was to show a willingness to accept Western economic aid in 1947. In addition to this there was growing opposition to the communist leadership from non-communist groups. All the non-communist members of the government resigned in February 1948. This move played into the hands of the communists, who presented it as an attempt to create an alternative right wing conservative coup. The highly respected President Benes agreed to support a communist-dominated government. In June 1948 he resigned and this left the pro-Moscow communists in complete control. The final step in the Moscow-driven take over of eastern Europe came with the creation of a communist-led East Germany in 1949.

Fig. 8 *Communists taking power in Czechoslovakia, 1948*

The formation of the Warsaw Pact

In 1955, the Soviet Union and most of the communist states of eastern Europe signed what was officially called the Treaty of Friendship, Cooperation and Mutual Assistance. This treaty brought into being what was known as the Warsaw Pact. Territories united in a pledge to defend one another should they be threatened by an external aggressor. In this case, the aggressor was specifically the forces of the North Atlantic Treaty Organisation (NATO), led by the United States. West Germany had entered NATO in 1955, and this alliance spurred the Soviet Union to create its equivalent defensive mass in the east.

The opening lines of the 1955 treaty presented the signatories in a benign light:

> Between the People's Republic of Albania, the People's Republic of Bulgaria, the Hungarian People's Republic, the German Democratic Republic, the Polish People's Republic, the Rumanian People's Republic, the Union of Soviet Socialist Republics, and the Czechoslovak Republic, 1 May 1955.
>
> The contracting parties,
>
> Reaffirming their desire for the organisation of a system of collective security in Europe, with the participation of all the European states, irrespective of their social and state systems, which would make it possible to combine their efforts in the interests of securing peace in Europe.

7

Yet as the treaty spelled out its various articles, it was obvious that the Warsaw Pact contained an implicit threat:

> *Article 4.* In the event of an armed attack in Europe on one or several states that are signatories of the treaty by any state or group of states, each state that is a party to this treaty shall, in the exercise of the right to individual or collective self-defence in accordance with Article 51 of the Charter of the United Nations Organisation, render the state or states so attacked immediate assistance, individually and in agreement with other states that are parties to this treaty, by all the means it may consider necessary, including the use of armed force. The states that are parties to this treaty shall immediately take council among themselves concerning the necessary joint measures to be adopted for the purpose of restoring and upholding international peace and security.
>
> In accordance with the principles of the Charter of the United Nations Organisation, the Security Council shall be advised of the measures taken on the basis of the present article. These measures shall be stopped as soon as the Security Council has taken the necessary measures for restoring and upholding international peace and security.
>
> *Article 5.* The contracting parties have agreed on the establishment of a joint command for their armed forces, which shall be placed, by agreement among these parties, under this command, which shall function on the basis of jointly defined principles. They shall also take other concerted measures necessary for strengthening their defence capacity, in order to safeguard the peaceful labour of their peoples, to guarantee the inviolability of their frontiers and territories and to provide safeguards against possible aggression.

8

The might of the Warsaw Pact's combined military muscle, opposed to that of the NATO countries, was the essence of the Cold War stand-off that would dominate European affairs for the next three and a half decades. Although the world never descended into the nuclear disaster people feared, both the Western and Eastern powers would express their military power in numerous 'proxy' conflicts dotted around the globe.

Summary questions

1. To what extent was the Grand Alliance still intact after the Yalta Conference?

2. 'The Soviet Union developed its influence in eastern Europe in the years 1945 to 1949 because it simply wanted to guarantee its security in the future.' How valid is this assessment?

2 The Origins of the USA's Globalism

In this chapter you will learn about:

- how the relationship between the USA and the Soviet Union deteriorated
- why the USA developed a foreign policy based on containment
- how the Soviet Union reacted to containment
- why the Cold War became a global issue.

With the end of World War II, the old days of empire were passing. In their place came the new era of the superpower nations. In the West, that superpower was the United States, a nation with awesome industrial output, economic wealth and military power. How it handled its position in relation to the other superpower, the Soviet Union, would determine international relations for the next 40 years.

Key dates

1946 February	Kennan's 'Long Telegram'
September	Novikov's 'Telegram'
1947 February	Britain withdraws aid to anti-communists in Greece
March	Truman Doctrine speech
June	The Marshall Plan is announced
September	Cominform is founded
1948 June	Berlin Blockade and allied airlift begins
1949 April	NATO established
May	Berlin Blockade ends
August	The Soviet Union successfully explodes an atomic bomb
September	The Federal Republic of Germany (West Germany) is founded
October	The German Democratic Republic (East Germany) is founded
	The People's Republic of China is created
1950 June	North Korea attacks South Korea – the Korean War starts
October	China enters the Korean War on North Korea's side
1951 April	The European Coal and Steel Community Treaty signed
1953 March	Stalin dies
July	The Korean War ends

An overview of US relations with Europe in 1945

The spectre of a divided Europe alarmed the USA. It had become very clear, very quickly, to the Americans that the USSR was not going to enter into any meaningful international dialogue over the future of eastern Europe. Roosevelt's position, grounded in self-determination for all nations and international security based on cooperation between states, had become increasingly untenable as the USSR strengthened its sphere of influence in eastern Europe by establishing pro-Soviet communist regimes. Truman's initial focus was on European reconstruction. US Secretary of State Stimson, in a report to Truman in July 1945, emphasised the importance of the restoration of stable conditions in Europe "for only thus can concepts of individual liberty, free thought and free speech be nurtured." There was no suggestion that the United States envisaged any long-term military or political entanglement in Europe beyond the time it would take to establish political and economic reconstruction there. Nor was there any clear indication that the USA regarded Europe as a springboard for the development of a global power role for the USA following the final destruction of European-centred world power.

What the USA was interested in was expanding its economic interests, not simply within war-torn Europe but also globally. At the end of the Second World War, the Americans wanted a world order in which their economic strengths could be enhanced. There would be international stability achieved through cooperation based on a collective desire to preserve peace. In this context, power based on military strength would no longer be relevant and the USA would be able to exploit its economic influence freely and on a global scale. This early American optimism was soon modified. Europe's power had been fundamentally damaged by 1945 and a power vacuum had emerged in international relations. America was an economically dominant western democracy and militarily the most powerful state on the globe. Given the increasing failure to establish any clear political agreement with the USSR, the USA was faced with two relatively straightforward policy options. It could either retreat into **isolationism** or it could project its power on a global scale. A major contributor to the final direction of US international policy came in the form of the Kennan Telegram.

Activity

Thinking point

Draw up a table with the words 'Isolationism' at the top of one column, and 'Global power' at the top of the other. Under these columns list first the strengths and then the weaknesses of each option for US foreign policy.

Key terms

Isolationism: this was the term used to describe US foreign policy after the First World War. It suggests that the USA did not regard it as in its interests to become involved in external conflict beyond its immediate neighbours. It would remain withdrawn from involvement in global and European issues.

George Kennan's 'Long Telegram', February 1946

The direction of US policy was already being moulded by Truman at the beginning of 1946. Stalin, as part of a strategy to consolidate Soviet security in the south, had demanded that Soviet military bases be established in Turkey. This would have given the USSR control of the Turkish Straits and the potential, thereby, to have a huge influence over the Mediterranean. In a note to Secretary of State Byrnes Truman, having ordered the US Sixth Fleet to the eastern Mediterranean, commented, "Unless Russia is faced with an iron fist and strong language another war is in the making. Only one language do they understand – how many divisions have you? ... I'm tired of babying the Soviets."

On 22 February 1946 George F. Kennan, a junior official in the US Embassy in Moscow, sent a lengthy despatch to the US State Department in Washington. Many historians, such as John Gaddis, regard the 'Long Telegram' as seminal in shaping US policy towards the Soviet Union and ultimately in determining the USA's role as a global power. US policy towards the Soviet Union would assume a global perspective rather than a purely European one because of the analysis Kennan presented of the motives of Soviet foreign policy.

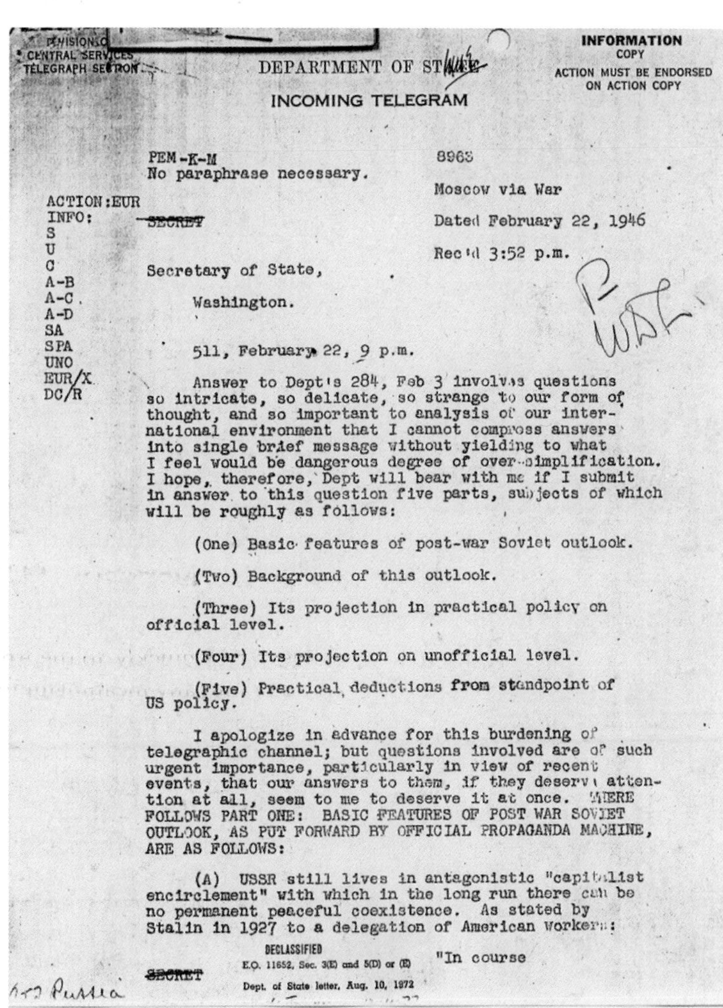

DIVISION OF CENTRAL SERVICES TELEGRAPH SECTION

DEPARTMENT OF STATE

INCOMING TELEGRAM

INFORMATION COPY
ACTION MUST BE ENDORSED ON ACTION COPY

PEM-K-M
No paraphrase necessary.

8963
Moscow via War
Dated February 22, 1946
Rec'd 3:52 p.m.

ACTION:EUR
INFO:
S
U
C
A-B
A-C
A-D
SA
SPA
UNO
EUR/X
DC/R

~~SECRET~~

Secretary of State,

Washington.

511, February 22, 9 p.m.

Answer to Dept's 284, Feb 3 involves questions so intricate, so delicate, so strange to our form of thought, and so important to analysis of our international environment that I cannot compress answers into single brief message without yielding to what I feel would be dangerous degree of over-simplification. I hope, therefore, Dept will bear with me if I submit in answer to this question five parts, subjects of which will be roughly as follows:

(One) Basic features of post-war Soviet outlook.

(Two) Background of this outlook.

(Three) Its projection in practical policy on official level.

(Four) Its projection on unofficial level.

(Five) Practical deductions from standpoint of US policy.

I apologize in advance for this burdening of telegraphic channel; but questions involved are of such urgent importance, particularly in view of recent events, that our answers to them, if they deserve attention at all, seem to me to deserve it at once. THERE FOLLOWS PART ONE: BASIC FEATURES OF POST WAR SOVIET OUTLOOK, AS PUT FORWARD BY OFFICIAL PROPAGANDA MACHINE, ARE AS FOLLOWS:

(A) USSR still lives in antagonistic "capitalist encirclement" with which in the long run there can be no permanent peaceful coexistence. As stated by Stalin in 1927 to a delegation of American workers:

"In course

DECLASSIFIED
E.O. 11652, Sec. 3(E) and 5(D) or (E)
Dept. of State letter, Aug. 10, 1972

~~SECRET~~

Fig. 1 *Kennan's 'Long Telegram', 22 February 1946*

Here are some extracts from the 'Long Telegram':

> It may be expected that the component parts of this far-flung (Soviet) apparatus will be utilised as follows:
>
> 1 To undermine general political and strategic potential of major Western powers.
>
> 2 Efforts will be made to weaken power and influence of Western powers over colonial, backward, or dependent peoples. Soviet dominated puppet political machines will be undergoing preparation to take over domestic power in colonial areas when independence is achieved.
>
> 3 Everything will be done to set major Western powers against each other.
>
> 4 The Soviet regime is a police regime accustomed to think primarily in terms of police power. This should never be lost sight of in gauging Soviet motives. (It is) desirable and necessary for our traditional way of life to be destroyed and the international authority of our state to be broken if Soviet power is to be secure.

1

Key profile

George F. Kennan, 1904–2005

Kennan was an American diplomat who was closely associated with eastern Europe and the Soviet Union during the inter-war years. Although he is closely linked to suggesting the idea of containment to Truman he did reject this link later. His influence continued beyond the 'Long Telegram'. In March 1948, as the Cold War intensified, he sent a report from Japan which argued that the USA should cultivate Japan as an ally. He served as US Ambassador to the Soviet Union in 1951 and to Yugoslavia between 1951 and 1963. Despite this he was, above all, an historian and an academic.

Kennan drew some clear conclusions for the direction of US foreign policy. He argued that the USA must be prepared to threaten the use of force and ensure unity among its allies. Significantly, he urged the USA to adopt a proactive role, particularly in Europe. His telegram referred to the urgency of action. "It is not enough to urge people to develop political processes similar to our own. (Europeans) are seeking guidance rather than responsibilities." Kennan added to his initial points by subsequently producing the so-called 'X' article. In this he called for a "long-term, patient but firm and vigilant containment of Russian expansionist tendencies." Kennan's analysis, founded on the conclusion that Soviet foreign policy was aggressive and ideologically driven, resonated with Truman's growing certainty that the Soviet Union was not only an enemy of western democratic values but also a threat to the USA's security. America's security had, by early 1946, become as powerful a force in the emerging post-war international relations as had that of the Soviet Union. Isolationism was not the way to preserve America's vital national interests and security in the new order of the post-war world. For Truman, the logic of his response was almost inescapable. The USA needed a clearly defined foreign policy framework and he provided it.

The Truman Doctrine: containment

Churchill's 'Iron Curtain' speech came hard on the heels of Kennan's telegram. This served to reinforce Kennan's analysis. Stalin needed a response to Kennan's communiqué and this came in September 1946 from the Soviet Ambassador in Washington, Nikolai Novikov. His striking conclusion was that "The foreign policy of the United States, which reflects the imperialistic tendencies of American monopolistic capital, is characterised in the post-war period by a striving for world supremacy." Novikov emphasised the link between the economic reconstruction of European states and US policy designed to "infiltrate their national economies." For Novikov the USA's aim was world dominance and he cited the massive increase in military spending as proof of this. Novikov underlined his analysis of an aggressively anti-Soviet American policy by saying, "The present policy of the American government is directed at limiting the influence of the Soviet Union from neighbouring countries. In so doing, it also attempts to secure positions for the penetration of American capital into their economies."

Fig. 2 *An American advertisement for refrigerators. US consumer power posed a great ideological threat to the communist Soviet Union*

Each side regarded the other not only as a threat to its national security, but also as being expansionist and a global strategic threat. By September 1946 the emergence of a Cold War was seemingly irreversible. East–West relations had developed a momentum which was grounded in mistrust and fear. These had always been characteristics of international relations but a new set of dynamics had been added after 1945. The USA was the dominant world economy and it intended to use this power as part of its foreign policy. This was a new approach for the USA. The Soviet Union had succeeded in establishing the beginnings of national security based on a system of satellite states in eastern Europe. It realised that its security could be further enhanced by developing its portfolio of pro-Soviet states and that meant expanding pro-Moscow communist-led regimes beyond Europe.

The catalyst that triggered a fundamental reorientation of US foreign policy came in Europe. Stalin had agreed that Greece should remain within the Western sphere of influence after the war. A civil war had erupted between the monarchists and Greek communists when Greece was liberated from Nazi occupation. Britain had been providing aid to the anti-communist forces in Greece but in February 1947 it announced that this aid was no longer available and appealed to the USA to assume the financial burden. Ironically, Stalin had not been aiding the Greek communists and there was no indication that he would start to do so when anti-communist British aid ended. Stalin was unsympathetic to indigenous communist revolutions because he could not ensure Moscow's control. Such realities had little impact on Truman. On 12 March 1947, Truman delivered his seminal announcement before the US Congress.

Here are some extracts from the Truman Doctrine:

> At the present moment in world history nearly every nation must choose between alternative ways of life . . . One way of life is based upon the will of the majority, and is distinguished by free institutions, representative government, free elections, guarantees of individual liberty, freedom of speech and religion, and freedom from political oppression. The second way of life is based upon the will of the minority forcibly imposed on the majority. It relies upon terror and oppression, a controlled press and radio, fixed elections, and the suppression of personal freedoms.
>
> I believe that it must be the policy of the United States to support free peoples who are resisting attempted subjugation by armed minorities or by outside pressures . . . I believe that our help should be primarily through economic and financial aid which is essential to economic stability and orderly political processes.

2

The Truman Doctrine was of fundamental importance in terms of the dynamics of international relations from 1947. As Richard Crockatt comments (*The Fifty Years War*, 1995), 'Bipolarity was not merely a matter of the structure of international relations but a state of mind.' International relations would be founded upon division, each side suspicious of the other. The Truman Doctrine institutionalised this as the working basis of East–West relations for at least the next 25 years. Significantly, Truman had not turned to the newly created United Nations as the arbiter of the dispute in Greece although this may well have been because he was convinced that the Soviet Union would use its veto power to prevent any UN peacekeeping intervention in the Greek civil war.

There are a number of motives which may be attributed to Truman's decision to introduce his Doctrine. The range includes:

- It was simply a rather blunt piece of diplomacy designed to keep the Soviet Union from aiding the Greek communist movement and it had no relevance to US policy beyond the Greek civil war.
- It was designed primarily to protect democracy and freedom and there was no aggressive intent towards any other state. It was a response to Soviet aggressive political, strategic and ideological expansionism in eastern Europe.
- Truman needed to demonise the Soviet Union and communism in the minds of the American public. He needed to present communism and the Soviet Union as an enemy of the USA in order to justify his aim of protecting the USA's vital national interests and turning the USA into a global power.
- Truman had to provoke the Soviet Union. His Doctrine was designed to make the USSR feel threatened by America's power. Truman wanted a Cold War to start because this would justify America's role as a defender of freedom but more importantly it would enable the USA to function as a world power.

- The Doctrine formed an important element of the USA's aim of developing its global economic power. By creating an enemy and presenting itself as the protector against that enemy, the USA would make other states not only militarily dependent on the USA but also economically dependent. These states would inevitably form close trade relations with the USA because they were close political allies.

The Truman Doctrine was the first step in the creation of containment as the basis of American post-war foreign policy. The next step came through a financial plan drawn up by George Marshall and designed to reinforce the Doctrine.

Activity

Group activity

Working in small groups prepare a presentation explaining why containment became the basis of US policy from 1947. Each group should focus on a particular motive outlined in the text and argue the case to support it.

Key profile

George Marshall, 1880–1959

Marshall was a career soldier and had served with US forces in Europe during the First World War. He later became a senior military adviser to President Roosevelt during the Second World War. After developing the European Recovery Programme he went into retirement, only to return as the US Defence Secretary from 1950 to 1951 during the Korean War.

Fig. 3 *Propaganda poster supporting the Marshall Plan*

The Marshall Plan, June 1947

In May 1947 Under-Secretary of State for Economic Affairs, William L. Clayton, returned from a fact-finding tour of western Europe. He reported that "Europe is steadily deteriorating." Clayton went on to conclude that "the immediate effects (of this) on our domestic economy would be disastrous: markets for our surplus production gone, unemployment, depression, a heavily unbalanced budget. These things must not happen." His analysis was alarmist and it exaggerated the economic importance of Europe to the USA but did illustrate the USA's rising concern about the nature of its long-term relationship with Europe. On 5 June 1947 Marshall unveiled his plan, known officially as the European Economic Recovery Plan (ERP), before an audience at Harvard University.

Here is an extract:

> Aside from the demoralising effect on the world at large and the possibilities of disturbances arising as a result of the desperation of the people concerned, the consequences to the economy of the United States should be apparent to all. It is logical that the United States should do whatever it is able to do to assist in the return of normal economic health in the world, without which there can be no political stability and no assured peace. Our policy is not directed against any country or doctrine but against hunger, poverty, desperation and chaos. Its purpose should be the revival of a working economy in the world so as to permit the emergence of political and social conditions in which free institutions can exist . . . Governments, political parties, or other groups which seek to perpetuate human misery in order to profit therefrom politically or otherwise will encounter the opposition of the United States.

3

Over the next five years the Plan provided $13.5 billion to 16 countries in Europe. This came not only in the form of money but also through goods as well.

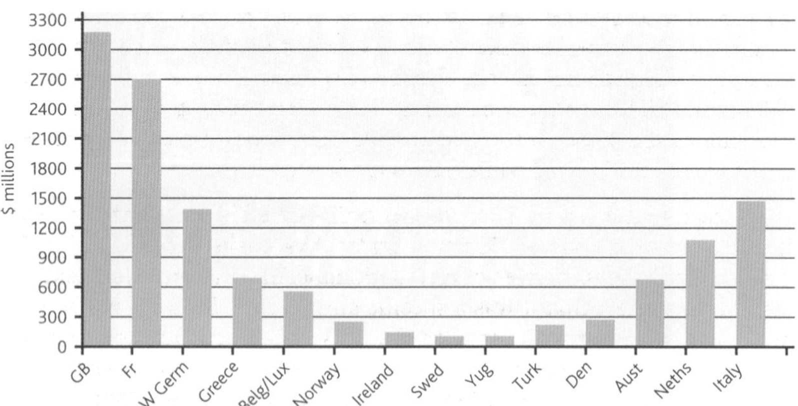

Fig. 4 *Marshall Plan aid to foreign countries, 1947–52 (all sums in $ millions)*

A condition of receiving the aid was that some of it had to be spent on importing goods from the USA. Recipients were also required to share economic information with the USA. The plan was part of a US economic strategy to benefit the US economy by helping in Europe's economic reconstruction but it also aimed at promoting European unity. A stable European bloc would be created which would reinforce Truman's idea of containment. The American vision for Europe rested in the creation of a single European market and historians have argued that the Marshall Plan contributed significantly to the creation of the European Coal and Steel Community and ultimately, therefore, to the existence of the European Economic Community from 1957.

The USA was profoundly concerned about political and economic stability in Europe, particularly in France and Italy. The French Communist Party had 1.7 million members in 1947. Continuing economic crisis could lead to growing support for the movement and this could result in the Soviet Union having an opening for influence in western Europe. The Soviets saw the Marshall Plan as a clear example of American economic imperialism. They believed that this influence may start to spread into eastern Europe and thereby undermine their sphere of influence and their security. The Plan certainly accelerated the division of Europe and, particularly, the division of Germany. The European Economic Recovery Programme was offered to all European states, including the Soviet Union. By 1947 Czechoslovakia and Hungary were not yet fully under communist control and there were still communist-dominated coalition governments with some interest in receiving Marshall Aid. This would have resulted in these states committing themselves to a restoration of **market economies** and a degree of integration of their economies with those of the west-European member states of the Organisation of European Economic Cooperation, the organisation responsible for allocating Marshall Aid. As Bideleux and Jeffries comment (*A History of Eastern Europe*, 1998), "The recipients would thus be drawn into the economic orbit of the richer Western capitalist economies." The Soviet Union saw this economic attraction as a clear threat to its influence in eastern Europe.

In July 1947 the Soviet Union walked out of the tripartite (three parties or elements) (ERP) Paris Conference and within four days had established the **Cominform**. The Soviet Union's perception of the Marshall Plan was clear. Czechoslovakia and those eastern-European states that had expressed an interest in Marshall Aid were ordered by Stalin to reverse their decision. The logic of the Soviet Union's position was inescapable. Greater tightening of Soviet control over eastern Europe was necessary. If the Marshall Plan was part of a US strategy to undermine the Soviet sphere of influence in eastern Europe and move these states closer to western democracy by integrating their economies with the rest of western Europe, it clearly failed. The Marshall Plan simply accelerated the division of Europe and further undermined the possibility of international relations being based on some degree of cooperation and consensus between the two superpowers.

At a speech to the United Nations General Assembly in September 1947, the Soviet Deputy Foreign Minister, Andrei Vyshinsky, accused the USA of renouncing the principles of international collaboration. Vyshinsky went on to suggest that it was a specific aim of the USA to split Europe and to revive the German economy as a base for American expansionism in Europe and ultimately to threaten the security of the Soviet Union. What motivated the Truman Doctrine was enshrined in the Marshall Plan. By late 1947 the USA's relationship with Europe had been firmly outlined. From this point the depth of the relationship increased.

The Berlin blockade, June 1948 to May 1949

It was an economic issue that appeared to be the immediate causal factor of what was seen as the most dangerous crisis in Europe since the war ended. The western allies had sought to create a stable and common

Key terms

Market economy: any economy in which the prices of goods and services are set by the forces of supply and demand, with minimal interference from the state.

Cominform: this was the Communist Information Bureau. Its purpose was to unite and coordinate the role and actions of communist groups throughout Europe in order that the Party functioned as a united whole. It aimed at spreading communist ideas and keeping the movement throughout eastern Europe united and acting collectively.

Activity

Revision activity

Write a newspaper article on either the Truman Doctrine or the Marshall Plan from

i) a Western

AND

ii) a Soviet perspective.

currency across their joint zones of occupation. By 23 June 1948 the newly created Deutschmark had been introduced into West Berlin.

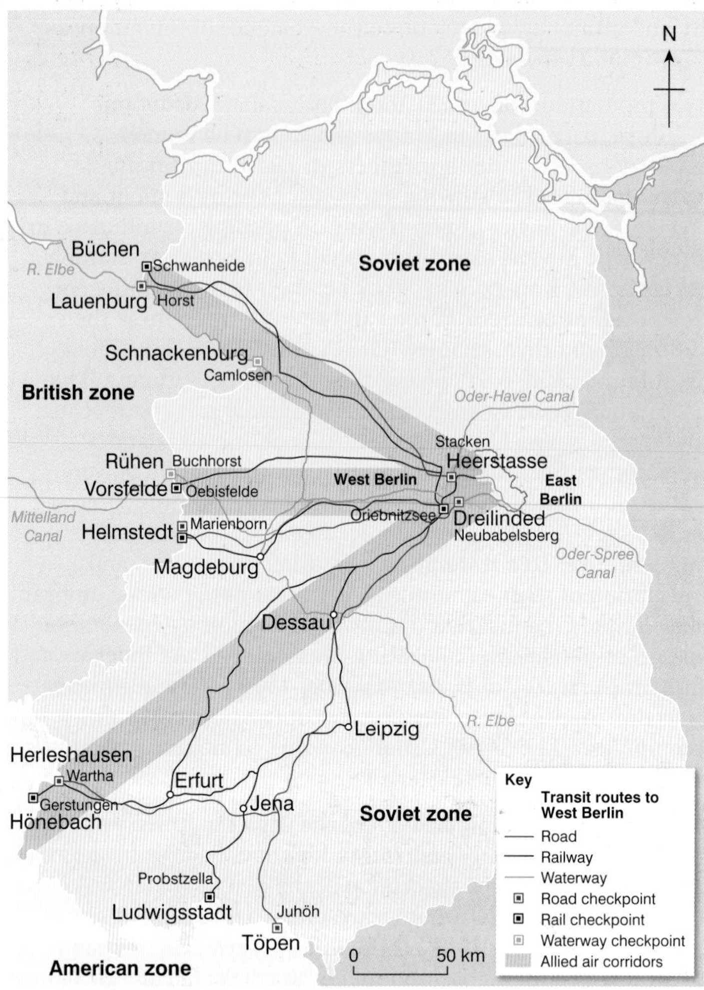

Fig. 5 *Map of transit routes to West Berlin, 1948*

On 24 June 1948 all road and rail links to the western zones and to West Berlin through the Soviet zone were blocked by the Soviet Union. British Foreign Secretary Ernest Bevin became the prime mover in driving the allied response to the Soviet blockade. Bevin argued that the Soviet Union's ultimate aim was to spread communism across the whole of Germany and their pressure to oust the Western powers from West Berlin was the first step in this process. At the very least a retreat from Berlin would hand a propaganda victory to the Soviet Union and illustrate that the first challenge to containment in Europe had succeeded. Bevin was adamant that the allies must not use military force to access West Berlin but must keep it supplied with essentials. US General Clay was committed to allied action. He said:

> When Berlin falls, western Germany will be next. If we mean to hold Europe against communism we must not budge . . . If we withdraw, our position in Europe is threatened. If America does not understand this now . . . then it never will, and communism will run rampant. I believe the future of democracy requires us to stay.

4

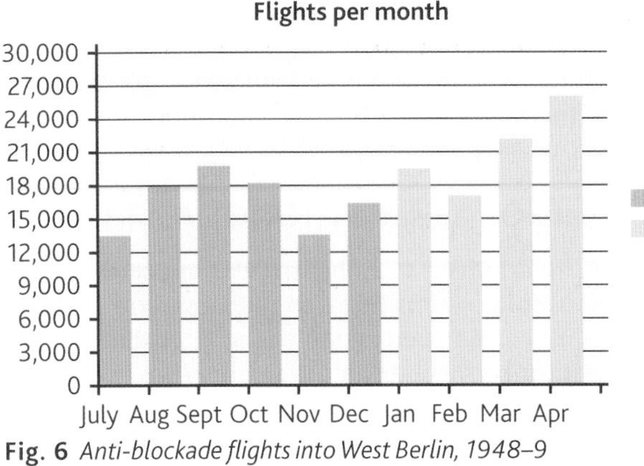

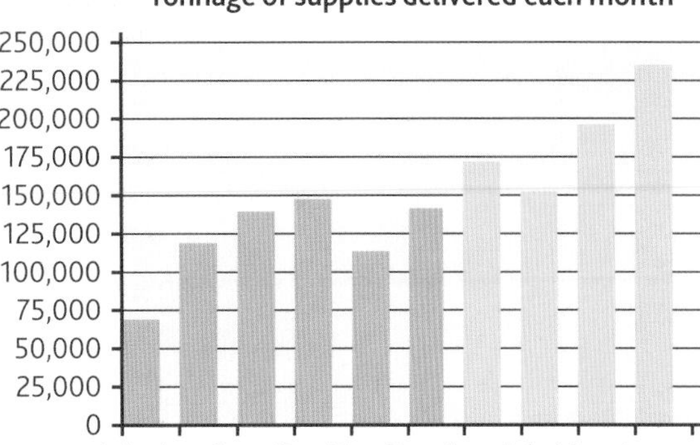

Fig. 6 *Anti-blockade flights into West Berlin, 1948–9*

In May 1949 Stalin ended the blockade. His aim had been to stop the creation of a separate West German state and he had failed. The policy of containment had proved a success and by 1949 Europe was finally divided as indeed was Germany. By October 1949 West Germany and East Germany had come into existence as two separate and independent states although the strategic and political realities were that neither was independent.

The blockade added to, and reinforced, America's certainty that it had to consolidate its relationship with Europe.

Fig. 7 *Berlin children greet a US transport plane during the airlift, 1948*

Germany and NATO

In fewer than 10 years, West Germany changed from an embryonic state under an occupation order into a major player in Europe and the Western Alliance system. Konrad Adenauer, the first Chancellor of the Federal Republic of Germany (FRG), recognised that the best way of reaccommodating his country was to win the support of the western world including a reconciliation with Germany's age-old enemy, the French. Reintegration was also supported by the USA who saw a strengthened West Germany as a safeguard against communist expansionism, while reliance on the US would prevent a resurgence of German nationalism and militarism which would have unsettled Europe. Adenauer's first important step in this process was made in the Petersberg (West Germany) agreements of November 1949, which allowed the FRG to join the Council of Europe as an associate member.

Exploring the detail

The Council of Europe

The Council of Europe was set up in 1949 as an association of European states committed to the principles of freedom, the rule of law and a safeguarding of the cultural heritage of Europe. The FRG became a full member in 1951.

The FRG was also given the right to set up consulates in other countries and to have direct representation on the Organisation of European Economic Cooperation (OEEC), the organisation which administered the Marshall Plan, and on the Board of the International Authority of the Ruhr.

The North Atlantic Treaty Organisation (NATO), April 1949

The USA's transition from isolationism to globalism was not certain, nor was it certain that the USA would commit itself to the long-term defence of western Europe. There was a strong perception in the USA that Europe should make a significant contribution towards its own defence. To some extent this process had already begun with the formation of a European defence organisation known as the Western European Union. Its members included Britain, France and the Benelux countries.

The Western European Union emerged from the Brussels Pact of 17 March 1948. Its overt aim was to prevent any form of German resurgence that might threaten the security of post-war western Europe. Many historians regard its creation as a major factor in the polarisation of the Cold War and of Europe becoming the focal point of Cold War confrontation. By its creation, European states were seen as signalling to the USA that West Germany and wider Europe were under threat from communist advance and that the USA must take a more proactive role in the development of a stronger regional defence system. This ultimately came in the form of the North Atlantic Treaty Organisation (NATO).

Exploring the detail

The Western European Union

The Western European Union was formed in 1948 as a defence pact among western European nations. By 1954 it had seven member states, with three more (Portugal, Spain and Greece) joining in the 1990s. It is also backed by various other 'Associate', 'Observer' and 'Member' countries. Although the WEU still exists, its responsibilities are largely controlled by the European Union and NATO.

For the USA the problem with this organisation was that it was 'too European', and too small to protect western Europe. It was not sufficient for the USA simply to join this union because it would have merely been protecting western Europe and having little direct input into policy making. Also, the burden of protection would have been heavier on the USA than on any other member of the union. The USA needed to create an Atlantic alliance rather than a regional European alliance if it was to have any real influence in, and certainty over, Europe and its defence against communist expansionism.

US thinking in the early stages of the creation of an Atlantic alliance was focused on the belief that the Soviet threat to western Europe was primarily a political rather than a military one. Given this interpretation it was essential that the USA could have a direct influence which would reinforce the confidence of western Europeans. In essence, the US view was that without an American presence in a defence system for western Europe, the region would be easy prey for ideological expansionism from the Soviet Union. The USA saw the alliance as a means not only of preventing western European states becoming communist, but also as a way of preventing them becoming neutral due to Soviet pressure. The alliance was in place to send a message to the Soviet Union highlighting the United States's determination not to accept any further expansion of Soviet influence into Europe. Membership of this alliance had to be extensive and certainly beyond that currently in the WEU.

In April 1949 NATO came into being. Its members were the United States, Canada, Britain, France, Belgium, the Netherlands, Luxembourg, Italy, Portugal, Denmark, Norway and Iceland. At this point the USA viewed its relationship with the Soviet Union in political and economic terms and NATO was primarily a political defence system. The Soviet Union objected to NATO on the grounds that it contradicted the principles upon which the United Nations had been founded. Why would such an alliance system be necessary if the United States was committed to international cooperation through the auspices of the UN? Only months after NATO's formation, the Soviet Union successfully tested its first atomic bomb. America's nuclear monopoly ended and NATO's initial political role very quickly transformed into a military role. Not only did NATO's raison d'être shift but so did the USA's application of containment. By 1950 the Cold War had extended to Asia.

Activity

Thinking point

Produce a report outlining the USA's options as regards involvement in Europe in 1949. Include an assessment of these options and recommend a final decision explaining why it is appropriate in terms of the USA's vital national interests.

A closer look

The United States and Japan

In August 1945 the war in Asia finally came to an end with the surrender of Japan. The USA's policy towards Japan mirrored to some extent its approach on Germany. In the early stages of reconstruction the Americans sought to remove the entrenched elites and institutions which had led to the rise of Japan's militarism in Asia during the 1930s. The USA wanted to democratise Japan and remove its capacity to produce heavy industrial goods. These occupation policies were largely abandoned by the USA by 1948. The USA needed to respond to the rise of communism in Asia in view of the imminent success of Mao Zedong's communist army in the ongoing civil war in China. Japan became the focal point of America's policy in Asia. Japan not only had to be reconstructed and stable, it also had to be pro-American; it rapidly became of crucial strategic importance for the USA's determination to limit the spread of communist influence in eastern Asia. By 1951 the USA had agreed a bilateral security treaty with Japan. Japan was able to regain its sovereignty and free itself from US occupation but only within the framework of a close alliance with the United States. Truman's administration was laying the foundations for the containment of communism in Asia and Japan was an integral part of this process.

Although the USA wanted West Germany in NATO, France at first resisted, and when the Foreign Secretaries of the USA, Britain and France met in New York in September 1950, the French put forward an alternative proposal, the 'Pleven Plan'. This plan, named after the French Foreign Minister René Pleven, would have allowed West Germany a limited number of troops, but only as part of a western European army, within a new European Defence Community (EDC). In December 1950, the USA, Britain and France approved, in principle, a German contribution to the defence of the West, although the British were still unhappy with the French scheme, and in May 1952, a General Treaty was signed in Bonn followed by another to set up an EDC in Paris.

Fig. 8 *Truman reassuring the USA's European allies of continued support, December 1947*

The General Treaty abolished the statute of occupation and recognised the full sovereignty of the Federal Republic, although a pledge to work for the future reunification of the whole of Germany was also included. All restrictions on the German economy and on German scientific research were lifted and Germany was allowed to set up a Bundeswehr to give a guarantee of security. However, the EDC arrangements collapsed when the French National Assembly refused to ratify the Treaty in August 1954. Adenauer, desperate to keep German involvement alive, voluntarily agreed to renounce nuclear weapons and to keep the West German army limited in size and under strict civilian control. As a result, the British plan, to admit Germany and Italy to the Brussels Pact and rename the European Defence Organisation as the Western European Union, was adopted.

The way was thus opened for West German rearmament. Since a proposed Four Power summit to discuss German reunification had been delayed after the power struggles following Stalin's death in 1953 and the GDR riots of the same year, the French reluctantly gave in to American pressure to accept West German membership of NATO. In May 1955, West Germany was admitted as a member. In retaliation, the USSR recognised the sovereignty of the GDR and created the Warsaw Pact with the GDR as a member.

The Korean War, 1950–3

By the late 1940s, events beyond Europe were taking on a significance of their own. In 1949 the Chinese communists were finally successful in their civil war with the non-communist nationalists. The Soviet Union was initially ambivalent about how close a relationship it should form with the Chinese. In December 1949 China's communist leader Mao Zedong travelled to Moscow to meet with Stalin. Upon his arrival

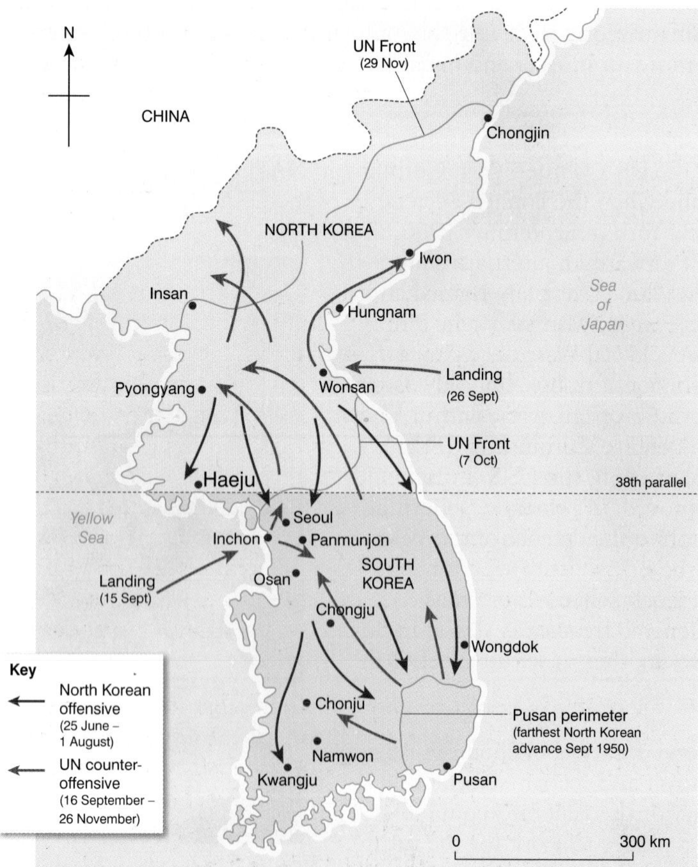

Fig. 9 *Korean War, 1950*

Mao was greeted not by Stalin but by Molotov. Despite Stalin's coldness, Mao left with most of what he wanted including loans, transfers of technology and military assistance. For Stalin's part, he did not view the Sino (Chinese)–Soviet alliance as a partnership of equals. China was to be the junior partner while the Soviet Union gained further political and military influence in the Far East. This reality did not go unnoticed by the USA. Significantly, Soviet support for China had heightened the certainty of a long-term Cold War relationship between China and the USA. The possibility of the USA developing a form of rapprochement with China had been greatly reduced by China's alliance with the Soviet Union.

In June 1950, communist North Korean forces invaded non-communist South Korea. Many western observers assumed that Stalin had encouraged the North Korean leader, Kim Il-sung, to carry out the attack. Modern research suggests that the idea to invade the South was Kim's although he desperately wanted Soviet endorsement and Stalin provided this. The logic underpinning this conclusion was that Stalin had to be seen to be proactive in promoting communism in the Far East or undermine his credibility in the face of Chinese influence. The Truman administration reacted almost immediately. The UN Security Council called upon member states to render every assistance to the UN in ensuring that the North Korean aggression ended. North Korea's invasion militarised containment and it indicated to the USA that the Pacific and parts of the Far East were now vulnerable to communist expansionism. Truman was keen to present US military interventionism, albeit under the auspices of the UN, as the USA using its resources to ensure that international relations were not based on a return to the rule of force. "The United States will continue to uphold the rule of law", announced Truman in a speech delivered on 27 June 1950. The USA was quickly presenting itself as a global policeman with communism as the global villain. Alternatively, as in Europe, the Far East and the Pacific region represented lucrative economic possibilities for America and any expansion of communism there would have undermined that. Truman's decision effectively institutionalised containment and made it the keystone of American foreign policy.

Activity

Thinking point

It is June 1950. You are given the task of justifying the USA's intervention in Korea. What points would you make to offer a rationale for US intervention?

Despite the fluctuations in the military outcomes, American forces under General MacArthur pushed north and reached the Yalu River by late October 1950. The initial UN resolution had called for a return to the status quo with the frontier based on the 38th parallel restored. In November the Chinese entered the war as an ally of North Korea. Their motives focused on, in the first instance, protecting Chinese security from a possible US invasion. By April 1951 American forces were back at the 38th parallel, having been pushed into South Korea earlier by the Chinese. MacArthur wanted to advance north and take the war into China itself. Truman, wishing to avoid an all-out war with China, ordered his recall to the USA. Any invasion of China would have shifted the balance of American foreign policy away from that of containment.

Negotiations to bring the conflict to an end began relatively early but it was Stalin's death in 1953 that accelerated events. He was followed by the more accommodating Malenkov. Truman's administration also came to an end in 1952 and a new President, Dwight D. Eisenhower, took control. In 1953 a cease-fire was finally agreed and the 38th parallel was restored as the border between North and South Korea.

Key profile

Dwight D. Eisenhower, 1890–1969

Eisenhower was a long-serving career soldier and served as head of the allied invasion of North Africa during the Second World War. He was Supreme Commander of allied forces during the Normandy landings in 1944 and lead US forces to the final victory over Germany in 1945. Between 1949 and 1950 he was Chairman of the Joint Chiefs of Staff (JCS) and went on to be head of NATO from 1950. In 1952 he resigned from the US Army and entered the Presidential election race, in which he was successful. He continued as US Republican President until 1960, having served two terms in office.

Fig. 10 *US troops capture Chinese soldiers in Korea, 2 March 1951*

The international significance of the Korean War

The war appeared to confirm the Cold War perception of the rise of monolithic communism. The Sino–Soviet alliance was the clear manifestation of the growth and unity of international communism. This was a perception reflected more by US public opinion rather than US administrations. US governments were not entirely convinced of the solidity of this Sino–Soviet alliance and there was the prospect of using China to weaken the rise of communism globally although this approach did not come into fruition for many years.

The war appeared to be a victory for containment. The spread of communism from North Korea had been halted and the USA had not opted to abandon containment by either destroying the communist regime in North Korea or, even more radically, push on into China itself. This reinforced the USA's commitment to containment which in turn necessitated a pronounced presence in Asia. The regional alliance system that had been created in Europe in the form of NATO now made sense in Asia. Ultimately, this had a negative impact on the Soviet Union. The assault of communism in Asia also emphasised the ongoing threat from communist expansion everywhere, especially in Europe. American military power was expanded in Europe and the way was paved for West Germany's rearmament.

A further complication for the Soviet Union came with China's growing confidence on the international scene through its central role in the Korean War. China increasingly viewed itself, rather than the Soviet Union, as the arbiter of communist influence in Asia. The relationship between China and the Soviet Union had been undermined because of the Korean War and this would have profound significance as China strengthened its status as a global superpower during the following two decades.

By 1953, as the Korean War ended, the principle features of the Cold War were in place and these were to determine the nature of international relations for almost 20 years. The Cold War had been globalised and containment had been militarised. An international alliance system had been established as the basis for this bipolar division. The crisis was further heightened by the technological context. Nuclear technology was advancing rapidly and both sides of the divide became engaged in a nuclear arms race.

The USA's 'special relationship' with Britain

Europe was vulnerable after the Second World War. A power vacuum existed and could not be quickly filled given the economic weakness of European states. To a large extent the USA did not want Europe to develop as a regional force that was independent of US influence. The USA's route into Europe came through its 'special relationship' with Britain. Britain represented a politically stable state amid other less stable mainland European states. The ties between Britain and the USA had been forged during the Second World War.

Britain was very much the driving force in preserving this relationship. For Britain there was a need to preserve its international status. This could only be achieved with the USA's support. Britain needed the USA to contribute to its security but it did not want this relationship to force Britain into the role of a second-rate power dependent upon the USA. The relationship became one of mutual support. The USA needed Britain and its role and influence in Europe just as much as Britain needed the USA to reinforce its own international status. In a Cold War environment each element of the bipolar framework had to have allies. The USSR established its allies through the creation of satellite states in eastern Europe. The USA had to form a relationship with the Western powers and Britain was the most receptive to these advances. Other western European states were faced with left-wing socialist political groups who appeared less reliable than the British Labour movement. Consensus politics were in place in Britain and this meant that Britain was a state that the USA needed and could do business with.

The USA as an economic and military power

Primary indicators of superpower status were the economic and military strengths of a nation. Nowhere was this more so than in terms of the USA. Alan Brinkley summed up the USA's economic condition when he noted:

> Alone among the major nations, the United States faced the future in 1945 with an intact and thriving industrial economy poised to sustain a long period of prosperity and growth. Gross National Product in the war years rose from $91 billion to $166 billion; 15 million new jobs were created, and the most enduring problem of the Depression – massive unemployment – came to an end; industrial production doubled; personal incomes rose by as much as 200 per cent.

5

The USA's capacity to function as a global power was made possible by its economic wealth. The Second World War had not only devastated the economies of the major European states, it also served to catapult America's economy to an almost unchallengeable level. The USA not only controlled the largest merchant fleet and owned two thirds of the world's gold stocks, but also had half the world's manufacturing capacity.

Key terms

Federal: relating to a whole nation rather than just the separate states or regions of that nation. For example, individual American states have their own governments, but these all come under the authority of the US federal government, headed by the US President.

The capacity of the government to inject money into the US economy was strengthened by the massive increase in tax revenue brought about by the increase in employment during wartime. By the end of the war **federal** revenue had reached the staggering level of $51 billion annually. In 1950 the national debt stood at $257 billion. This spending power enabled the USA to underwrite its international power and ensure the nation's economy remained strong. One of the primary objectives of the USA after the war was to ensure that there would be no return to the economic depression of the 1930s. The post-war world gave the USA an ideal opportunity to work towards this goal. The economic prosperity the war had brought to the USA could be preserved by ensuring that the USA expanded its global economic influence. The USA needed to establish lasting spheres of economic influence. The Marshall Aid programme was the first step in achieving this objective. It followed from this that the USA had a vested economic interest in promoting a Cold War relationship with the East. By establishing a situation where western states became dependent upon the USA for their protection, they became locked into an economic relationship. This benefited the USA as much as it offered any benefits to non-communist western states. This whole process reinforced the strength of the USA's economic power and therefore strengthened its global power.

Summary questions

1. How far did the North Korean invasion of South Korea increase the globalisation of the Cold War?
2. 'A Cold War was necessary if the USA was to become a global superpower.' How valid is this assessment of the motives which underpinned America's foreign policy between 1945 and 1953?

Economic power was central to the exercise of the USA's military power. The USA had the means to deploy large military forces on a global scale. This reality was a primary factor in driving Europe's quest for protection from the communist threat in the east. The fundamental military power that the USA possessed was its nuclear capability. Until 1949 the USA commanded a technology that no other state could compete with. In 1949 the Head of the Policy Planning Staff defined a defence policy which was labelled NSC-68. This proposed a spending programme that was to reach $45 billion annually. This underlined the USA's approach to the Cold War. There was to be no return to isolationism or any form of diplomatic consensus such as appeasement. The USA was to adopt a militaristic stance and use its military power to support containment. US militarism became the foundation of the confrontational nature of the Cold War.

3 The Cold War Stalemate

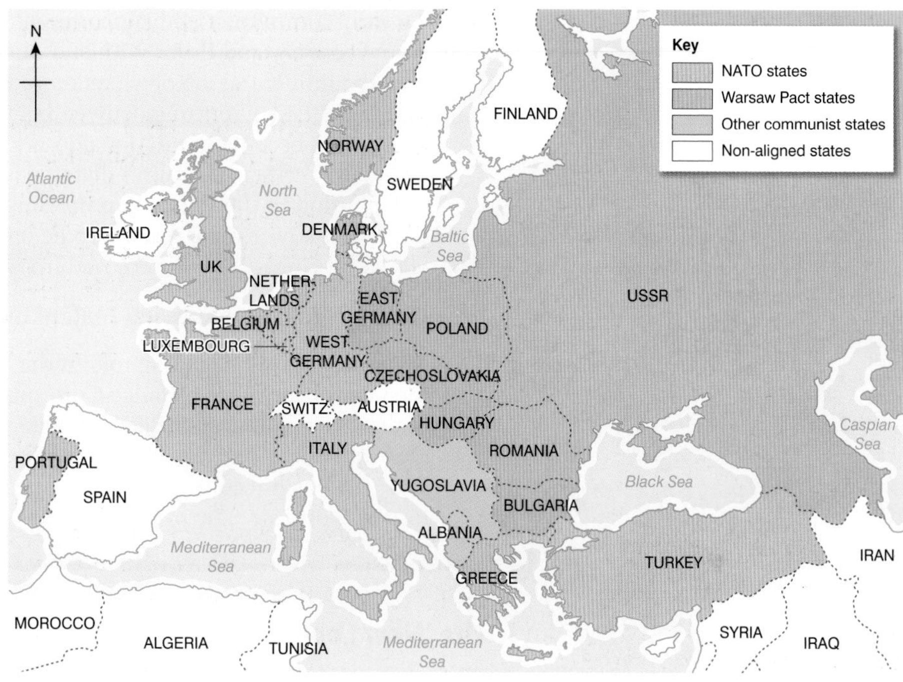

Fig. 1 *Map of Europe and its alliances, 1949*

In this chapter you will learn about:

- the concept of peaceful coexistence from 1953 to the 1960s
- the place of Germany in the Cold War
- the nuclear arms race in the years 1949 to 1962.

In 1960, the US Presidential election saw the candidates make passionate statements on the threat of Soviet communism. John F. Kennedy, who would go on to win the election, put his case in the boldest terms, "The enemy is the communist system itself – unceasing in its drive for world domination. This is a struggle for supremacy between two conflicting ideologies: freedom under God versus ruthless, godless tyranny." The Cold War was hotting up.

The role of Khrushchev and peaceful coexistence, 1953–60

1953 appeared to be a year that opened a new era of opportunity for progress towards redefining the nature of international relations and even the possibility of bringing the prevailing Cold War relationship to a close. Truman, the architect of containment, had ended his presidency. His successor, Dwight D. Eisenhower, had an opportunity to forge a new relationship with the Soviet Union and the communist East. This opportunity became more pronounced when, on 5 March 1953, Stalin died, and was replaced by Nikita Khrushchev who was soon to denounce the worst excesses of the Stalinist regime. Soon after Stalin's death, the chairman of the Council of Ministers, Malenkov, called for peaceful coexistence abroad, stating, "we stand as we have always stood, for the peaceful coexistence of the two systems." He went on to suggest to the USA that "there is no dispute or outstanding issue which cannot be settled peacefully." Also in July 1953 the war in Korea was finally brought to an end, thus removing a major source of international tension.

Key profiles

Nikita Sergeyevich Khrushchev, 1894–1971

An early communist and supporter of Stalin, Khrushchev became Party Secretary and Prime Minister of Ukraine in 1944. In 1949 he held the influential job of Secretary of the Central Committee. By June 1957 he had outmanoeuvred his rivals Beria, Malenkov and Molotov to become the national leader. His 1956 speech, in which he publicly criticised Stalin's dictatorship, was seen as a major contribution to the Hungarian uprising and he almost took the world to the brink of nuclear war when he ordered nuclear missiles to be placed on Cuba. He was removed from power in October 1964.

Georgy Maksimilianovich Malenkov, 1902–88

Malenkov played a leading role in the USSR's war effort as a member of the State Defence Committee. On Stalin's death Malenkov became the Prime Minister. He actively promoted the idea of peaceful coexistence and easing of relations with the West. In 1955 he was forced to resign as Prime Minister and he went into a form of political exile in Kazakhstan.

The 'New Look'

A key figure in Eisenhower's administration was his Secretary of State, John Foster Dulles.

Key profile

John Foster Dulles, 1888–1959

Dulles was a member of the US delegation at the Treaty of Versailles in 1919 and he helped to draft the UN Charter towards the end of World War II. Between 1953 and 1959 he was Eisenhower's Secretary of State. He was instrumental in developing regional alliances in order to prevent the further spread of communist influence. These included the South East Asia Treaty Organisation (SEATO) and the Central Treaty Organisation (CENTO).

Cross-reference

For more on the policies of nuclear retaliation, see page 51.

Dulles loathed communism and criticised Truman for a half-hearted response to communist expansionism. He advocated "the liberation of these captive peoples" of eastern Europe. He argued in favour of a forceful American policy which would 'rollback' Russian occupation and dismantle the Iron Curtain. Dulles also introduced the concept of 'massive retaliation' as an ultimate nuclear deterrent strategy and security guarantee for the USA. This collective policy direction became known as the 'New Look'. In essence, it was a commitment to the idea that containment would not allow nations to restore democracy if they were controlled by pro-Soviet communist regimes. Nor would it provide a watertight security system for the USA in the face of an ever accelerating nuclear arms race between the USA and the USSR. American foreign policy appeared to be moving to a more proactive, and even aggressive, position. However, Eisenhower was keen to develop more cordial relations with the Soviet Union and although he endorsed the 'New Look' the reality was that containment, and its relatively non-aggressive position, remained the cornerstone of American foreign policy. When the administration was faced with actually rolling back the Russians in Hungary in 1956 they did nothing other than express loud protests. A similar response had followed in June 1953, when a strike by East Berlin construction workers turned into an uprising across East Germany, which was suppressed by Soviet armed forces. Rollback was nothing more than a paper tiger and did little to impede improved East–West relations. There was scope for change in US–Soviet relations and ultimately the potential lay in the characters of the new leadership in both the USA and the Soviet Union.

Exploring the detail

Hungary, 1956

Hungary had been under Soviet-influenced communist control since the end of the Second World War. Many urban industrial workers felt that the Stalinist model of communism had failed to respond to their economic needs and nationalists wanted a political system that responded to the specific needs of Hungary and its people. In October 1956 mass disturbances quickly developed into a popular revolt. The leaders demanded that Hungary withdraw from the Warsaw Pact. The USSR used military force to restore 'normality'. Thousands of Hungarians were killed and many more forced into exile. No aid was given during the revolution from any Western powers.

Fig. 2 *John Foster Dulles meeting Churchill, 4 February 1953*

Although committed to the 'New Look' initiative, Eisenhower was level-headed and reasonable. In practical terms the 'New Look' did not move the USA dramatically away from containment. As such there was the scope to adopt a moderate and non-confrontational relationship with the Soviet Union. Eisenhower was keen to reduce the risk of nuclear war and this stimulated his willingness to consider a better relationship with the USSR. He was conscious of the fact that the USSR, although lagging behind in terms of the scale of its nuclear capability, was beginning to catch up with the USA. He was also aware of the implications of the creation of the Warsaw Pact in 1955 in terms of its potential to deepen Cold War relations between East and West.

Fig. 3 *A captured Russian tank in Hungary, 1956*

Peaceful coexistence

Khrushchev gradually established himself as the sole leader of the Soviet Union and in 1956, in a speech delivered at the 20th Congress of the Soviet Communist Party, he was able to feel confident enough to denounce Stalinism and emphasise that Soviet foreign policy should move from confrontation to coexistence.

Khrushchev had very clear foreign policy imperatives:

- The Soviet Union must remain as the unchallenged leaders of the socialist community, both within eastern Europe and in the face of growing competition from China and its leader Mao Zedong.
- A firm grip must be maintained over the eastern bloc satellite states.
- Germany must be prevented from rearming and becoming a future threat to the Soviet Union.
- The USSR must continue to expand its nuclear capability and thereby stay firmly implanted in the nuclear arms race between East and West.
- Spending on military security had to be reduced as did Soviet conventional forces in eastern Europe.
- International tension had to be defused and care had to be taken not to unnecessarily provoke the USA.

This final point underpins the aims of the Soviet Union under Khrushchev. Post-Stalinist Soviet leadership proposed to meet, and counter, the growing power of the USA through a policy of peaceful coexistence. This was a means to an end. It was not a move to end the Cold War but it was a strategy to consolidate Soviet international power and security by existing in a less volatile environment. Khrushchev also rationalised this policy by saying in 1959, "In our day there are only two ways, peaceful coexistence or the most destructive war in our history. There is no third way." In November 1960, the World Communist Declaration announced:

> Peaceful coexistence of countries with different social systems does not mean conciliation of the socialist and bourgeois ideologies. On the contrary, it means intensification of the struggle of the working class for the triumph of socialist ideas. Ideological and political disputes between states must not be settled through war.

1

Activity

Talking point

Explain why the Soviet Union pursued a policy of peaceful coexistence. How likely was it to succeed?

This mood of cooperation was seen initially over the future of Austria.

The Austrian State Treaty, 1955

Soviet policy towards Austria had been closely linked to the policy towards Germany. Immediately after the end of the war the USSR had favoured a unified German state that was neutralised and could offer no threat to the Soviet Union. Like Germany, Austria had been divided into occupation zones and the USSR had focused on receiving economic aid from Austria as they had from the eastern zone of Germany. To some extent, Austria had the potential to become as great an issue dividing East and West as Germany had been until 1949. Austrian leaders in the western zones promoted the idea that Austria could easily be absorbed into the Soviet sphere of influence in the way that Czechoslovakia had been a few years earlier. Some observers even referred to Austria as 'Europe's Korea'.

By 1955 the USSR began to show serious intentions of embarking on negotiations over the future of Austria. By May 1955, the four occupying powers had reached agreement in the form of the Austrian State Treaty. It led to the withdrawal of all occupying powers and the declaration that Austria would be a neutral state. This was in line with the USSR's willingness to accept both Finland and Yugoslavia as neutral states and therefore not liable to be subjected to joining the Soviet sphere of influence.

This agreement not only showed a serious intent towards mutual cooperation between the Cold War powers, it also removed a major source of potential conflict. Agreement over Austria eased the path towards further cooperation between East and West. Following this agreement the Western powers removed their occupation forces from West Germany. This cooperation consolidated the East–West position and was very much the essence of peaceful coexistence. The next significant step in the process was taken with the decision to resume **summit** diplomacy.

The Geneva Summit, 1955

Background

Khrushchev accepted the need for flexibility in Soviet policy. Although the Soviet Union was still closely involved in a nuclear arms race there was a real incentive for Khrushchev to slow the race down. Russia needed extensive **conventional forces** to ensure compliance among the eastern bloc states and to contribute to their security. Khrushchev also needed to promote internal economic development in the Soviet Union. A less confrontational relationship with the West would significantly contribute to achieving these objectives and protect the Soviet Union's national security and global superpower status at the same time. Khrushchev was a pragmatist of the first order. A further incentive which brought Khrushchev to the summit was the fact that in May 1955 the Federal Republic of Germany was admitted into NATO and rearmament began. In order to reassure the French that any resurgence of Germany militarism would be addressed, the USA agreed to place a large and permanent force of troops in Europe. This caused concern for Khrushchev and increased the urgency of organising a summit.

The outcomes

On the two major issues which the Geneva Summit discussed – nuclear disarmament and the future of Germany – no satisfactory outcome was reached.

The 'Open Skies' proposal

Eisenhower presented this proposal as part of an attempt to end the deadlock over the issue of the superpowers inspecting each other's nuclear arsenals and thereby taking a step closer to disarmament. Eisenhower called for each side to provide details of military installations and allow aerial reconnaissance. Eisenhower even suggested that "each plane would be authorised to include in its crew one or more representatives of the nation under inspection." Khrushchev, however, rejected the proposal, because he was aware of the existence of the American U-2 spy plane and the fact that the Soviets had nothing comparable.

The future of Germany

Eisenhower also proposed a reunified Germany, free elections and Germany's freedom to ensure its own security, which effectively meant it would become part of NATO. Khrushchev, however, would only contemplate reunification if a future Germany was demilitarised and neutral. He also refused to discuss the future of the eastern bloc states. Out of the summit emerged an agreement on the principle of free elections but no procedures were set up to make this progress become reality.

Key terms

Summit: a meeting of the leaders of various governments.

Conventional forces: these are traditional non-nuclear based forces. Such forces would be of the kind that were deployed during the Second World War, for example, and based on ground troops and mechanised and armoured troops along with airforces which were made up of warplanes acting as fighters and bombers.

Fig. 4 *Khrushchev's problem*

Exploring the detail

U-2 spy planes

The U-2 was a jet-powered reconnaissance plane that was capable of flying to altitudes of more than 70,000 feet. No spy satellites were available until the early 1960s so this plane was an invaluable asset to the USA. It was used to photograph Soviet military and industrial activities. It carried three static cameras and its first flight over Soviet territory took place in the summer of 1956.

Activity

Talking point

Was Khrushchev's attitude at the Geneva Summit unreasonable? Explain your views.

Cross-reference

For information on the operational use of the U-2 spy plane in the Cuban Missile Crisis, see Chapter 4.

Activity

Research exercise

Research the challenges to the success of peaceful coexistence after 1955. You could consider the Hungarian uprising of 1956, the creation of regional alliances such as SEATO and problems in the Middle East, e.g. Egypt, 1955–7.

Overall, the summit's value lay not in its practical outcomes but in the fact that it appeared to mark the beginning of a dialogue between the superpowers. It seemed to mark a point of calm in international relations and it suggested that the foundations of peaceful coexistence were firmly in place. In the years that followed the summit a number of crises placed peaceful coexistence under huge strain.

Fig. 5 *The representatives of the USSR, USA, France and Great Britain at the Geneva Summit: Boulganin, Eisenhower, Faure and Eden, September 1955*

Exploring the detail

The status of Germany in 1961

Germany was divided into two sovereign states and had been since 1949. No formal treaty had been arrived at, therefore Germany was still subject to the Four Power control established at Potsdam in July 1945. West Berlin, controlled by the Western powers, was in the communist controlled DDR. Access to West Berlin was what made it a potential target for superpower confrontation and bargaining.

Cross-reference

See page 52 for more on the political implications of the Sputnik mission.

The problems over Berlin and Germany, 1958–61

As in 1945, the position of the two Germanies became a pivotal issue in international relations. By 1958 the future of Germany re-emerged as a test of peaceful coexistence. The Sputnik space missile convinced Khrushchev that the USSR finally dominated the missile race. He needed a further issue to reinforce the USSR's status compared to that of the USA. Since 1955 West Germany had been a fully fledged member of the Western Alliance through joining NATO. Khrushchev feared that the USA may deploy nuclear missiles in West Germany as part of its programme of building up short-range nuclear missiles which could reach the USSR from Western Europe. There was an urgency to minimise Western power in Europe and to gain guarantees from West Germany that it would not accept missiles.

Khrushchev was also mindful of the fact that relations between the Soviet Union and China were turning sour. Moscow had failed to support China in its conflict with the breakaway non-communist Taiwan in 1958. Communist China was attempting to recover islands in the Formosa Straits. As a consequence, the Soviet Union needed to reinforce its credibility as a leader in the communist world. This could be achieved by showing greater support for its allies in Europe. One such ally was the German Democratic Republic (GDR – the official name for East Germany). Its leader, Walter Ulbricht, believed that the GDR had reached a crisis point in its economic future. There was an open boundary between East and West Berlin and this had enabled a haemorrhage of talent to migrate to the more prosperous West. Between 1949 and 1958 about 188,000 trained, skilled or professional people had left East Germany. Any kind of outcome which protected the GDR and caused the USA to back down could only be seen as a propaganda coup.

In November 1958 Khrushchev referred to Berlin as "a smouldering fuse that had been connected to a powder keg. Incidents arising here, if they seem to be of local significance, may, in an atmosphere of heated passions, suspicions and mutual apprehensions, cause a conflagration which will be difficult to extinguish." Khrushchev's tactic was to declare an ultimatum. The West had six months to recognise the existence of the DDR and accept West Berlin as an independent political entity and a free city. If this did not happen then the Soviet Union would surrender its control of its zone to the DDR. This would mean that the East Germans would control all access to West Berlin. Access to West Berlin would be determined by the DDR. In effect, this would force the USA to formally recognise the DDR as an independent state – something that had not yet happened. Up to this point the USA regarded the DDR merely as the Soviet zone in the post-war settlement. Also it would oblige the USA to accept the permanent post-war division of Germany and remove its troops from West Berlin.

The Western powers effectively ignored the Soviet threats and Khrushchev's bully-boy tactics failed. However, in March 1959 Britain's Prime Minister, Harold Macmillan, proposed a summit on Berlin and the issues of European disengagement and disarmament. Khrushchev withdrew his ultimatum and declared, "I believe that the US, Britain and France do have lawful rights for their stay in Berlin."

Khrushchev became the first Soviet leader to visit the USA, when he participated in the Camp David talks with Eisenhower in September 1959. During the discussions, Einsenhower and Khrushchev discussed a number of issues, including disarmament and the situation in Berlin. They also agreed to settle international issues by diplomacy rather than force. In many respects, this was a reaffirmation of Khrushchev's faith in peaceful coexistence. It was likely that the visit caused a deterioration in the Soviet Union's relations with China and reinforced the West's certainty that a communist power bloc had not been created by any alliance between these two communist leaders. The Camp David talks served to calm the German issue and they led directly to the Paris Peace Summit in May 1960.

The Paris Summit, May 1960

Khrushchev was heavily committed to peaceful coexistence. He faced major opposition from both the Chinese and many in the Soviet hierarchy. Not only did Khrushchev want a deal over Berlin, but he also wanted an agreement to prohibit nuclear weapons in the Pacific and a ban on such weapons in Germany. This balancing act was destined to fail when China announced that it would not consider itself bound by any agreement that it had not been involved with. China's nuclear arsenal was very close to completion by 1960.

The summit collapsed with the news that an American U-2 spy plane had been shot down while on a mission over the Soviet Union. The incident gave Khrushchev the opportunity to calm opposition from China.

1961 heralded the arrival of a new President for the USA. John F. Kennedy had been elected as the USA's new Democratic Party President. Kennedy declared in his inauguration speech, "Let every nation know, whether it wishes us good or ill, that we shall pay any price, bear any burden, meet any hardship, support any friend, oppose any foe to assure the survival and the success of liberty."

Exploring the detail

The Formosa Straits Crisis

The 1958 Formosa Straits Crisis originated in mainland China's bombardment of the Formosan islands of Quemoy and Matsu. The United States used military force against China, resulting in clashes between US and Chinese aircraft. A cease-fire was declared on 6 October.

Cross-reference

See Chapter 4 for more details about the post-war US relationship with Cuba.

Activity

Research activity

Choose one of the meetings referred to in this section: the Camp David talks, the Paris Summit or Khrushchev's meeting with Kennedy in June 1961. Find out more about this meeting from the internet and/or books and give a class presentation on the importance of the particular occasion in the context of the Cold War.

Key profile

John F. Kennedy, 1917–63

John F. Kennedy came from an affluent Boston Roman Catholic family which had significant political influence. His father had been US Ambassador to Britain before the Second World War. Kennedy was elected to Congress (1947–53) and then served as a Senator for Massachusetts. He was elected President in 1961, having defeated Eisenhower's Vice President, Richard Nixon. His primary interest was foreign policy and many of his contemporaries came to regard him as a Cold War warrior. His greatest success came with the Cuban Missile Crisis but his political career was prematurely cut short with his assassination in November 1963.

Kennedy's agenda seemed to damn the future of peaceful coexistence. He increased the defence budget and promised more flexible conventional forces. He favoured an expansion of the USA's nuclear arsenal and its Polaris missile submarine force. Khrushchev and Kennedy met for the first time in June 1961 in Vienna. Little of any substance was achieved although Khrushchev came away from the meeting convinced that Kennedy was a young and politically vulnerable leader whom he could easily manipulate. The recent Bay of Pigs debacle – an unsuccessful attempt by the US to aid the overthrown of Fidel Castro's communist government in Cuba – had reinforced this view. The issue that continued to haunt US–Soviet relations was that of the future of Germany.

Kennedy's refusal to compromise on the status of Berlin and accommodate Khrushchev's demand that Berlin should cease to be an 'escape route' for East Germans confirmed a stalemate in East–West relations in Europe. Kennedy told the American people that, "The immediate threat to free men is West Berlin but that isolated outpost is not an isolated problem. The threat is world wide." Berlin was a symbol of Cold War confrontation. It was also a symbol of the global differences between the superpowers. After Vienna, Kennedy asked Congress to increase defence spending, call up army reservists and reactivate ships about to be scrapped. On 25 July Kennedy called for a build-up of NATO forces.

Fig. 6 *The Berlin Wall under construction, August 1961*

The Berlin Wall, August 1961

On 13 August Soviet troops and East German police began to seal off East Berlin from West Berlin. The initial wire fences were eventually replaced with a 30 mile concrete wall with only four recognised crossing points. The Cold War symbolism of the Berlin Wall was immortalised when Kennedy visited West Berlin in June 1963 and famously declared that "all free men, wherever they may live, are citizens of Berlin" and therefore "as a free man I take pride in the words 'Ich bin ein Berliner'." The wall dramatically slowed down the loss of skilled East Germans and soon brought it to a complete halt. Despite attempts by the Soviet Union to present the wall as a necessary block to stop western spies infiltrating East Berlin and consequently East Germany, the wall was a failure for Khrushchev. It was also a propaganda disaster. No one was convinced by the Soviet propaganda. The only rational conclusion that could be reached was that it was designed to keep East German citizens trapped in a communist state. Despite this, the West had taken no action to stop the wall from being erected. This may have encouraged Khrushchev to believe that he could drive a wedge through NATO in the face of this lack of resolve. Although the wall became an abiding symbol of the Cold War, it also eased Cold War tensions over Berlin; a kind of status quo had been established.

The 'bomb' and the nuclear arms race, 1949–62

Table 1 *The nuclear technology race up to the early 1960s*

Weapon	Date of testing or introduction to the arsenal	
	USA	USSR
Atomic bomb	1945	1949
Intercontinental bomber	1948	1955
Jet bomber	1951	1954
Hydrogen bomb	1952	1953
Intercontinental ballistic missile	1958	1957
Submarine-launched ballistic missile	1960	1964

The USA used atomic bombs over Japan in August 1945 and this effectively accelerated Japan's willingness to surrender. America maintained what was a nuclear monopoly until 1949. The primary influence of this monopoly was to stimulate the USSR into developing its own nuclear weapons. In the rapidly developing Cold War environment, which had become founded on a bipolar international relations power base, the USSR reacted in a predicable fashion. In response to any technological breakthrough by one side there was an urgency to create some degree of balance. Nuclear technology suggested that conventional fighting forces were becoming relatively unimportant compared to the destructive power of nuclear weapons. Suddenly, the USSR's mighty ground and air forces were neutralised. If the USA had nuclear weapons then so must the USSR. This was the simple and logical start to the nuclear arms race. The process became one of action and reaction. Each side responded to what the other side did in terms of nuclear developments by equalling it and then advancing the technology further. It was a race to stay on top.

The race began in August 1949 when the USSR carried out the first tests on it own atomic bomb. The USA learned of it the following month. Significantly, Truman and his advisers did not take the view that mutual control of such devastating weaponry would lead to any level of mutual deterrence by the USA and the USSR. This was a crucial step in the development of the arms race. Both sides had identical weapons of mass destruction. Both sides knew the potential scale of the destruction. Truman did not accept that this would deter the

Did you know?

Once construction of the Berlin Wall began, its existence caused many people in East Berlin to plan their 'escape'. Numerous ways were devised to get past the wall. These included tunnelling under it and, more audaciously, attempting to fly over it. There were many temporary barriers set up to distance people from getting too close to the wall. One such was a series of road blocks set as low-level bars across roads. One intrepid group cut the top off a car and deflated the tyres to a point where the car could still move. They then drove under the barriers. For many others in the early days, it was simply a matter of running at the barriers and trying to avoid capture by the guards.

Activity

Group activity

Set up two groups. It is 1 September 1961: one group will act as Soviet representatives, the other will act as US representatives. Each group should draw up their rationale for the building of the Berlin Wall. Each group also needs to explain to the other what that rationale is and what it sees as the likely impact of the construction.

Exploring the detail

NSC-68

The new Cold War environment and the implications of the Truman Doctrine convinced the USA's strategic military planners that a coordinated security system needed to be devised. A single department responsible for running all the different military services was set up under the 1947 National Security Act. This also set up the National Security Council (NSC) which was to advise the President on all defence and security issues. An intelligence gathering agency was established. This was the Central Intelligence Agency – the CIA. These innovations illustrated the importance of foreign policy to the USA and how far the USA had moved away from its pre-war isolationism.

USSR from using the technology against the USA. The 1950 strategic assessment, known as NSC-68, concluded that:

> When the Soviet Union calculates that it has sufficient atomic capability . . . to make a surprise attack on us, nullifying our atomic superiority and creating a military situation decisively in its favour, the Soviet leadership might be tempted to strike quickly and by surprise. The existence of two large atomic capabilities in such a relationship might well act, therefore, not as a deterrent, but rather as an incitement to war.

2

By the time the Truman administration left office in 1952 some important principles had been laid down:

- The USSR would not hesitate to use nuclear weapons if it was to its advantage.
- Such an attack would come by stealth. It would be a surprise attack.
- In a situation where war between them was deemed to be imminent, then the USA was committed to carrying out a pre-emptive strike against the USSR (an attack made to prevent an attack by the enemy).
- This necessitated accurate intelligence gathering upon which any assessment of the need to carry out such a strike would be made.
- The USA must also devise anti-nuclear defence systems. Nuclear strategic planning would be based on an assessment of the danger, a readiness to carry out a first strike attack and the creation of a defence system which would effectively protect the USA's nuclear retaliation capability.

Fig. 7 *US F-102A Delta Dart fighter, another symbol of US military power during the early years of the Cold War*

Emergence of the H-bomb

Between November 1952 and August 1953 the USA and the USSR successfully advanced the destructive capability of nuclear weapons by developing hydrogen bombs. These bombs are also referred to as thermonuclear weapons. The destructive power of the atomic bomb dropped on Hiroshima in 1945 was equivalent to 12,500 tonnes of high explosive. The hydrogen bomb successfully tested by the USA in November 1952 was equivalent to 10.4 million tonnes of high explosive. The era of the megaton nuclear weapon had emerged. The USSR had caught up by August 1953. The memoirs of a leading Soviet nuclear physicist, Andrei Sakharov, who was closely involved with the development of the H-bomb for the USSR, illustrated the attitude of the Soviet Union in late 1953. Sakharov recalled a Soviet official, Malyshev, announcing immediately after the test that, "The chairman of the Council of Ministers, Georgy Malenkov, has just telephoned. He congratulates everyone who has helped build the hydrogen bomb – the scientists, the engineers, the workmen – on their wonderful success. Georgy Malenkov requested me to congratulate and embrace Sakharov in particular for his exceptional contribution to the cause of peace."

This may be viewed purely as a piece of political rhetoric. However, in the newly emerging post-Stalinist era the notion of deterrence had become central to Soviet thinking on nuclear technology. The Stalinist perception that war between the capitalist West and the communist East was inevitable was rapidly fading. After Stalin's death nuclear weapons were seen by the USSR as the key to preventing future war. Malyshev's reference to 'peace' was consistent with the revised Soviet perspective. The prevention of war was all important. However, the USSR had not naïvely reached the conclusion that possessing nuclear weapons would protect them from American nuclear aggression. The USSR needed to maintain a balance of nuclear power with the USA and the West in order to ensure that it was in a position to fight a nuclear war should the USA use, or threaten to use, nuclear weapons against them. With this position in mind, it was inevitable that the USSR would continue to be an active participant in the nuclear arms race.

The USA and 'massive retaliation'

During the Eisenhower administration a shift in emphasis on nuclear policy took place. Truman's policy had been uncertain. It lacked specific detail in exactly what a pre-emptive nuclear strike would involve. What scale would it assume? The concept of massive retaliation was established as the basis of American nuclear policy. The policy was first formulated through National Security Council document NSC-162/2 produced in 1953. The report recognised that the death of Stalin in 1953, and the emergence of new Soviet leaders, including Khrushchev, had not diminished the determination or the capacity of the Soviet Union to conduct a nuclear attack against the USA. American intelligence suggested that Soviet nuclear capacity was actually growing. The report concluded that the United States must develop 'a strong military posture, with emphasis on the capability of inflicting massive retaliatory damage by offensive striking power.' In part, this approach was adopted because US policy makers wished to keep the economic costs of defence at a level which would not weaken the US economy or undermine US prosperity. The threat of massive retaliation was a clear deterrent strategy adopted by the USA. It was designed to convince the Soviet Union that any threat of a nuclear kind they made would be met with an extreme nuclear response.

Eisenhower's administration had committed itself to maintaining the Truman Doctrine but, as John Foster Dulles commented in 1954:

> It is not sound economics, or good foreign policy, to support permanently other countries; for in the long run that creates as much ill will as good will. Also, it is not sound to become permanently committed to military expenditures so vast that they lead to 'practical bankruptcy'.

3

Activity

Talking point

How far did US policy contribute to the escalation of the nuclear arms race?

In essence, the aim of the massive retaliation policy was to preserve US global security at a cost-effective price, not to undermine the relationship with America's allies (and therefore the USA's essential global superpower links) by abandoning the commitment to containment and to ensure the long-term security of the USA against a Soviet nuclear attack. American policy was founded, therefore, on a reliance on deterrence. The Soviet Union had to understand that a nuclear attack would cause them more damage than it would cause the USA, therefore it was not worth undertaking. Dulles summed the policy up quite simply when he said, "We want, for ourselves, and the other free nations, a maximum deterrent at a bearable cost." This policy was a significant move away from Truman's position and it necessitated an expansion of the USA's nuclear arsenal and technological improvements in the delivery systems for nuclear weapons. It represented a stark warning that conventional forces were significantly less important as a means of conducting warfare than they had formerly been. A conventional attack could, and would, be met with massive nuclear retaliation.

The USSR and the USA were comparable in nuclear bomb technology by 1955 but not in terms of their delivery systems. The US had access to military bases in Europe and Japan and were easily able to target Soviet cities. In addition to this advantage they increased spending on intercontinental range jet bomber development. By 1955 the B-52 Stratofortress had been deployed. The USSR responded in 1956 with the Tu-20 Bear.

Khrushchev placed his faith in missile development. This was done partly to gain a position of strength in the problem over Germany and Berlin. It was also seen as a means of projecting an image of Soviet power in the minds of non-aligned developing countries in an era of increasing decolonisation. By May 1957 the Soviet Union had developed a long-range nuclear missile system with its development of what became known as Intercontinental Ballistic Missiles (ICBM). These could travel about 3,000 miles in approximately 30 minutes. They would leave the earth's atmosphere and split into multiple nuclear warheads. The technology (based on delivering nuclear weapons by manned aircraft) had been surpassed by this accelerated long-range missile delivery technology.

The Sputnik, 1957

In October 1957 the Soviet Union launched the first satellite to orbit the earth successfully. The USA perceived this move as clear evidence that the USSR was superior in the long-range missile field. There was no known defence against a nuclear missile attack from space. Eisenhower's Republican administration came under increasing pressure from Democratic Senators who accused it of allowing the Soviet Union to gain the lead in nuclear technology in order to save money. The massive retaliation programme was under immense pressure.

The Democrats' position was summed up by Senator Stuart Symington when he commented:

> The recently announced launching of an earth satellite by the Soviet Union is but more proof of the growing Communist superiority in the all-important missile field. If this now known superiority over the United States develops into supremacy, the position of the free world will be critical.

The USA had to catch up in terms of its missile technology. Even shortly before the launch of Sputnik in 1957 an influential NSC study was undertaken. This was known as the Gaither Report. The report anticipated a huge expansion in Soviet nuclear capability but its findings were based on assumptions of Soviet strength rather than on any concrete evidence of such strength. Gaither concluded that the Soviet economy was growing faster than that of the USA and that expenditure on nuclear technology would double that of the USA within a decade. He suggested that the Soviets had the capacity for 1500 nuclear weapons and that they had developed an arsenal of short- and medium-range ballistic missiles, sophisticated early warning systems which could readily intercept US missiles and, most significantly, the Soviets "probably surpassed us in ICBM development." Gaither was not far from the truth in his assessment of this final point.

Gaither recommended a rapid increase in ICBM expansion and all other medium- and short-range missile development. He also suggested developing interception technology through an Anti-Ballistic Missile (ABM) programme. In addition to this, the report also called for a huge civil defence programme based on constructing nuclear fallout shelters for US citizens. The Sputnik launch merely confirmed Gaither's worst fears of a Soviet lead in the nuclear arms race. Eisenhower was restrained in the commitment he showed to the report. Some historians even suggest that he rejected it. The shelter proposal was rejected but there was some movement on the rest, albeit on a limited scale. One of the contributors to the report later noted that:

> The high priority recommendations of the report were carried out ... In the course of the next few years we perfected our early warning capabilities and put a substantial part of our Strategic Air Command bomber force on fifteen minute alert, deployed our first Atlas ICBM squadron, successfully flight tested the Titan ICBM, accelerated the Minuteman ICBM development programme, and placed two nuclear weapon launch Polaris submarines at sea.

The position by 1962

The reality of the nuclear balance between the USA and the USSR was not one of Soviet superiority. The SS-6 rocket used to launch Sputnik in 1957 was inadequate as a nuclear missile delivery system. More importantly there was a stark gap between Soviet nuclear capability and that of the USA. America had been aware of the Soviet Union's continuous attempts to catch up in the arms race but was convinced that this would become a reality and that the USSR's nuclear capability could eventually surpass that of the USA. US estimates suggested a

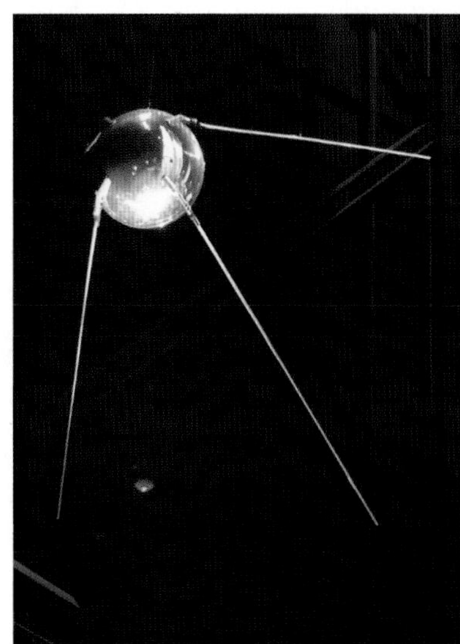

Fig. 8 *Sputnik1, October 1957*

Soviet ICBM deployment of 500 in early 1961 and 1,000 by 1962. The USA had only 70 in 1962. In fact, the USSR had only 50 ICBMs by 1961 of which only four were ready and deployed. Khrushchev was fully aware of the disparity despite the years of Soviet propaganda which reinforced the myth of Soviet nuclear superiority.

Under Kennedy the USA recognised that even though the Soviets trailed in the arms race they still had the capacity to survive a first strike and reply to it. Despite this, the nuclear arms race was a contributor and a consequence of the Cold War. The Cold War by the early 1960s was firmly founded on mutual suspicion. The USA still held the view that the Soviet Union must be judged on its potential to act aggressively rather than solely on its ability to do so. The Soviet position by the early 1960s was founded on the idea of preventing war but at the same time being ready to engage in one effectively. Essentially this was a defensive position rather than an aggressive one but it necessitated ensuring that the USSR had sufficient capacity to defend itself. These positions were to have great significance in the Cuban Missile Crisis, which was looming on the horizon by the start of 1962.

Learning outcomes

Through your study of this section you should now understand why the wartime alliance between the communist east and the capitalist west collapsed. You should have developed a knowledge of the policies and actions that each of the superpowers and their allies undertook in the years immediately following the war, and be able to evaluate the relative importance of these as contributory factors in the development of the breakdown in relations.

You should also be able to consider other factors in the collapse of relations, such as the significance of ideological differences and the existence of the atomic bomb. You should be aware of political developments in the 1950s and early 1960s thus enabling you to understand why international relations remained tense.

'Peaceful coexistence failed by 1961 because neither the East nor the West was fully committed to it.' How valid is this assessment?

This is a fairly open-ended question which enables you to examine not only the levels of commitment but also the motives which existed on each side of the early Cold War. You may argue that the Soviet Union had no real direct interest in peaceful coexistence or it would not have contributed so aggressively to the nuclear arms race. Equally, you might argue that Khrushchev was a very different man from Stalin and he was interested in easing the Cold War. The key issue in terms of technique is to ensure that you define an argument at the start and sustain it throughout the answer. The best place to make the argument clear is in the introduction.

2 From Cold War to Détente, 1962–81

4 The Cuban Missile Crisis

In this chapter you will learn about:

- the background to the crisis from 1958
- the reasons why the Soviet Union decided to place nuclear missiles on Cuba
- the significance of the Soviet action and how the crisis was brought to a peaceful conclusion
- the impact of the crisis.

Fig. 1 *Castro and Khrushchev at the UN General Assembly, 21 September 1960*

Key terms

Protectorate: a state that is placed under the military or diplomatic protection of another state. The protectorate is technically sovereign and independent, but in reality its status can range from being protected by a powerful friend through to being a virtual colony.

In October 1962, the world came the closest it has ever been to a nuclear war. The nuclear forces of the United States and the Soviet Union were on full alert, ready to launch devastating strikes against each other's major cities. Civilians on both sides of the 'Iron Curtain' read the news in genuine fear. Politicians scrambled to stop the situation spiralling out of control. The cause of this tension lay on the island of Cuba, which lay only 90 miles from the coast of the United States.

Key dates

1959 Batista is overthrown and replaced by a Castro-led regime

1960 Period of deteriorating Cuban–US relations

1961 April: US supported Bay of Pigs invasion by anti-Castro rebels
November: Kennedy authorised Operation Mongoose

1962 March: USA launched military manoeuvres in Caribbean and Operation Quick Kick
May: Khrushchev decides to send nuclear missiles to Cuba
August: US intelligence observes 'activity' on Cuba
September: SAM sites discovered by USA on Cuba
14 October: American U-2 spy planes discover Soviet missile sites on Cuba
16 October: ExComm has its first meeting
22 October: Kennedy announces the 'quarantine' of Cuba
25 October: Soviet ships begin to withdraw en route to Cuba
27 October: US U-2 spy plane shot down over Cuba
29 October: Khrushchev decides to withdraw missiles
November: Withdrawal is completed and the immediate crisis ends

1963 August: The Partial Test Ban Treaty

The origins of the crisis

Historical background, pre-1959

The Caribbean was regarded by the USA as its own 'back yard'. As such, America was determined to maintain stability there in order to protect its own national interests. This American policy directly affected the island of Cuba at the end of the 19th century. In 1898 the USA went to war against Cuba's colonial ruler, Spain, in order to bring an end to the instability developing due to Spanish misrule in Cuba. US forces occupied Cuba until 1902 but until the events of 1959 Cuba was, in effect, little more than an American **protectorate**. The Cuban constitution gave the USA rights of intervention and required Cuba to provide land for naval bases – hence the US base at Guantanamo Bay today. The USA had a huge influence in the affairs of this apparently independent state but presented its relationship with Cuba as a benign and benevolent one.

The historian Samuel Flagg Bemis wrote in 1943:

> If ever there was an emblem of pride on the escutcheon of American idealism, it is the attitude in our century of the Continental Republic toward Cuba. The urge to annex was there for a century, but it was bridled, curbed, and halted by a great and historic self-denial, checked by the common people of the United States and their opposition to imperialism.

1

Fig. 2 *Cuba, 1962*

Inevitably this smug and paternalistic (father-like) attitude adopted by America generated opposition among many nationalistically minded Cubans. This had little real impact on the wider sphere of international relations for much of the first half of the 20th century. However, it did have an impact on an individual who was to become a key player in international relations at the height of the Cold War. His name was Fidel Castro (Ruz) and his primary enemy in Cuba was Fulgencio Batista, the pro-American military dictator.

Castro, after a period in exile, returned to Cuba in December 1956 with his brother Raul, Ernesto 'Che' Guevara (an Argentine revolutionary) and 79 supporters.

Key profiles

Fidel Castro (Ruz), 1927–present

Castro was a nationalist revolutionary. From the successful revolution of 1959, he assumed the title of Prime Minister until 1976, when he became President of Cuba. He developed Cuba as a communist state once it was clear that the USA was unwilling to cooperate with him and he needed some form of external support. He is credited with raising the standard of living of many Cubans, but his regime is seen as a dictatorship.

Ernesto 'Che' Guevara, 1928–67

Guevara trained as a medical student, but became committed to social revolution and communism. He joined Castro and formed the '26 July Movement' in Cuba. After Batista's overthrow he held office in the Cuban administration but resigned in 1965 and became a guerrilla leader in Bolivia. He wrote a book entitled *Guerrilla Warfare*. A committed communist and freedom fighter, he was executed in 1967. He became an icon of 1960s resistance.

Castro and his followers were dubbed *los barbudos* – the bearded ones. After a guerrilla campaign conducted against the Batista regime, Castro's supporters began to swell. On 1 January 1959 Batista's regime collapsed and Castro rode triumphantly into Cuba's capital city, Havana. The immediate question was how would the USA respond to this revolution and what impact would the response have on international relations in general?

Early developments, 1958–60

America had shown little significant support for the Batista regime during Castro's revolution. While the revolution looked like a home grown, nationalist, non-communist uprising with no direct external aid from communist states, the USA was willing to let it run its course. In May 1958 Vice President Richard Nixon had conducted a goodwill visit to a number of Latin American states, which led to a shift in US policy towards the region. Economic stability became a target and the USA supported the creation of a regional banking institution, the Inter-American Development Bank, and regional common markets. Eisenhower also agreed not to offer unconditional American support to dictators. He ordered an embargo on further arms shipments to Batista.

Some of Castro's key supporters, however, such as Osvaldo Dorticos, Anibal Escalante and Blas Roca, were communists. He could not allow these men to become his rivals for power, nor could he let them deliver Cuba into the hands of either China or the Soviet Union. He needed the support of a great power in order to manage the inevitable US response to his plans to reduce US economic and political influence in post-revolutionary Cuba. Castro had to maintain his own authority, Cuba's independence and avoid alienating powerful internal and external allies.

In May 1959 Castro introduced a programme of agrarian reform which led to considerable amounts of American-owned property being seized by the state. These early reforms were more moderate than revolutionary and did not instantly generate a hostile US response. US fears of Cuba becoming a Soviet satellite in the Caribbean and a base from where pro-communist regimes could be managed across Latin America were heightened when the Soviet First Deputy Premier, Anastas Mikoyan, visited Cuba in February 1960 and arranged $100 million dollars in credits with Castro. This inevitably tied Cuba into not only an economic relationship with the Soviet Union, but also a political one. Ironically, it was the Soviet version of the Marshall Plan and it had a similar impact on the USA as the Marshall Plan had had on the Soviet Union in 1947.

Key profile

Anastas Mikoyan, 1895–1978

A close ally of Stalin from early on in the Bolshevik revolution, Mikoyan had a particular skill in terms of commerce and trade. He loved Castro's revolution, saying it reminded him of his youth. He remained in office under Khrushchev and when he was removed, his successor, Brezhnev, allowed him to stay on in government.

Activity

Research activity

Was Castro a communist? Castro himself was quite ambiguous about his beliefs. Find out all you can in answer to this question and share your views with the rest of the class.

The first shipment of crude oil arrived in Cuba in April 1960 and when US-owned oil companies refused to refine it, Castro nationalised them. America immediately imposed economic sanctions on Cuba and reduced their imports of Cuban sugar by 95 per cent. This downward spiral in US–Cuban relations continued when Castro seized $1 billion of US assets on Cuba in October 1960. Castro needed the Soviet Union for both foreign and domestic reasons. He was not simply a victim of American aggression; however, he was proactive in instigating it himself. By 1961, the USA decided that the time had come to remove Castro and his regime from Cuba.

The Bay of Pigs invasion and Operation Mongoose, 1961

Fig. 3 *Cubans celebrate the failed Bay of Pigs invasion, April 1961*

The Bay of Pigs invasion plan had been initiated during the Eisenhower administration and it was President Kennedy who inherited it. Essentially the plan was to enable about 1500 anti-Castro exiles to land on Cuba and carry out a military coup to remove him. Kennedy chose to support this CIA-inspired attack to land these exiles at the Bay of Pigs. It was an unmitigated disaster and a profound humiliation for Kennedy; it also confirmed the Soviet Union's and Castro's fears about the USA's intentions for Cuba. The affair also ensured that Castro's power in Cuba was affirmed and consolidated. He had protected Cuba from an American imperialist assault.

On 30 November 1961 Kennedy authorised Operation Mongoose whose aim was 'to help Cuba overthrow the communist regime.' The plan included the option of using military force but the primary methodology was the use of **covert operations** within Cuba to destabilise the regime and facilitate an anti-Castro revolt from within. Kennedy appointed General Edward Lansdale to head the operation.

Operation Mongoose's prospects for success were slim and this reality was acknowledged as another military invasion plan was developed in parallel with Mongoose. Kennedy's military advisers developed an air strike plan known as OPLAN 312 and a land-based invasion plan known as OPLAN 314. The Soviet Union had been supplying Castro with arms shipments for some time but the USA did not intervene in this because there was no suggestion that such arms could or would threaten the USA. In March 1962 the USA undertook one of the largest military manoeuvres in its history. This was Operation Quick Kick and it happened in the Caribbean. It was a show of US military might and it made Khrushchev's Defence Minister, Rodion Yakovlevich Malinovsky, conclude that in the face of a determined US attack, Cuba would stand for no more than a week. Khrushchev adopted a new stance. He decided to deploy Soviet nuclear missiles on Cuba in 1962.

Key terms

Covert operations: These involve gathering intelligence information, forms of economic sabotage and psychological intimidation through propaganda. These are all acts that take place secretly and are designed to have a collectively damaging impact on the state where they are applied.

The Soviet decision to deploy nuclear missiles: Operation Anadyr

The code name 'Anadyr' was used for the Soviet decision to deploy nuclear missiles in Cuba because it was the name of a river in the north-east of the USSR. Soviet planners wanted to heighten their security by selecting a code that might suggest the operation was connected to action in the Arctic rather than the Caribbean. The Soviets chose to send a huge range of nuclear and military equipment to Cuba; this is shown in the table.

Activity

Talking point

Write a newspaper editorial about the Bay Of Pigs incident for either an American or Cuban newspaper.

Table 1 *Equipment audit planned for deployment*

Strategic nuclear weapons		
	R-12 MRBMs	R-14 IRBMs
Numbers	36	24
Launchers	24	16
Warhead capacity	200 kilotons to 1 megaton	200 kilotons to 1 megaton
Range	1,100–1,300 miles	2,200–2,800 miles
Ground forces		
Conventional ground troops	14,000	
Luna missiles	6	Short-range nuclear missiles (range: 40 miles) with 2-kiloton warheads
Air forces		
Il-28 jet light bombers	42	Range 600 miles with 8–12 kilotons nuclear bomb capacity
MiG-21 fighters	40	
Anti-aircraft missile launchers	72	
Anti-aircraft missiles	144	
FKR–1 cruise missiles	80	Launchers: 16; 5–12-kiloton warheads; range: 125 miles
S-2 'Sopka' missiles	Launchers: 2	Conventional high-explosive warheads; range: 50 miles

The Soviet rationale

Khrushchev's decision to deploy these missiles was to have profound consequences for international relations and it was extremely unlikely that he would have been unable to predict all of them. In trying to anlyse the rationale behind his decision, historians have considered the following motives:

The defence of Cuba

In December 1962, only a few weeks after the crisis had ended, Khrushchev declared:

> Our purpose was only the defence of Cuba. Everybody saw how the American imperialists were sharpening the knives and threatening Cuba with a massed attack . . . We saw a possibility of defending the freedom-loving people of Cuba by stationing missiles there . . . We were confident that this step up would bring the aggressors to their senses and that they, realising that Cuba was not defenceless . . . and American imperialism not omnipotent, would be obliged to change their plans.

2

This is a deceptively obvious reason. Khrushchev restated the objective of protecting Cuba as his primary reason for deploying missiles in his memoirs published in 1971. There was overwhelming evidence of the hostility of the US government towards Cuba and a determination to translate that hostility into direct action. What did Khrushchev have to gain by defending Cuba with nuclear weapons?

Some historians regard the nuclear option as comparable to using a sledge hammer to crack a nut. If defence was Khrushchev's sole, or primary, motive he could have opted for something far less provocative to the USA and infinitely less risky in terms of world peace. They argue that Khrushchev could have used a protective force of conventional Soviet forces configured purely for defence purposes. The USA would have had no legitimate reason to present to the international community to suggest that America's vital national interests were under threat. No one would have been threatened by such a deployment on the Soviet's part. The fact that Khrushchev opted for a nuclear deployment rather than a conventional defence system may suggest that he had some other motive in deploying missiles.

Despite this, there was strong evidence to suggest US military aggression. Paterson (*The Defense-of-Cuba Theme and the Missile Crisis*, 1990) argues that the United States made concerted efforts 'to harass, isolate, and destroy the radical government in Havana' and that in the absence of this approach 'there would not have been a Cuban Missile Crisis'. This view presents the USA as the primary causal factor in the crisis and Soviet actions as being relatively benign and purely defensive. The nuclear option made sense because it was purely a deterrent and never a threat.

Bridging the missile gap

Despite Khrushchev's rhetoric suggesting a Soviet lead in the nuclear arms race the reality was that, by October 1961, the dominant nuclear power in world affairs was the USA and not the Soviet Union. Events such as the launch of the Soviet Sputnik satellite and the first successful manned orbit of the earth in April 1961 appeared to suggest Soviet dominance in rocket technology. Khrushchev had commented that the Soviet Union was producing long-range intercontinental ballistic missiles 'like sausages'.

Cross-reference

For more information about the nuclear arms race and the position by 1962, see Chapter 3.

The reality was that a Soviet lead in the so-called 'missile gap' was inaccurate. The 'missile gap' favoured the USA and Moscow knew this. The Soviets had not only lost the atomic leverage in international relations that they had exploited for years but also this power had now moved into the hands of the USA.

Fig. 4 *The Kennedy–Khrushchev struggle*

Some historians have argued that given this knowledge Khrushchev's only hope of rapidly redressing the Soviet–American missile imbalance was to place nuclear missiles on Cuba. Geo-strategically, Cuba was manna from heaven for Khrushchev who acknowledged that it could take at least a decade for the Soviet Union to establish parity with the USA's long-range missile capability. Historians Munton and Welch *(The Cuban Missile Crisis*, OUP 2007*)* see the missile gap and Cuba's defence as being of equal importance to Khrushchev in his decision to deploy nuclear missiles on Cuba. They comment, "The evidence suggests that Khrushchev cared deeply about both. If we were to judge on the basis of the weight of the evidence and testimony, we would have to conclude that these were the two main motives".

Reducing the missile gap would also have been a supplement to Khrushchev's wider aims for military planning. A more developed strategic status would have contributed to Khrushchev's objective of reducing spending on conventional military forces. In addition to this, the deployment would have enabled Khrushchev to direct more resources into the expansion and modernisation of the Soviet nuclear arsenal and still have resources left to invest in the non-military civilian economy. It had become increasingly clear that the economic developments in eastern Europe that had been promised by the pro-Moscow communist regimes had not materialised and the Soviet Union's hold over these vital satellite states was becoming increasingly fragile.

Despite the apparently logical and convincing nature of the missile gap explanation there was no attempt made by the Soviets to camouflage the missile sites. Equally, there appears to have been little regard for the ability of the USA, using its U-2 spy plane system, to identify the missile installation points. If bridging the missile gap was so important to the Soviets, why did they take such little precaution to ensure the missiles' secrecy?

The need for friendship in view of the Chinese situation

J. L. Gaddis (*The Cold* War, Penguin 2005) rejects the idea that redressing the missile imbalance was Khrushchev's primary motive for the deployment. He writes, "It is now clear that this was not Khrushchev's principal reason for acting as he did. Khrushchev intended his missile deployment chiefly as an effort to spread revolution throughout Latin America." Castro's seizure of Cuba was the first time an apparent Marxist–Leninist revolt had succeeded in establishing control of a state since Mao Zedong's revolution in China in 1949. China was a significant factor in Khrushchev's attitude towards Cuba and its revolution. By 1962 the Sino–Soviet alliance had degenerated into a Sino–Soviet split.

One of Khrushchev's priorities was to address the challenge that China had mounted against the Soviet Union's leadership of international communism.

Key profile

Mao Zedong, 1893–1976

Mao Zedong was the Chinese political leader who succeeded in establishing a communist regime in China in 1949. He was a Marxist and as such wanted communism to spread globally. He found himself at loggerheads with Khrushchev, particularly during the period of peaceful coexistence. He was a firm suppporter of communist revolutionary movements in developing nations.

Khrushchev's redirection of Soviet relations with the West had become based on peaceful coexistence. China exploited this to suggest that it showed that Khrushchev was reluctant to back revolutionary movements, particularly in developing countries. Placing nuclear missiles in a newly revolutionised developing country 90 miles from the American border represented a spectacular move and one which would clearly neutralise Chinese anti-Soviet propaganda. Essentially, the deployment would contribute significantly not only to the protection of Cuba but also to the preservation of communism in the Latin American region and this wider protection would be facilitated by Soviet actions.

There was a further incentive for Khrushchev. In March 1962 Castro purged Anibal Escalante and his pro-Soviet 'micro-faction' because he feared Escalante as a potential rival to his leadership. This could suggest that Soviet influence in Castro's regime was diminishing and there may have been an opening for China's influence to become established. Missile deployment would reaffirm the Soviet Union's commitment to Cuba and tie Castro to a Soviet–Cuba alliance more firmly.

A link to Berlin

Some historians have suggested that Khrushchev saw intervention in Cuba as a way of putting pressure on the powers over Berlin. Khrushchev may have hoped to develop a **linkage** strategy between Cuba and Berlin where, despite considerable efforts between 1958 and 1961, he had failed to remove the Western power. Not only was this Western presence a political embarrassment to Khrushchev; it also had significant implications in terms of the security of the communist bloc in eastern Europe.

Key terms

Linkage: in the diplomatic sense, linkage relates to linking concession in one field for concessions in another.

Cross-reference

For more on the issues relating to Berlin during the early Cold War, see Chapter 3.

The deployment of nuclear missiles to Cuba might divert American attention from Berlin. This could in turn put pressure on the unity of the NATO alliance if other NATO members felt that the USA was placing its own regional interests above those of the Western Alliance. Ultimately, the Cuban issue might present the USA with a hemispheric threat that they viewed as being serious enough to impel them to withdraw from Berlin in return for Soviet concessions in Cuba.

Although this linkage rationale makes some sense there is little tangible evidence to substantiate it. Significantly, Khrushchev never made any direct efforts to seek concessions over Berlin as part of a missile withdrawal deal with the USA. Despite this, the crisis illustrated the way in which a problem in one area could be used to solve a problem in another. This was a very characteristic device in international relations and appears throughout the Cold War era.

Fig. 5 *Kennedy with the Soviet Foreign Minister, Gromyko, and the Soviet Ambassador to the USA, Anatoly Dobrynin*

US missiles in Turkey

The USA's commitment to NATO was amply illustrated when, in May 1962, its programme of missile deployment in Turkey was completed. Jupiter intermediate-range ballistic missiles were placed in Turkey to supplement NATO's defensive nuclear umbrella. Once again there is a linkage factor. Khrushchev's response to this deployment may have been linked to his decision to place missiles on Cuba. The Cuban missiles would have given Khrushchev a bargaining tool to use against US missiles in Turkey.

The development of the crisis

In the early summer of 1962, Castro agreed to Khrushchev's request for the deployment of Soviet nuclear missiles on Cuba. The early historiography of the crisis, limited as it was by a lack of access to Soviet and Cuban sources, presents Kennedy as a strong and resolute leader who forced Khrushchev to back down after his opportunistic challenge to USA's nuclear and global strategic power. Kennedy's brother, Robert, produced the best known example of this approach with what has been referred to as a 'masterpiece of spin', when he wrote *Thirteen Days: A Memoir of the Cuban Missile Crisis* (New York, Norton, 1969). Later literature suggests Kennedy overreacted and that his actions risked a nuclear war erupting. James Nathan presents such an analysis in *The Missile Crisis: His Finest Hour Now* (World Politics, Vol. 27, 1976). A substantial re-examination of the roles of all three major protagonists has been produced by Aleksandr Fursenko and Timothy Naftali, *One Hell of a Gamble: Khrushchev, Castro and Kennedy, 1958–1964* (New York, Norton, 1997).

Kennedy's failure in the initial stages of the unfolding crisis lay in his certainty that Khrushchev would never carry out such a reckless plan as to deploy nuclear missiles so close to the USA. Kennedy failed to assess the reaction choices that both Castro and Khrushchev could have had towards the Bay of Pigs incident, Operation Mongoose, US military 'training' in the Caribbean and the very clear attempts to isolate Cuba economically and diplomatically. He failed to have a range of strategies in place to respond to whatever the possible reactions were. To some extent, Kennedy operated an approach based on crisis management. He dealt with the problem when it arose rather than anticipating it in advance and having a viable strategy in place to address it.

Activity

Group activity

Take one of the possible motives for Khrushchev's decision to deploy nuclear weapons in Cuba and research it in more detail. Produce a critical evaluation of the motive and present your findings to the group.

Follow this up with a discussion or essay agreeing with, or challenging, the view that the benefits outweighed the costs for the Soviet Union.

The apparently chaotic nature of international relations was also evident in Khrushchev's approach. There was no clear evidence to suggest that Khrushchev understood how Kennedy might react to the deployment of nuclear weapons so close to the US mainland. He seemed to have gravely overestimated the attitude of both Kennedy and the international community on the validity of having Soviet missiles so near to the USA. Munton and Welch summarise this well by commenting that, 'He failed to see that by attempting to sneak missiles into Cuba, others would conclude that his intentions were offensive and aggressive, rather than largely defensive, or that they were driven by a sense of need rather than a perception of opportunity'.

Castro's position was slightly different. With Soviet missiles on Cuba the island was safe from attack from the USA. It could be argued that Castro was a reckless and dangerous opportunist who rose to the chance to humiliate the USA by having a major nuclear capability on Cuba. Such an argument would suggest that he used both the Soviet Union and the USA to advance Cuba, through risky gambling.

By mid July the Soviets began shipping men and equipment to Cuba. The *Maria Ulyanov* arrived on 26 July, 1962. The US used photographic detail from U-2 spy planes to gather information about what was arriving in Cuba. By 5 September there had been three flights but the deployment of missiles was not sufficiently advanced to be discovered at this point. Kennedy came under increasing pressure to be proactive. On 11 September he announced, "If at any time the Communist build-up in Cuba were to endanger or interfere with our security in any way" or if Cuba were to "become an offensive military base of significant capacity for the Soviet Union, then the United States would do whatever must be done to protect its own security and that of its allies". The Soviet Union's response came on 21 September when Foreign Minister Andrei Gromyko made a speech to the UN in which he warned that an attack on Cuba would mean war with the Soviet Union.

The Soviet deployment had depended on a major nuclear build-up taking place without the USA realising it had happened. This secrecy ended on 14 October when a U-2 spy plane flight produced unmistakable evidence of an R-12 missile site at San Cristobal.

Fig. 6 *The San Cristobal medium-range ballistic missile site, 1 November 1962*

Kennedy immediately assembled an advisory committee known as ExComm, otherwise formally called the Executive Committee of the National Security Council.

Kennedy and ExComm were faced with a range of constraints in their response to the deployment. They could do nothing which might risk splitting the NATO alliance by appearing to ignore the interests of Europe in favour of a purely American policy. Anything that remotely exposed Europe to a Soviet nuclear response would be unacceptable to both Europe and the USA. Given the increasing detail coming from the U-2 photographs it became clear that any kind of air strike against the installations was unfeasible. As the scope of any potential air strike widened, the likelihood that a military response would be undertaken narrowed. Kennedy opted for a naval blockade that would stem the flow of missiles entering Cuba. There were simply too many missiles to guarantee the destruction of all of them before any Soviet retaliatory action against the USA. Kennedy announced the quarantine to the American people on 22 October. Despite this, only the day before this announcement Kennedy had confided to one of his aides, Arthur Schlesinger, that the crisis must not escalate out of control. He is reported as having commented, "We will have to make a deal in the end. We must stand absolutely firm now. Concessions must come at the end of negotiation, not at the beginning".

The quarantine was not Kennedy's sole response. US bases were put on maximum alert in preparation for a possible military strike against Cuba. Kennedy had not lost sight of the possibility of a Soviet attack against West Berlin. Kennedy's speech to the American people on 22 October represented what became a seminal statement in the Cold War.

The speech (edited)

Neither the United States of America nor the world community of nations can tolerate deliberate deception and offensive threats on the part of any nation. Should these offensive military preparations continue, thus increasing the threat to the hemisphere, further action will be justified. It shall be the policy of this nation to regard any nuclear missile launched from Cuba against any nation in the western hemisphere as an attack by the Soviet Union on the United States, requiring a full retaliatory response upon the Soviet Union. I call upon Chairman Khrushchev to halt and eventually to eliminate this clandestine, reckless and provocative threat to world peace and to stable relations between our two nations. I call upon him further to abandon this course of world domination, and to join in an historic effort to end the perilous arms race and to transform the history of man.

3

The next day the Security Council met and the US Ambassador to the UN, Adlai Stevenson, condemned the Soviet deployment and referred to Cuba as "an accomplice in the communist enterprise of world domination". Astonishingly, neither the Soviet Ambassador to the UN, Valerian Zorin, nor the Ambassador to the USA, Anatoly Dobrynin, had been told of the deployment by Moscow. Khrushchev called the blockade "an act of aggression . . . pushing mankind toward the abyss of a world missile-nuclear war". The blockade did have an impact. By 24 October the first Soviet ships to reach the quarantine either stopped dead in the water or turned around. ExComm member Dean Rusk remarked that

Exploring the detail

ExComm was formally established on 22 October 1962. Along with the President and Vice President, other key players in the group included Secretary of State Dean Rusk, Defence Secretary Robert McNamara, Treasury Secretary Dillon, Attorney General Robert Kennedy and the Chairman of the Joint Chiefs of Staff, General Maxwell Taylor along with other lesser individuals. The group's main role was to consider options and the consequences of such choices. Maxwell Taylor summed up the overall view when he commented, "Our strength anyplace in the world is the credibility of our response. If we don't respond here in Cuba (our) credibility is sacrificed".

Exploring the detail

The Blockade (Quarantine)

A blockade of Cuba would have constituted an act of war so the USA referred to it as a quarantine. Its purpose was to enable Kennedy to buy time and focus on a diplomatic solution to the growing crisis. It also forced the Soviet Union to decide whether it would recognise the quarantine or not. Doing so would weaken Khrushchev's position. Not doing so would force the USA to take action. This was a classic example of brinkmanship.

Activity

Group activity

Divide into groups and each take a day in the crisis beginning with 22 October and ending with 28 October. Each group will need to research and present its detail and observations of the events of their day. Each group might prepare a card of facts and these could be displayed to give an overall chronology.

Cross-reference

Brinkmanship is also referred to and developed in Chapter 3.

"We're eyeball to eyeball and I think the other fellow just blinked". This was a classic observation on the brinkmanship that was so fundamental to the crisis as a whole.

The end in sight

Despite the skilful efforts made to avoid a direct military confrontation, neither Kennedy nor Khrushchev had presented any significant offer as a basis for a diplomatic settlement. Brinkmanship was a high-risk strategy in international relations and could only be successful if both sides recognised that any form of military confrontation in a nuclear age would clearly be the least desirable approach. Khrushchev certainly began to rethink his position. If, as he often declared, his aim had been to protect Castro's regime from US aggression by deploying nuclear missiles, he had clearly not succeeded. Cuba appeared to be in the greatest danger of US invasion. Equally, Kennedy's covert manoeuvring on the issue of removing the Jupiter missiles from Turkey was never going to be sufficient to end the crisis.

The essence of effective international diplomacy lay in compromise. Even as late as 26 October, Kennedy was keeping his options open although he had not rejected the idea of compromise as he said, "We will get the strategic missiles out of Cuba only by invading Cuba or by trading". Using force to overthrow Castro and remove the missiles remained an essential policy option for Kennedy. Perhaps significantly the drive towards compromise and a diplomatic solution came from two individuals not connected directly with the upper levels of government in either the Soviet Union or the USA. The KGB station chief in the Soviet embassy in Washington, Aleksandr Feklisov, contacted an ABC reporter, John Scali. They discussed the idea that Soviet missiles would be withdrawn from Cuba and no further missiles would ever be deployed there. In return for this concession, the quarantine would end and the USA would agree not to invade Cuba. Scali immediately reported to the US State Department. At a second meeting, Scali was able to tell Feklisov that he was empowered "by the highest authority" to indicate US interest in the proposal.

On this same day, Friday 26 October, Khrushchev sent a long and rambling letter to Kennedy. In essence, Khrushchev was looking for a way out of the crisis. The basic proposal that Khrushchev was making was that if the USA made a non-invasion pledge then the Soviet Union would remove its military presence on Cuba. From the US point of view this was a perfect scenario. The blockade was having no impact on the weapons systems already on Cuba. The nuclear threat was real and it was in place. A military solution was still a real option for Kennedy. A peaceful resolution was made more difficult at this point by the actions of Castro. He was convinced that an American attack was imminent. He recalled in 1992, "On the night of the 26th we saw no possible solution. We couldn't see a way out. Under the threat of an invasion, of an attack, with enormous propaganda using all the mass media, and an international campaign talking about this very serious problem, we really couldn't see any solution". On 26 October Castro ordered Cuban anti-aircraft forces to start firing on low-level reconnaissance planes. He said "We cannot tolerate these . . . overflights".

To add to the deepening crisis, on 27 October Khrushchev sent another communiqué to Kennedy which shifted the conditions under which the Soviet missiles may be removed from Cuba.

> You are disturbed over Cuba. You say that this disturbs you because it is 90 miles by sea from the coast of the United States of America. But Turkey adjoins us; our sentries patrol back and forth and see each other. Do you consider, then, that you have the right to demand security for your own country and the removal of the weapons you call offensive, but do not accord the same right to us? You have placed destructive missile weapons, which you have called offensive, in Turkey, literally next to us. How then can recognition of our equal military capabilities be reconciled with such unequal relations between our great states? This is irreconcilable.

4

This linkage between US missiles in Turkey and Soviet missiles in Cuba had the potential to undermine any moves towards a mutual compromise agreement. ExComm vehemently opposed the trade-off. News came through to ExComm that a U-2 spy plane had been shot down over Cuba and the pilot, Major Rudolf Anderson, had been killed. Kennedy and ExComm had already committed themselves to responding to such attacks with US air attacks against Soviet S-75 anti-aircraft emplacements on Cuba. The crisis appeared to be on the brink of escalating out of control. Kennedy's strategy to recover was to ignore Khrushchev's second letter and simply reply to the first. Kennedy needed to ensure that Khrushchev would accept this response. A meeting was summoned with the Soviet Ambassador, Anatoly Dobrynin, during which Robert Kennedy was authorised to inform Dobrynin that the President was willing to remove the US missiles in Turkey – but not immediately. Such a concession could not be incorporated into any formal, public settlement of the crisis. Kennedy recognised the fairness of such a trade-off but could not allow the USA's NATO allies to view it as a concession to Soviet pressure. So important was this that NATO was told explicitly that no secret agreement had been reached. McGeorge Bundy, an ExComm member, later commented, "We denied in every forum that there was any deal . . . we misled our colleagues, our countrymen, our successors, and our allies."

The diplomacy was a success. On Sunday morning, 28 October, Khrushchev agreed to remove the missiles. Kennedy praised Khrushchev's 'statesmanlike decision'. The immediate crisis was over. Castro was incensed at what he saw as a humiliating betrayal by Khrushchev. He refused to allow inspections of the missile sites once they had been dismantled. Such checks were an essential element of the US–Soviet agreement and were only fulfilled as Soviet ships removing the missiles revealed the contents of their cargoes to US inspectors.

A closer look

International relations theories in history

Studying theories of international relations in history is an important means by which to understand how people in their own time think about the world. In the second half of the 20th century, the major theories for understanding the international system were called 'realism' and 'idealism'. 'Realism' was developed as a theory of international relations based upon the notion that nation-states pursue power as a primary interest. Competition among a few 'great powers' has the effect of balancing the international system into what is called the 'balance of power', signalling that no single power

Activity

Talking point

Prepare for a group discussion based on the proposition that 'The Cuban Missile Crisis was a triumph for Russian rather than American statesmanship'. The group should split into two sections, one arguing that the crisis was a triumph for the USA, and the other that it was a triumph for the Soviet Union.

gains significant ground over another. In his textbook *Politics among Nations* (1948), Hans J. Morgenthau looked at the history of the balance of powers and declared the use of power to be at the core of international relations. Realist ideas were central in Professor E. H. Carr's *The Twenty Years' Crisis* (1939). He distinguished 'the visionary hopes of the first decade' after World War I (1919–29) from the 'grim despair of the second' (1929–39) and insisted that the study of the history of international relations contained the keys to the solution of present problems. Carr considered that international relations were a constant power struggle among groups organised as the nation-state. He coined and popularised the word 'realism' to describe these positions. In the years following World War II and the collapse of the international order, academics took an increasing interest in the idea of integration and cooperation that would prevent a similar series of events from occurring. The American scholar John H. Herz called this position 'idealism'. Schemes for regional integration in Europe and the North Atlantic were prevalent in the 1950s and 1960s among scholars in the US such as Karl W. Deutsch, Ernst B. Haas and Joseph Nye. At the same time, a variant of realist thinking emerged that emphasised the anarchic quality of the international system and that war was a result of the breakdown of a balance of power. In 1957 Morton Kaplan, a professor of political science at the University of Chicago, introduced 'systems analysis' as a theoretical approach to the study of international relations. According to this, wars waged for the maintenance of the balance of power were just; his conclusion explicitly justified military action against the Soviet Union if the Soviet government upset the post-war balance of power.

The impact of the crisis

The crisis brought the world closer to a nuclear war than had ever happened at any other time. However, despite the critical nature of the crisis there was little evidence to suggest that Khrushchev or Kennedy were taking irresponsible actions that could have led to a loss of control. What the crisis did show was that international relations cannot be conducted through crisis management methods. It was also quickly accepted that it was insufficient to see the crisis as the epitome of crisis management and a model, therefore, of how any future crises may be managed. The immediate response to this reality was the creation, in 1963, of a so-called 'hot line' connecting the Kremlin and the White House. The frequency of the hot line's usage is unknown. Some historians have taken the view that its symbolic value has been greater than its practical application.

Fig. 7 *Poster advertising the film* Dr Strangelove*, 1963. The film satirised the absurd international relations of the nuclear era*

The crisis also led to a growing awareness of the need to create some control over the nuclear arms race by placing restrictions on nuclear tests. In October 1963 a partial test ban treaty, known more formally as the 'Treaty Banning Nuclear Weapons Tests in the Atmosphere, in Outer Space and Under Water' came into force. It was Khrushchev who first proposed nuclear test ban negotiations as early as 30 October 1962. The outcome of the negotiations has been described as 'a watershed, marking an important new era in arms control' but 'while it represented a genuine step toward reducing superpower tensions and building mutual confidence, it fell short of the comprehensive test ban that many had advocated' (Munton and Welch, 2007). The treaty contained no provisions for underground tests or for periodic review and inspection. This implicit sanctioning of the testing of nuclear weapons underground encouraged weapon proliferation among the major nuclear powers. In addition to this the signatories, after three months, could restart testing if they thought that their vital national interests were at stake by not doing so. There was no obligation on states to sign up; consequently, China and France did not do so. They continued to test nuclear weapons in the atmosphere. Despite its many shortcomings, the treaty was a major contributory factor in the development of **détente** later in the decade. On this R. Crockatt commented, 'Détente itself showed the impress of the missile crisis.'

The crisis had seen the USA using its superior military power to pressure the Soviets to withdraw the missiles. This was perceived as a humiliation for the USSR. America's actions may be viewed as an offensive use of military power. The Soviet Union had been forced to respond rather than being deterred from taking action. The outcome had been a Cold War defeat for the Soviet Union and a constraint on Soviet freedom of action in the international arena. The Soviet Union had strategic parity with the USA, and despite the moves towards détente and controls over nuclear testing, the USSR emerged from the crisis with a determination to restore its international status.

At the end of the crisis Cuba remained a communist state in the USA's 'back yard'. The US commitment to containment and the Truman Doctrine had failed. This began to raise the issue of its validity by the 1960s but not to the point where the missile crisis had fundamentally undermined American Cold War policy in international relations. US intervention in South Vietnam was only just beginning to develop as the missile crisis came to an end. Cuba's survival may be seen as a spectacular success for Khrushchev. The missile crisis proved to be more than a clash between the USA and the USSR. It was part of a process of revolutionary change within developing countries. In 1975 Castro sent troops to Angola in support of that state's revolutionary regime following the withdrawal of Portugal from Africa.

Not only did the crisis ensure the survival of Cuba and its communist regime, it also ensured the survival of West Berlin as an outpost of western capitalist democracy in the heart of the communist bloc in eastern Europe. Ultimately, aspects of the dynamics of international relations and Cold War interaction had shifted and moved the bipolar world closer towards greater cooperation prior to the era of détente which was to follow.

Key terms

Détente: literally means a relaxation of tensions. In terms of international relations it came to describe the idea of easing relations between states.

Cross-reference

For an extended discussion of détente, see Chapter 5.

Activity

Revision activity

Create a table with three columns headed 'Causes', 'Events' and 'Results'. Under these headings, map out the development and effects of the Cuban Missile Crisis.

Summary questions

1. 'The conclusion of the missile crisis was absolute proof that the USA's strategy of containment had failed.' How valid is this assessment?
2. 'Placing nuclear missiles on Cuba was a reckless piece of international gambling by Khrushchev that achieved nothing of significance for the USSR.' How valid is this view?

5 The Emergence of Détente

In this chapter you will learn about:

- the development of détente from 1962
- the improvement in Sino–American relations to 1972
- SALT I and II and the summit meetings of 1972–4.

By the late 1960s western Europe and the United States had faced the Soviet Union in nuclear standoff, each side bristling with nuclear weapons. Yet by a process of negotiation, by the early 1970s President Nixon and the Soviet leader Leonid Brezhnev were proclaiming a new era of 'peaceful coexistence'. The world was attempting to build peace, but it rested on fragile foundations. The process started by Nixon was continued by his successor, Gerald Ford.

Fig. 1 *US–Soviet harmony in 1974*

The idea of détente

The USA's interpretation of détente

The Nixon administration regarded détente as a process based on negotiation rather than confrontation. Nixon summed up his view when he said:

> The Soviet Union will always act in its own self-interest; and so will the United States. Détente cannot change that. All we can hope from détente is that it will minimize confrontation in marginal areas and provide, at least, alternative possibilities in the major ones.

1

Nixon and his key adviser, Henry Kissinger, saw détente as a strategy rather than as an objective.

Cross-reference

For a definition of détente, see the previous chapter, page 69.

He said, "Détente is a means of controlling the conflict with the Soviet Union." Both Nixon and Kissinger aimed to draw the Soviet Union into a state of interdependency with the USA. Fundamentally, the American perception of détente was that it represented a strategy designed to prevent a nuclear conflict as the Soviet Union became increasingly more powerful. Détente was about creating a network of mutually advantageous relationships so that it would not be in the Soviet Union's interest to base its policies on confrontation with the USA. The Soviet Union would have more to gain by cooperation rather than confrontation. In this way the USA would be in a position to 'manage' Soviet international power. Kissinger summed this up when he said, "By acquiring a stake in this network of relationships with the West the Soviet Union may become more conscious of what it will lose by a return to confrontation. Indeed, it is our expectation that it will develop a self-interest in fostering the entire process of relaxation of tensions."

Key profiles

Richard Milhous Nixon, 1913–94

Nixon trained as a lawyer and after service in the US Navy during World War II he was elected to the US Senate. Two years later he stood as Eisenhower's running mate in the Presidential elections. He quickly developed a reputation as a committed anti-communist. After being Vice President to Eisenhower he lost the 1960 Presidential election to Kennedy. He developed a policy which became known as the Nixon Doctrine. This was based on the idea that US forces abroad should be reduced and smaller nations should be helped to defend themselves. Nixon and his closest adviser, Kissinger, embraced détente. Ultimately his career was ended through an internal political scandal known as the Watergate Crisis. Faced with the real prospect of impeachment he resigned his office as President on 9 August 1974.

Henry Alfred Kissinger, 1923–present

Born in Germany, Kissinger arrived in the USA in 1938. He was an intellectual and after gaining a doctorate in 1954 from Harvard he joined the staff there. He became deeply involved with international relations throughout his time at Harvard. In 1969 he was appointed Assistant to the President for National Security Affairs and remained in the post until 1975; he was Secretary of State from 1973 to 1977.

The Soviet Union's interpretation of détente

Brezhnev saw détente as a means of overcoming the Cold War and the route by which normal, equal relations could be restored between states. Disputes would be resolved not through the use of threats or force but through peaceful means via negotiation. The legitimate interests of each side would be recognised and respected by the other. Brezhnev also regarded détente as mutually advantageous to both the East and the West.

Key profile

Leonid Ilyich Brezhnev, 1906–82

Upon the removal of Khrushchev, Brezhnev became First Secretary of the Communist Party and by 1969 his political dominance was complete. In 1968 he drew up what became known as the Brezhnev Doctrine. This emphasised the right of the Soviet Union to intervene to protect any other communist regime under threat of being undermined by capitalist forces. Brezhnev was committed to détente and he was present at all the significant meetings that moved détente forward.

From the Soviet perspective, détente was made possible because the Soviet Union, by the late 1960s, had established nuclear equality with the USA. By that point, the Soviet Union had reached a strategic balance with the USA in terms of nuclear capability. This equality put the Soviet Union in a position to cooperate with the West and it necessitated such cooperation as far as the West was concerned. The Soviet Union took the view that the USA was no longer the dominant world power and the Soviet Union was now in a position to gain by being able to cooperate with the USA. In essence, détente was the means by which the Soviet Union could preserve world socialism and protect it from the threats posed by Western capitalism and imperialism. Brezhnev summed up the Soviet thinking on the role of détente in an article published in the Soviet state newspaper, *Pravda*, in June 1975. He said:

Activity

Group activity

Working in small groups draw up your own definition of the key differences in the perceptions of détente held by the USA and the Soviet Union.

> Détente became possible because a new correlation of forces in the world arena has now been established. Now the leaders of the bourgeois world can no longer seriously count on resolving the historic conflict between capitalism and socialism by force of arms. The senseless and extreme dangers of furthering increasing tension under conditions when both sides have at their disposal weapons of colossal destructive power are becoming ever more obvious.

2

Sino–American relations, 1969–72

During the twenty years after the communist takeover of China in 1949 the USA had simply refused to recognise the legitimate existence of the People's Republic of China (PRC). The Sino–American relationship in this period had been one of mutual confrontation and isolation. With the arrival of Richard Nixon and his principal adviser, Henry Kissinger, there came a new realisation that the USA could gain by bringing China into the global political arena through improved Sino–American relations. Equally, the Chinese came to realise that self-imposed international isolation was of no advantage to them.

A further impetus behind improved Sino–American relations was worsening Sino–Soviet relations. Although China and the Soviet Union shared a communist outlook, this did not bring unity. During World War II and the late 1940s, Mao resented Stalin's attempts to interfere in the revolutionary war. With the establishment of the PRC, Stalin equally resented China's attempts to become a leader in advancing world communism, or at least communism in east Asia. Hostility between the two countries increased and become publicly open from 1960. Mao later criticised the Soviets over backing down in the Cuban Missile Crisis, and even claimed that the USSR had slipped back into capitalism. By the late 1960s, there were clashes between Soviet and Chinese troops on the Sino–Soviet border. Sensing its international isolation, China made an understandable move to ease relations with the West.

Fig. 2 *President Nixon visits Mao Zedong in Peking, 21 February 1972*

Nixon was a prime mover in changing US policy towards China. As early as 1968, when he was selected as the Republican Party Presidential candidate, he commented, "We must not forget China. We must always seek opportunities to talk with her. We must not only watch for changes. We must seek to make changes." Nixon realised that China was a developing nuclear power and a major political and strategic force in Asia. Most importantly, China was a communist power which was independent of the Soviet Union. The first tentative steps in improved relations came in July 1969 when the USA removed some trade controls and relaxed some travel restrictions. These were part of what was termed the 'artichoke' approach. This was based on the gradual peeling-off of restrictions layer by layer rather than wholesale removal of controls. Nixon also managed a number of diplomatic contacts through France, Romania and Pakistan. The aim of these was to use their diplomatic connections with China to promote the idea of a US willingness to work towards improving Sino–American relations. By early 1970 some initial diplomatic connections between China and the USA had been established in Warsaw.

For its part, China was also making some progress in improving relations. A crucially important development came in August–September 1970 when Zhou Enlai, China's Prime Minister, achieved a major victory (led by Lin Biao and Zhen Boda) over those opposed to China opening improved relations with the USA. There was a policy shift away from dual confrontation with both the Soviet Union and the USA towards a recognition that the former was the greater threat to China. This shift was not publicly acknowledged until 1972. There was clearly a significant shift towards Sino–American détente underway as early as 1970. A fundamental issue in China's moves towards détente with the USA was Mao Zedong's realisation that there was a changing balance of power between China, the USA and the Soviet Union. Mao did not reject the USA as a threat to China, he simply saw the Soviet Union as the greater and more immediate threat and therefore it made sense to form détente with the USA in order to address, in the short term, the immediate threat from the Soviet Union.

In his Presidential Report on Foreign Policy, issued in February 1971, Nixon stated, "We are prepared to establish a dialogue with Peking" and "there could be new opportunities for the People's Republic of China to explore the path of normalisation of its relations with its neighbours and with the world, including our own country." What slightly delayed developments was American military action in Cambodia in May 1970 and the subsequent action in February 1971 in Laos as part of the US military strategy in the conflict in Vietnam. These did not have a fundamental impact as the USA had already begun a policy of troop withdrawals from Vietnam.

Exploring the detail

China's international role since 1949

The most significant factor in China's place in international relations came in 1962. By that point it was clear that a split had occurred between China and the Soviet Union. Khrushchev was reluctant to enable China to become a nuclear power and he was concerned about Mao Zedong's apparent determination to spread communism on a global scale. This Sino–Soviet split offered an opportunity for the USA to shift the dynamics of the Cold War by bringing China into the equation. Certainly by the end of the 1960s, China was an established nuclear power despite Soviet opposition.

A closer look

Nixon and Vietnam

Richard Nixon inherited a crisis when he came into office as US President in January 1969. The USA had been involved in a long and costly war in South Vietnam since 1965, fighting against communist insurgents and the army of North Vietnam. Nixon's predecessor, Johnson, had escalated US military involvement and this had led to rising casualties and rising domestic opposition to the government's stance in Vietnam. Nixon was determined to withdraw from the entanglement in Vietnam in a manner that would lead to 'peace with honour'. He was committed to not losing the war and to preserving South Vietnam as a non-communist state. This attitude had been firmly established after the Tet Offensive in 1968. The pro-communist and nationalist Vietcong lauched attacks across the country against the US forces and their allies, the South Vienamese Army. From then it was clear to Nixon that a military victory in Vietnam was highly unlikely. Despite this he was not prepared to abandon militarism. He saw militarism as a means to an end rather than an end in itself. He was fully aware of the development of détente in Europe and he hoped to use the new phase of mutual cooperation as a way out of Vietnam. He realised the importance of China in the diplomatic dynamics of the early 1970s and he saw China as a possible form of pressure on communist North Vietnam.

Nixon's strategy for withdrawal depended on his policy of Vietnamisation. This meant the gradual withdrawal of US forces and handing the conduct of the war over to the South Vietnamese themselves. He supported this strategy by adopting a policy of aggressive militarism which involved extensive bombing of North Vietnam and attacks on the neighbouring states of Cambodia and Laos. Ultimately Nixon's attempts to put military pressure on North Vietnam failed. The 1973 peace talks resulted in an American withdrawal in 1975 and South Vietnam was finally reunited with the north under a communist political system, something Nixon had always intended to resist.

In April the Chinese gave an important signal to the US administration when they invited the US team to participate in the 31st World Table Tennis Championship match in Peking. The team was formally received by Zhou Enlai. In July 1971 Kissinger visited Peking. Perhaps the most significant outcome of this trip was an agreement to establish a Presidential visit and a Sino–American summit meeting in early 1972. A further barrier to Sino–American détente was removed with the unexpected death of Mao's designated successor and opponent of Sino–American relations, Lin Biao, in September 1972. This simply strengthened Mao's and Zhou's ability to improve relations with the USA. In October 1971 Kissinger made a second trip to Peking in preparation for the Nixon visit.

Nixon's visit to China was a significant step in promoting positive Sino–American relations and this inevitably reinforced the possibility of triangular diplomacy between China, the USA and the Soviet Union. Nixon, in a toast he made at the end of the visit, hailed it by declaring, "This was the week that changed the world." Until the Nixon years the USA had committed itself to a policy based on 'two Chinas'. In addition to mainland China there was also Taiwan. Part of this policy involved having US troops on Taiwan. As a result of the Nixon visit the USA became committed to a policy aimed at "the ultimate objective of the withdrawal of all US forces and military installations on Taiwan as the tension in the area diminishes." In return for this significant US concession and a commitment to promote the unification of China, the US had drawn China into its own commitment to ease 'tensions' in the area. What this amounted to was gaining China's cooperation in ending the war in Vietnam. This was a fundamental objective of the Nixon administration.

Ostpolitik and the development of European détente

West Germany held a significant place in the development of détente in Europe. The traditional Cold War stance taken by West Germany had been established by Chancellor Konrad Adenauer from 1955. Adenauer adopted the Hallstein Doctrine. This stated that West Germany would not recognise the independent existence of East Germany (the GDR) and, therefore, would not establish diplomatic relations with any state that did recognise East Germany. The only exception to this was the Soviet Union. This Doctrine, and Adenauer's commitment to the reunification of Germany, came to represent a profound barrier to any future détente in Europe.

The appointment of Willy Brandt as Chancellor in October 1969 triggered a new phase in European relations. Brandt started a new approach to East–West European relations. Brandt had experienced at first hand the sufferings brought about by the division of Germany when he was mayor of West Berlin at the time of the Berlin Wall's construction. Subsequently as Foreign Minister from 1966 and in turn Chancellor from October 1969, he was able to put his belief in Ostpolitik – reducing the consequences of division – into action. His overall objectives were to recognise East Germany and the territorial changes that had occurred at the end of the Second World War, particularly the creation of the Oder-Neisse border with Poland. Brandt's strategy was to negotiate with the Soviet Union, settle the frontier with Poland and finally to negotiate with the GDR.

Fig. 3 *The German–Poland Treaty, 7 December 1970*

Activity

Thinking point

Draw up a list of motives that explain why the USA and China wanted to 'normalise' their relationship from 1969. Think about economic, political and military motives, and what each side wanted to achieve in the context of the Cold War.

Activity

Research activity

Find out more about Willy Brandt's career and why he won the Nobel Peace Prize using the Key profile on page 76 as an outline guide.

Key profile

Willy Brandt, 1913–92

Brandt began his political career in 1948 within the Social Democratic Party and he became a member of the Berlin House of Representatives. Between 1957 and 1966 he was the Mayor of Berlin and became Chairman of the Social Democratic Party of Germany (SPD) in 1964, a position he held until 1984. Between 1966 and 1969 he was Foreign Minister and Chancellor from 1969 until 1974. As leader of the SPD, he played a key role in shaping the party as a moderate socialist force and in 1971 he won the Nobel Peace Prize. His active political career ended in 1987.

Fig. 4 *Brandt and Koygin sign the Soviet German Treaty*

Brandt's talks with the Soviet Union led to a joint Non-Aggression Pact signed in August 1970. On 7 December 1970 a treaty was signed with Poland which recognised the post-war Oder-Neisser border. These important steps towards establishing Ostpolitik and the eventual mutual recognition of the two Germanies was furthered in May 1971 when the Communist Party chief in East Germany, Walter Ulbricht, resigned and was replaced by Erich Honecker. Ulbricht had been regarded as 'the last Stalinist'. With this shift in leadership came a shift in relations. It became possible to accommodate the East German idea of two states with the West German notion of 'two states within one German nation.' A major breakthrough in the development of European détente came in December 1972 when the two Germanies signed an agreement formally recognising each other. The Hallstein Doctrine was dead. This had a significance that extended beyond Europe. Kissinger realised that the USA must develop an American détente with the Soviet Union in order to prevent a West German driven détente from marginalising US influence in Europe and possibly splitting the Western Alliance. The USA's superpower influence was not to be undermined by initiatives taken by West Germany.

Key profile

Erich Honecker, 1912–94

Honecker was head of East Germany, the GDR, between 1971 and 1989. He was a committed communist and joined the Party in 1929. He was imprisoned by the Nazis during the war. In 1946 he was a member of the Socialist Unity Party which became the leading force of the GDR. In 1958 he joined the **Politburo** and in 1961 was the pricipal mover in the construction of the Berlin Wall. He lost touch with reality by 1989, failing to respond to his country's economic problems or opposition pressure. He was forced to resign but escaped a criminal prosecution through ill health.

Key terms

Politburo: the supreme policy making body of the Communist Party. It was made up of the most senior and powerful members of the Party and the government. It ceased to exist with the collapse of the Soviet Union in 1991.

The Berlin Agreement, September 1971

An agreement on Berlin would greatly advance the prospects of American–Soviet détente and both sides were keen to reach a consensus on Berlin's future and status within East–West relations. When Brandt took over as Chancellor, the Soviets expressed an interest in holding talks to discuss Berlin. By early 1971 Kissinger and President Nixon were keen to use the Soviet interest in Berlin as a means of advancing SALT (Strategic Arms Limitation Treaty). Honecker's appearance on the diplomatic scene in 1971, replacing the aging Ulbricht, also facilitated an agreement on Berlin. The Quadripartite Agreement on Berlin was signed on 3 September 1971.

The Soviets guaranteed Western access and the West German presence in Berlin was reduced, although cultural and economic ties between West Germany and West Berlin were recognised. The West recognised that East Berlin was now an integral part of East Germany and not merely the Soviet occupation zone. Equally, it was agreed that West Berlin would remain separate from West Germany, and Berlin as a whole would retain the Four Power presence established in 1945. The Berlin Agreement effectively neutralised a continuing source of conflict between East and West and in doing so it opened the way for further progress to be made for Ostpolitik. It created a positive climate for wider American–Soviet détente.

Cross-reference

For full details of SALT I and II, see pages 80–1.

Activity

Thinking point

Explain why an agreement on Berlin was reached in 1971.

The Basic Treaty

The Basic Treaty of 21 December 1972 was another important moment in the development of Ostpolitik and the relations between East and West Germany. The label 'Basic Treaty' (in German *Grundlagenvertrag*) was a contraction of 'Treaty concerning the basis of relations between the Federal Republic of Germany and the German Democratic Republic'. As the full title suggests, the treaty was an attempt, in some measure, to normalise relations between the two Germanies.

Fig. 5 *The signing of the Basic Treaty*

The groundwork for the the Basic Treaty was laid throughout 1971 and 1972, key players being Egon Bahr and Michael Kohl (Under-Secretaries of State for West and East Germany respectively) and Federal German Chancellor Willy Brandt. Both sides faced some serious resistance from hardliners opposed to any sort of thawing in relations, but in the end the treaty was signed on 21 December in East Berlin. The first three articles alone of the treaty illustrate its political importance:

> Article 1
> The Federal Republic of Germany and the German Democratic Republic shall develop normal, good-neighbourly relations with each other on the basis of equal rights.
>
> Article 2
> The Federal Republic of Germany and the German Democratic Republic will be guided by the aims and principles laid down in the United Nations Charter, especially those of the sovereign equality of all States, respect for their independence, autonomy and territorial integrity, the right of self-determination, the protection of human rights, and non-discrimination.
>
> Article 3
> In conformity with the United Nations Charter, the Federal Republic of Germany and the German Democratic Republic shall settle any disputes between them exclusively by peaceful means and refrain from the threat or use of force.
>
> They reaffirm the inviolability now and in the future of the frontier existing between them and undertake fully to respect each other's territorial integrity.

3

Embedded within these three articles alone was the commitment to potential economic relations, the recognition of the sovereignty of the FRG and GDR and their territorial 'inviolability'. Further articles promised to seek peaceful methods of conflict resolution.

The Basic Treaty was a critical moment in European détente. It not only settled relations, comparatively at least, between East and West Germany, but it also provided the route by which other European nations could establish relations with the GDR. Following the signing (although the treaty actually came into official effect in June 1973), certain nations established diplomatic relations with the GDR:

Table 1 *Nations that established diplomatic relations with the GDR*

Nation	Date diplomatic relations opened with GDR
Australia	December 1972
United Kingdom	February 1973
France	February 1973
Netherlands	February 1973
Federal Republic of Germany	February 1974
United States	December 1974

By the end of September 1973, both the FRG and the GDR were members of the United Nations. The groundwork had been laid for a furthering of European détente.

The Helsinki Accords, 1973–5

European détente reached its high point with the convening of a European security conference which led to a fundamental agreement being reached in 1975. The conference took place in Helsinki and was known formally as the Conference on Security and Cooperation in Europe (CSCE). Preparatory talks began in Helsinki in November 1972 which laid the groundwork for the official opening of the CSCE in July 1973. A total of 35 states participated and these included the whole of Europe, except Albania, and also the USA and Canada. Each had the power of veto at its disposal. The work of the conference lasted two years and reached its finale at a summit-level meeting between 30 July and 1 August 1975. The outcome was known as the Helsinki Accords or, more formally, the Final Act. The main parts of the agreement were divided into what became referred to as 'baskets'. Each basket was linked to a specific package of agreements:

Basket I: Security in Europe

This basket led to a Declaration on Principles Guiding Relations between Participating States which consisted of ten principles that were to be applied to inter-state relations:

1 Respect for sovereignty and equality among states.
2 The rejection of the threat or use of force.
3 The peaceful settlement of disputes.
4 Recognition of existing frontiers.
5 Territorial integrity to be recognised and acknowledged.
6 Non-intervention in the internal affairs of other states.
7 Respect for human rights and fundamental freedoms.
8 Equal rights and self-determination of peoples.
9 Cooperation among states.
10 The fulfilment of international obligations.

A further agreement was reached on the obligation to provide advanced notification of large military exercises and other similar plans in order to reinforce mutual confidence.

Basket II: Cooperation in the Field of Economics, of Science and Technology and of the Environment

This addressed trade and industrial cooperation, transportation, science and technology, the promotion of tourism, the environment and issues concerning migrant labour.

Basket III: Cooperation in Humanitarian and Other Fields

This focused on cultural and educational exchange and the wider issue of contacts among peoples. It sought to encourage the freer movement of people, information and ideas.

The Final Act was not seen as the last step in European détente. Plans were laid to have follow-up meetings and the first was planned to take place in Belgrade in late 1977.

The Soviet position

The Soviets had three main interests in the CSCE:

1 To expand Ostpolitik and develop wider acceptance of the status quo in central and eastern Europe.

2 To decrease barriers between states in order to increase economic activity and trade.

3 To further the process of East–West détente.

The Soviets were less interested in the details of human rights issues. There was a real concern about external interference in the internal affairs of the Soviet Union and other communist states in eastern Europe. There was some initial reluctance to accept the provisions on advanced notice of military exercises. It was the Soviet commitment to the wider aim of promoting East–West détente that led them to accept these conditions in the Final Act.

The American position

The USA was not fully committed to accepting the political status quo in eastern Europe which the Final Act seemed to recognise as a permanent reality. They also feared that as western Europe came to feel more secure there was the real possibility that its support for reduced military programmes within NATO member states would be reduced.

Activity

Thinking point

Was the Final Act likely to be a major contributor to the future of détente?

Despite the reservations the superpowers had over the Final Act, there was a common recognition that East–West confrontation in Europe was relaxing and both sides welcomed this. Some commentators regarded the Helsinki Accords as the high point in détente. The accords offered a political solution to European security and cooperation.

SALT I and SALT II and strategic arms limitation in the 1970s

Commonly known as SALT, these negotiations and the agreements that followed became seen as the foundations of détente. The SALT negotiations began in 1969 and were finalised in May 1972. The two fundamental agreements were the Anti-Ballistic Missile (ABM) Treaty and the Interim Agreement on Measures with Respect to Strategic Offensive Weapons.

Fig. 6 *Carter and Brezhnev agree SALT II*

The ABM Treaty limited both the Soviet Union and the USA to constructing two fields of anti-ballistic missiles, each with no more than 100 missiles. One of these could be set up around a capital city while the other was to protect intercontinental ballistic missile sites. This significantly restricted the strategic value of ABMs. It meant that there would be no significant competition to further develop ABM defence technology. It also made the race to develop offensive strategic nuclear weapons less critical. The ABM Treaty did show that both of the superpowers recognised the other's destructive power and therefore each side had an interest in preventing what would be a mutually destructive conflict.

The Interim Agreement on offensive weapons established a freeze on strategic missiles. This amounted to:

- 1,054 intercontinental ballistic missiles (ICBMs) for the USA and 1,618 for the Soviet Union.
- 656 submarine launched ballistic missiles (SLBMs) for the USA and 740 for the Soviet Union.
- 450 strategic bombers for the USA and 140 for the Soviet Union.

The Treaty was to be current for 5 years.

This agreement made no provision for limitations on newly developing technology, particularly the multiple independent re-entry vehicles (MIRVs). Similarly there were no defined limits on cruise missile systems. The agreement was only interim and it was at SALT II that these deficiencies would be addressed further. Nevertheless, SALT I was an opportunity missed by the superpowers. Despite these limitations SALT I was a significant step towards strategic arms control. Perhaps most importantly the SALT agreement contributed to a relaxation of tension which opened the way for more developed détente agreements between the USA and the Soviet Union.

Some argue that SALT I acted as a catalyst in the détente process. It was a crucial step towards détente. The talks were politically beneficial to both Nixon and Brezhnev and reinforced the political advantages to be gained by national leaders if they backed policies which created greater stability and the prospects of international peace. In June 1972 President Nixon announced the significance of SALT to the US Congress:

> Three-fifths of all people alive in the world today have spent their whole lives under the shadow of a nuclear war which could be touched off by the arms race among the great powers. Last Friday in Moscow we witnessed the beginning of the end of that era which began in 1945. We took the first step toward a new era of mutually agreed restraint and arms limitation between the two principal nuclear nations. With this step we have enhanced the security of both nations. We have begun to check the wasteful and dangerous spiral of nuclear arms which has dominated relations between our two countries for a generation. We have begun to reduce the level of fear, for our two peoples and for all peoples in the world.

4

SALT was more than merely an arms limitation agreement. It was the foundation of a political achievement which made détente possible. SALT opened the way for an era of negotiation rather than confrontation. By accepting SALT the USA accepted nuclear parity between itself and the Soviet Union. US nuclear dominance had faded and the two major nuclear superpowers were of equal status. This was a fundamentally important step in international relations because it meant that both sides had something to gain from détente. In effect a balance of power had been acknowledged and this necessitated the construction of a new non-confrontational relationship. That relationship was to be détente.

Activity

Thinking point

Explain the importance of SALT I for the development of détente between the superpowers.

The Nixon–Brezhnev Moscow Summit, May 1972

In addition to the finalising of the SALT agreements the May 1972 Moscow Summit also produced agreements to expand American–Soviet cooperation in science and technology as well as in areas such as the environment and health, and in space exploration. Most importantly the summit also set out the guidelines for American–Soviet relations. 'The Basic Principles of Relations Between the United States and the Union of the Soviet Socialist Republics' acted as a code of behaviour in terms of the relations the two powers had with each other.

The Basic Principles Agreement

There were 12 principles agreed but the three most fundamental and significant were:

1 It was agreed in the first Basic Principle that the United States and the Soviet Union 'will proceed from the common determination that in the nuclear age there is no alternative to conducting their mutual relations on the basis of peaceful coexistence.' They were also committed to develop 'normal relations based on the principles of sovereignty, equality, non-interference in internal affairs and mutual advantage.'

2 The second Basic Principle focused on a determination to avoid situations developing that could damage their commitment to peaceful coexistence. This led to an agreement to avoid military confrontations and prevent the outbreak of nuclear war. The text of this second principle read, 'They will always exercise restraint in their mutual relations and will be prepared to negotiate and settle differences by peaceful means.' Each power rejected the idea that it should be free to gain at the expense of the other. Peaceful relations were to be based on the recognition of the right of each state to protect its security interests based on the rejection of the use of force.

3 In the third Basic Principle there was an acceptance of a 'special responsibility . . . to do everything in their power so that conflicts or situations will not arise which would serve to increase international tensions' and 'to promote conditions in which all countries will live in peace and security and will not be subject to outside interference in their internal affairs.'

Activity

Group activity

Split into two groups. One group should identifiy and explain the strengths of the outcome of the Moscow Summit while the other identifies and explains its weaknesses. Each group should argue its case to the other.

The basic problem with the agreement was that the Principles had no legal status. Everything depended upon each side abiding by the guidelines. As far as America was concerned the Basic Principles represented a set of aspirations rather than a solid basis for future détente. The Soviet Union reacted differently to the agreement. It considered the Basic Principles to be of fundamental importance. SALT and now the Basic Principles Agreement recognised parity between the USA and the Soviet Union and this was the foundation of détente as far as the Soviet Union was concerned.

The Nixon–Brezhnev Washington Summit, June 1973

Both the USA and the Soviet Union wished to see further developments in détente. For the Americans détente was not simply a commitment to achieve international peace and cooperation. Détente had been developing in Europe since the emergence of Brandt's policy of Ostpolitik. Kissinger was eager to ensure that America should not have its influence in Europe sidelined by European détente. He wanted to bring Europe and China into close relations with the USA so that they could be used in the USA's strategy of influencing global diplomacy. He did not want Europe making unilateral agreements with the Soviet Union. The objective failed and European détente was strengthened during 1973. Kissinger's and Nixon's policy illustrates the reality that they were primarily interested in protecting the USA's global power rather than simply backing any international developments that might reinforce world peace.

The Washington Summit convened in June 1973. The summit was held partly in Washington and at Camp David, and partly in San Clemente, California. There were agreements on agriculture, cultural exchanges and transport. The summit also considered the current situation in the

Middle East. Brezhnev pushed for joint support of a Soviet proposal to make Israel withdraw to the frontier that had existed before the 1967 Arab–Israeli War. America was not willing to back such a proposal at that stage. Brezhnev was keen to push the Americans to guarantees that American–Soviet relations would come before Sino–American relations. He emphasised the importance of the USA not forming any military alliances with China as part of the increasing process of Sino–American improved relations. Some efforts were made to create further guidelines for the next round of SALT negotiations. There were no detailed discussions on the differences that still existed between both sides on SALT issues. However, one major new agreement was reached. That was the Agreement on the Prevention of Nuclear War.

Cross-reference

For a study of the Arab–Israeli conflicts of the 1970s, see Chapter 6.

The Agreement on the Prevention of Nuclear War, 1973

Both sides agreed that the object of their policies was to be the removal of the danger of nuclear war and the use of nuclear weapons. There was a commitment to avoid military confrontations and the threat of force. If a situation arose which could move nations towards nuclear war, then the USA and the Soviet Union agreed to enter into urgent consultations to avert such an outcome. This commitment to consult before a crisis developed amounted to a crisis prevention strategy shared by the two superpowers. In doing this, the Prevention of Nuclear War Agreement built on the Basic Principles signed at the Moscow Summit the previous year. In his memoirs Kissinger referred to this agreement when he commented, "we eventually agreed in June 1973 on a bland set of principles that had been systematically stripped of all implications harmful to our interests." The Americans had been reluctant to agree to the non-use of nuclear weapons for some time prior to the Washington Summit. They feared that it would remove a vital deterrent in international conflicts.

Many in the Soviet Union also had reservations about the Prevention of Nuclear War Agreement and détente as a whole. They feared it might weaken Soviet defences and lead to divisions within the Soviet sphere of influence in eastern Europe. There was also the idea that the Soviet Union would lose its ability to support developing countries seeking to break free from Western control. Détente was seen as tying the Soviet Union down and restricting its freedom to act globally in socialist interests.

Despite their misgivings the Americans went along with the idea. Like the Soviets, the Americans came to see the Prevention of Nuclear War Agreement as a benefit. The Soviets saw it as a way to ensure that the USA would be unable to threaten the use of nuclear force in situations around the world. This would, to some extent, restrict their global influence. The USA saw it as a necessary incentive for the Soviets to keep them committed to détente.

The Third Soviet–American Summit, June–July 1974

This was an opportunity to develop some progress on the SALT II agreement. However, neither side could agree on the levels of MIRVs. The Americans knew that they had superiority in MIRVs and they were unwilling to see this superiority undermined by allowing the Soviets to catch up. For their part, the Soviets rejected the idea that the USA should maintain a permanent advantage. There was some desire to keep SALT alive and in order to do that both sides agreed to reduce the number of permitted anti-ballistic missile sites from two (which had been set under the terms of the ABM Treaty) to one.

The summit did produce some agreements. A ten-year agreement was reached on economic, industrial and technical cooperation. Consular links were also set up. The summit, despite its limited outcomes, did further consolidate détente as the basis of superpower relations. It reaffirmed that summit meetings should be the forum for addressing progress in peaceful relations. What it did not do was to make any real progress on laying the foundations for meaningful SALT II to get underway. The next attempt at this came in Vladivostok.

The Vladivostok Accord, November 1974

This meeting was preceded by a visit to Moscow in October by Henry Kissinger. Gerald Ford had succeeded Nixon after the Watergate scandal, but he retained Kissinger as the US chief negotiator with the Soviet Union. Kissinger talked with Brezhnev about numbers of strategic missile launchers and MIRVs and there was some movement in the positions held by both sides.

At the Vladivostok Summit, agreement was reached on a framework for a ten-year plan; this was seen as the preliminary move towards a future SALT II treaty. The Soviets had agreed to equal levels of ICBM launchers and SLBM launchers. Despite internal opposition in the USA linked to the high levels of weapons being retained and the apparent gains made by the Soviet Union, Congress passed resolutions supporting the Vladivostok SALT Accord by February 1975. However, when the SALT II negotiators met in Geneva it became increasingly clear that a smooth transition from Vladivostok to SALT II would not happen. One problem was that the USA argued that the limit on air-to-surface missiles applied only to ballistic missiles while the Soviet Union argued that it also included cruise missiles. Other similar issues or clarification also emerged in Geneva. Although there had been some progress, the two sides were still far away from a finalised agreement that could be ratified through SALT II.

Fig. 7 *Ford and Brezhnev at the Vladivostok Summit, 24 November 1974*

A closer look

Watergate

This political scandal in America took its name from the building in Washington DC that housed the headquarters of the Democratic Party campaign during the 1972 Presidential elections. The Republican Committee to Re-elect the President had been formed to ensure that Richard Nixon was returned to the White House. Five individuals associated with this committee were caught after breaking into the Watergate building. They had sophisticated electronic surveillance equipment in their possession that was used to spy on the Democratic Presidential campaign.

By August 1974 President Nixon was being closely implicated in the affair. He was accused of using his power as President to obstruct the investigation and lying about his involvement. Much of the detail was revealed by two investigative Washington Post journalists – Bob Woodward and Carl Bernstein. The Senate Investigating Committee gained valuable evidence from Nixon's aids. Dean, Erlichman and Haldeman all provided vital detail that led to the recommendation to **impeach** Nixon. Another important witness was Alexander Butterfield. He announced that Nixon had taped all his conversations

Key terms

Impeach: charge someone (usually a public official or politician) with a crime, aiming to have that person removed from office.

in the White House. The tapes directly linked Nixon to the cover-up. All these factors forced Nixon to resign before he was impeached. Politically the Watergate scandal weakened the Presidency and created a more general distrust of Washington.

This scandal had a serious impact on détente. The power of the Presidency to carry out executive decisions on foreign policy was significantly undermined. The opponents of détente suddenly found themselves in a much stronger position, as détente was now associated with an undermined adminstration. Nixon was replaced by Gerald Ford.

Key profile

Gerald Rudolph Ford, 1913–2006

Ford was Richard Nixon's Vice President and when Nixon resigned in August 1974, Ford succeeded him as President. He entered the House of Representatives in 1949 and was nominated by Nixon as his Vice President upon the resignation of Spiro Agnew. His aim in foreign affairs was to maintain US power and prestige after the collapse of South Vietnam in 1975. During his administration détente continued. Ford was defeated in the 1976 Presidential elections by the Democratic candidate, Jimmy Carter.

When Kissinger returned from Vladivostok he faced significant opposition from Rumsfeld and General Brown, Chairman of the Joint Chiefs of Staff (JCS), and many others. New proposals were forced on to Kissinger and backed by Ford. Brezhnev rejected the new approach and it was clear that a further SALT agreement would not be achieved in 1976, particularly since this was a Presidential election year and Ford was the nominated Republican candidate.

The Carter Administration, 1977–81

1977

In January 1977 Jimmy Carter, the Democratic Presidential electoral candidate, replaced Ford as US President.

Key profile

James Earl (Jimmy) Carter Jr, 1924–present

Carter was born in Plains, Georgia and spent some time managing the family peanut farm. In 1970 he was elected Governor of Georgia. He was nominated as the Democratic candidate for the Presidential elections in July 1976. He was a champion of human rights. In 1978 he brought the Egyptian and Israeli leaders together and they signed the Camp David Accord. Although he participated in the SALT II agreement he did not seek Senate approval for its ratification after the Soviet invasion of Afghanistan. He was blamed for the failure to negotiate the freeing of US embassy officials who had been taken as hostages in Teheran in November 1979. His apparent soft approach against terrorism and communism contributed greatly to his defeat in the 1980 Presidential elections.

The Carter administration began by trying to establish a far more ambitious arms reduction programme for the SALT II agreement than had been laid out in the Vladivostok Accord during Ford's brief stay in the White House. By March 1977 Carter was considering substantially reduced levels of heavy ICBMs, new limits on testing and a ban on new types of ICBMs. Carter was not interested in simply completing Kissinger's unfinished business from Vladivostok. The details of the new proposals were unveiled to the Soviets on 28 March 1977. They included:

- reducing the strategic systems from the 2,400 level agreed at Vladivostok to between 1,800 and 2,000
- reducing the number of launchers for missiles with MIRVs from 1,320 to 1,100
- reducing modern ICBMs to 150 and the number of launchers for ICBMs with MIRVs to 550
- a ban on the development, testing and deployment of new ICBMs
- a ban on all types of cruise missiles with a range above 2,500 kilometres
- air-launched cruise missiles with a range of 600–2,500 kilometres which would be restricted to heavy bombers.

Not only did these proposals have a greater impact on the Soviet Union than they did on America, Brezhnev regarded the Vladivostok agreement as binding and that Carter was acting in a unilateral and, therefore, unacceptable manner. The proposals demanded a disproportionate reduction in Soviet forces compared to those of the USA. Brezhnev simply rejected them. It appeared as if the USA was abandoning several years of hard won progress in the SALT process. Foreign Minister, Andrei Gromyko, summed up the Soviet response when he commented, "One cannot talk about stability when a new leadership arrives and crosses out all that has been achieved before." Gromyko certainly felt that the American proposals undermined the security of the Soviet Union and its allies. Towards the end of 1977 the USA modified the proposals and the key differences between the Vladivostok, and the early Carter, proposals were resolved. It certainly appeared as if SALT II was back on track.

Key profile

Andrei Andreyevich Gromyko, 1909–89

Between 1946 and 1948 Gromyko led the Soviet delegation at the UN. In 1949 he became the deputy Soviet Minister of Foreign Affairs until 1952. He reappeared as Deputy Foreign Minister in 1957. From 1973 he began to have a major influence on Soviet foreign policy through his membership of the Politburo. His role as Soviet President, which he held from 1985, was taken by Mikhail Gorbachev in 1988. Gromyko was renowned for his rather austere appearance and he was given the nickname 'grim Grom' by many who came into contact with him.

The difficulties facing the SALT II agreement and détente generally were added to by Carter's commitment to human rights issues. Early in his Presidency Carter launched a drive for human rights focused on the situation in the Soviet Union and eastern Europe. In January 1977 the US Department of State accused Czechoslovakia of violating human rights and harassing the signatories of Charter 77. At the same time the USA showed direct support for the Soviet dissident Andrei Sakharov.

Did you know?

Charter 77 was a human rights manifesto signed by more than 700 intellectuals and politicians in Czechoslovakia. The charter, inspired by the CSCE talks, forced a crackdown by the communist government, resulting in arrests and persecution.

In March Carter welcomed the exiled Soviet dissident Vladimir Bukovsky to the White House. These steps were part of a sustained process of human rights recognition directly aimed at the Soviet Union and its allies. In July 1977 both Helmut Schmidt, West Germany's Chancellor, and the Canadian Prime Minister Pierre Trudeau cautioned Carter on the risks imposed on East–West détente by adopting too robust a human rights stance against the Soviet Union. Carter failed to appreciate the implications of challenging the internal affairs of the Soviet Union.

Carter faced conflicting advice on how America's attitude towards the Soviet Union and détente should develop. This tended to make Carter's approach uncertain and sometimes ill-defined. Cyrus Vance, Carter's Secretary of State, supported détente. He saw SALT II as an asset for the USA. At the very least the increased and sustained Soviet–American peaceful coexistence would be prevented from backing extremist Arab regimes in the Middle East. The other influence on Carter's thinking was Zbigniew Brezinski, America's National Security Adviser. He had less faith in détente. His approach was aimed at developing America's strategic superiority over the USSR and developing Sino–American relations in order to marginalise the Soviet Union. SALT II was important to Brezinski but it was not the primary route to ensuring American power and the protection of the USA's vital interests.

1978

The USA's relationship with China became an increasing issue in the SALT II process. Carter decided to turn to China in order to retaliate against what he regarded as expansionist Soviet activity in developing countries. China was increasingly receptive to American moves because it was facing problems with Vietnam and feared a Soviet–Vietnam alliance in some form. Carter intended the development of a relationship with China and what became known as the 'China Card', to counter Soviet and Cuban activities in Africa. The aim was to promote the 'normalisation' of Sino–American interests. Astonishingly, Carter failed to realise that this would significantly damage Soviet–American relations at a crucial point in the SALT II development process.

Activity

Research activity

Research either Vance or Brezinski. In either case try to develop an evidence bank that helps you to arrive at a conclusion on how important each man was in influencing Carter and the effects of that influence. A group discussion could follow this research work.

1979

Despite the China factor both the Soviet Union and America wanted the SALT II agreement to proceed. The Treaty was finally announced on 9 May 1979. It was to be signed and finalised at the Vienna Summit in June 1979. This signing was the main concrete achievement of the Vienna Summit but the fact that such a summit could take place at all meant that the Soviet and American leadership could talk and communicate directly with each other rather than through intermediaries. However, some historians take the view that the summit merely interrupted the decline in détente and the irreversible deterioration in relations between the two superpowers.

Activity

Group discussion

As a group, consider the significance for détente and SALT II of Carter's decision to normalise relations with China.

Summary questions

1. 'European détente was a quite separate development from détente between the superpowers.' How valid is this assessment?
2. To what extent did America's relationship with China undermine the development of détente with the Soviet Union?

6 Détente under Pressure

In this chapter you will learn about:

- the Arab–Israeli conflict in 1973 and its impact on détente
- the civil war in Angola and the response of the superpowers
- the Soviet Union's invasion of Afghanistan in 1979 and its effect on détente.

Did you know?

Israel was formed in 1948 and was immediately faced with opposition from surrounding Arab states. One of the leaders of this opposition was Egypt. Israel and Egypt had been involved in a series of wars, the most recent before 1973 occurring in 1967. Egypt was convinced that only through external support could Israel be removed as a threat to Egypt's security. The 1973 war against Israel was a deliberate ploy by Egypt to involve the USA and the Soviet Union in a lasting peace process.

Exploring the detail

Israel's occupation of the Sinai

During the 1967 Six-Day War Israel had taken control of the Sinai peninsula. This was a significant in-road into Egyptian territory and made Egypt vulnerable to further Israeli attacks of the kind that followed in 1973.

'In the mid-1970s the policies of reducing military tension through negotiations and agreements came under increasing pressure in international affairs and within the superpowers themselves. Within a few years the optimistic climate of the early part of the decade had been replaced with what some scholars see as a second Cold War . . . it was conflict over changes in developing countries that brought the détente process to a halt.' (Hanhimaki and Westad, *The Cold War*, 2003.)

Arab–Israeli conflict: The October War, 1973

At the summit meeting in Washington in June 1973, détente appeared to be in a healthy state. Four months later a war in the Middle East caused more confrontation between the two superpowers than at any time since the Cuban Missile Crisis. The crisis in the Middle East in October 1973 had a profoundly damaging impact on the whole policy of East–West détente.

Fig. 1 *Israel and the occupied territories, 1973*

The basis of the conflict that erupted in October 1973 lay with Egypt's President Sadat's determination to end the Israeli occupation of Egyptian Sinai, taken after the Six-Day War of 1967. His strategy was to embark on a limited war against Israel in order to bring international pressure to bear against Israel. On 6 October 1973 Egyptian and Syrian forces attacked the Sinai. Both the USSR and the USA had a shared objective of preventing themselves being drawn into the war and also preserving their détente relationship. Initially both powers supplied their client state with arms. The Soviets helped Egypt and the USA backed Israel. Despite this the two powers were able, by 22 October, to persuade Egypt and Israel to accept a cease-fire. America's primary aim was to ensure it emerged as the driving force in brokering peace in the Middle East. Kissinger wanted to "demonstrate that the road to peace led through Washington." Soviet objectives were less grand. They wanted to retain Arab confidence and have a share in the peace process. America was not inclined to share the diplomatic influence that came with managing the peace process. By the time the cease-fire was declared Kissinger commented that, "We had created the conditions for a diplomatic breakthrough. We had maintained a relationship with key Arab countries and laid the foundations for a dominant role in post-war diplomacy."

Key profile

Anwar Sadat, 1918–81

Sadat became President of Egypt in 1970, upon the death of Nasser. His conduct of the 1973 October War against Israel restored morale in Egypt and in 1974 his plans for social, economic and political reforms were unanimously accepted in a national referendum. In 1977 he visited Israel as part of a reconciliation process and this led to him sharing the 1978 Nobel Peace Prize with Israel's Prime Minister, Menachem Begin. In 1981 he was assassinated by **Islamic fundamentalists**.

Key terms

Islamic fundamentalists: Muslims who believe that all societies should be governed according to a strict interpretation of the Islamic holy scriptures, the Koran and the Sunnah.

DEFCON: this acronym stands for Defence Readiness Condition, a scale used by the US armed forces to state its level of alert. DEFCON 5 is the lowest level of alert, while DEFCON I implies that the US forces are ready for imminent war.

Superpower confrontation

Within hours of the cease-fire being agreed it was violated. Israel launched a major attack against the Egyptians. For the USA this was a critical point. How could the USA retain influence with even the most moderate Arab state in the Middle East if, having sponsored and managed a cease-fire, it did nothing to end this Israeli assault? The Soviet Union proposed sending Soviet and US troops into the region to enforce the cease-fire. This was the source of the confrontation. Kissinger commented, "We had not worked for years to reduce the Soviet military presence in Egypt only to cooperate in reintroducing it. Nor would we participate in a joint force with the Soviets, which would legitimise their role in the area." The aim was to exclude Soviet influence in the region, not facilitate it. Kissinger was even willing to use force to stop any such Soviet military presence in Egypt. There was the real possibility that the Soviets would act unilaterally if the Americans refused to cooperate. Kissinger used the possibility of Soviet unilateral intervention in order to show that the USA would, and could, take a firm stand against the USSR. He also used the threat of Soviet intervention to put pressure on Israel to accept the cease-fire. Both actions presented the USA as the prime mover in Middle Eastern affairs. The Soviet Union's influence was being increasingly marginalised.

Kissinger convened a National Security Council meeting and a general **DEFCON**-3 military alert was declared. This included the Strategic Air Command (SAC) and the North American Air Defence Command (NORAD). The aircraft carrier *Franklin Delano Roosevelt* was moved to the eastern Mediterranean to join the *Independence* and the carrier *John F. Kennedy* was moved to the Mediterranean. The crisis was defused when it was agreed that a UN international force, excluding Soviet and American troops, would be sent in to manage the cease-fire. The crisis ended without any fundamental disruption to the American–Soviet relationship. However, it did raise issues about the Soviet and American perceptions of détente.

The impact of the Middle East Crisis on détente

There was some sustained criticism of the Soviet Union's position during the crisis. In *The Soviet Union and the October 1973 Middle East War: The Implications for Détente*, Kohler, Goure and Harvey comment, "There is no doubt, on the basis of the evidence, that the Soviet Union violated both the letter and the spirit of the agreements signed at the Moscow and Washington Summit Meetings." However, both the superpowers supplied arms to their respective client states and neither power did all it could to defuse an increasingly dangerous situation in the Middle East. Equally, both sides breached the Basic Principles by seeking to gain a unilateral advantage in the crisis. Significantly, neither the USA nor the Soviet Union accused the other of violating the principles of détente in 1973.

Fig. 2 *Israeli troops in Syria, 1973*

In his memoirs, Kissinger presents a revealing view of détente. He commented:

> Our policy to reduce and where possible to eliminate Soviet influence in the Middle East was in fact making progress under the cover of détente. Détente was not a favour we did the Soviets. It was partly necessity; partly a tranquilizer for Moscow as we sought to draw the Middle East into closer relations with us at the Soviets' expense; partly a moral imperative of the nuclear age.

1

Since 1971 the Russians had interpreted détente as building on the cooperation that had been established with the USA. They were also committed to the idea that 'progressive' developments in the world should proceed without direct Soviet or US involvement. The October War had raised serious questions about America's perception of détente, based as it was on a determination to remove the Soviet presence and influence in the Middle East. This inevitably raised a question for the Soviet Union: was détente with the USA serving Soviet interests? An issue for the Soviet Union lay in the reality that many Arab states were sceptical of the idea that Soviet–American détente was compatible with the Soviet Union's claim to support the progressive and national liberation struggle facing many developing countries.

The two superpowers did cooperate in bringing the warring states together at a conference in Geneva in December 1973. This turned out to be the final effort to work effectively together in order to achieve a comprehensive settlement. From this point the USA resumed its own diplomatic efforts among key Arab states and the Israelis. This became known as 'shuttle diplomacy'. In the period 1974–5 Kissinger succeeded in arranging a number of disengagements and partial Israeli withdrawals not only with Syria but also with Egypt. During 1974 diplomatic relations were restored between the USA, Syria and Egypt. On 18 March the Arab oil embargo imposed on the USA during the October War was lifted. Kissinger's shuttle diplomacy gave the USA a pivotal role in the Middle East and it excluded the USSR from significant diplomatic action. The Soviet's strategy was to develop their relationship with Syria and Iraq. In addition to this, the Soviet Union also fostered closer relations with Libya and the **Palestine Liberation Organisation (PLO)**. The latter was officially recognised in August 1974. The October War had created new strategies towards the Middle East by both the USA and the USSR and this inevitably put increased pressure on the validity of détente.

The October War also fuelled opposition to détente within the USA. Prominent among the opponents were those who were friends of Israel. Fears grew that Soviet–American cooperation would lead to agreements that could result in trading Israeli occupied territory for peace between Israel and its Arab neighbours. US–Soviet détente had, on the whole, succeeded during the October War and it was that which alarmed the anti-détente lobby. The war had generated a growing, and influential, body of opponents to détente who feared the implications of continued US–Soviet cooperation would only be harmful to Israel. The détente relationship was about to be further undermined by events in Africa and western Asia.

Key terms

Palestine Liberation Organisation (PLO): an Arab organisation founded in 1964. Its aim was to bring about the creation of an independent Palestinian state. From 1969 its leader was Yasser Arafat. Initially the PLO wished to see the destruction of the state of Israel although this was later modified to one of establishing an independent Palestine alongside Israel.

Neo-colonialism: colonialism refers to the act of a state creating and enforcing colonies abroad. Neo-colonialism is used to describe developed nations exerting their influence over weaker developing nations.

Activity

Talking point

What impact did the Middle East Crisis have on the future of détente?

Angola, 1974–6

Some historians argue that it was conflict over changes in developing countries that brought a halt to the détente process. A critical challenge to the integrity of détente came through instability in developing countries during the 1970s. The Soviet perception was very much focused on the view that this instability was inspired by American **neo-colonialism**. Those Americans who were doubtful of détente and its value to US global interests viewed Soviet policy in a similar way. A fundamental issue in many crises in developing countries was nationalism and independence from external control. The crisis that emerged in Angola was a classic example of how problems in developing nations affected détente; it also revealed the nature of US–Soviet competition.

Fig. 3 *Map of Angola, 1974*

The Angolan Civil War, 1975–6

In April 1974 a revolution in Portugal led to the creation of a left-wing military junta taking power. The new government announced its decision to grant its southern African colony of Angola independence the following year and an end to all offensive military action against the Angolan nationalist opposition in May 1974. A scramble for power between the three Angolan nationalist groups was well underway by November. The issue dividing the sides was essentially which of the three groups would assume power of the newly independent state of Angola. The three groups were:

1 MPLA – the Popular Movement for the Liberation of Angola
2 FNLA – the National Front for the Liberation of Angola
3 UNITA – the National Union for the Liberation of Angola.

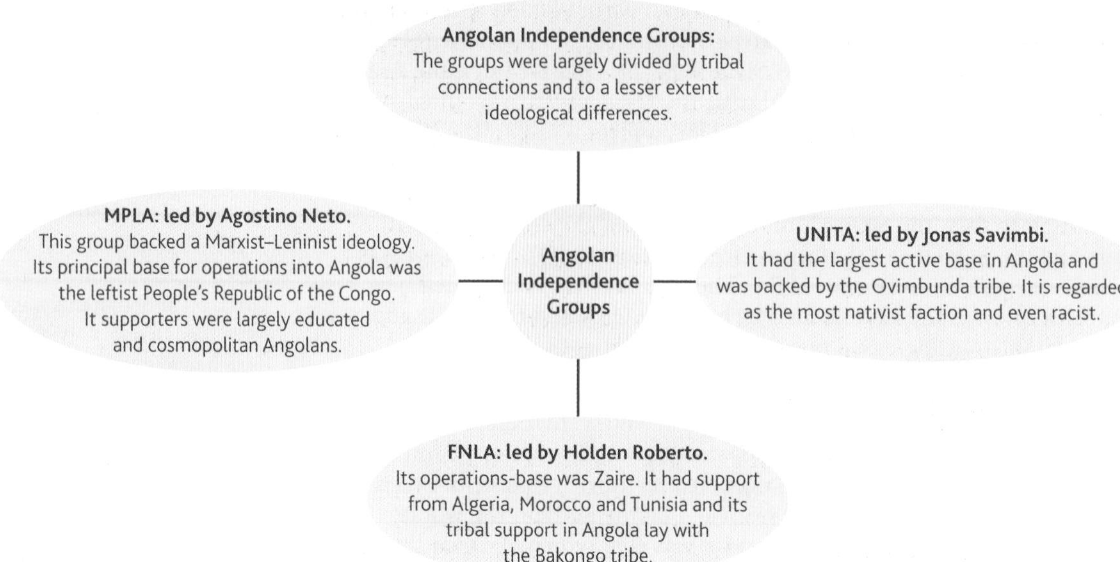

Fig. 4 *Angolan Independence Groups*

Attempts to manage a rivalry that might degenerate into a civil war were finalised through the Alvor Accords of January 1975. The three groups agreed to cooperate with a transitional government. This was the high point of attempts to manage a peaceful transition to independence. Very quickly external powers began to intervene. In June 1974 China had sent 120 military advisers to Zaire to aid the FNLA. In July the USA increased covert funding to this group and this was further increased after the Alvor Accords. The MPLA received funding and arms supplies from the Soviet Union from October 1974, and civil war quickly flared up.

Table 1 *Principal events and their significance*

Date	Event	Significance
February 1975	FNLA began a military campaign against the MPLA	Fundamentally undermined the Alvor Accords
March 1975	The Soviet Union increased its arms supplies to the MPLA	Kissinger acknowledged this as "merely part of an effort to strengthen that group so it could compete militarily with the much stronger FNLA"
May 1975	Cuba sent 230 'military advisers' to support the MPLA	By the summer of 1975 the MPLA launched a major assault against the FNLA and it became clear that the military advantage had shifted to them
July 1975	Zaire and Zambia asks the United States for assistance in preventing the "Soviet Union and Cuba from imposing a solution in Angola, becoming a dominant influence in south-central Africa, and threatening the stability of the area" (Kissinger)	United States increases military aid to the FNLA
August 1975	South Africa enters the conflict	South Africa becomes another ally of the FNLA

By late January 1976 there were about 12,000 Cuban troops supporting the MPLA and these significantly aided the MPLA to reach a final victory by March 1976. The MPLA proclaimed the creation of the Peoples' Republic of Angola (PRA) as early as November 1975 although it was not formally recognised by other African states through the Organisation of

African Unity until February 1976. Relations with both the Soviet Union and Cuba developed well. In October 1976 the Soviet Union ratified a twenty-year Treaty of Friendship. Cuba began the removal of its troops in early 1977 but promised military aid should the PRA face external threats, particularly from South Africa. The USA was less compliant with the PRA. In June 1976 it vetoed Angola's application for membership of the United Nations, but in November it abstained. The strongest and most consistent support for the PRA and President Agostinho Neto's control of it came from Cuba. Cuban troops were used to support Neto's suppression of an attempted coup by Nito Alves, a pro-Soviet rival. Cuba's role in ending this coup reinforced Angolan–Cuban relations and served to weaken Neto's links with the Soviet Union.

The USA's position

Until Cuba, aided by the Soviet Union, began large scale military intervention in Angola in November 1975 the USA did not regard the involvement of the superpowers as being compatible with détente. By the summer of 1975 it was becoming increasingly clear that the FNLA was not going to win the power struggle. One option open to the USA was to do nothing and simply allow events to take their course. This would avoid a costly involvement in a situation over which the USA may not be able to guarantee total control. This was particularly significant given the position in Vietnam by that time. Non-intervention would also protect the USA from international criticism and it would avoid any further antagonisation of the MPLA. The likely outcome of neutrality would be that Neto would be able to establish a dominant position and Angola would move further to the political left while Zaire would conclude that the USA was not interested in the region and move towards a stronger anti-American position. Increasingly, by the summer of 1975, the USA began to question whether Soviet aid to the MPLA was consistent with détente.

Despite this, even by November 1975, the USA did not regard Angola as a direct threat to its economic and strategic interests. Kissinger said in November of that year, "The United States has no national interest in Angola." The USA had no overwhelming objection to the MPLA. It had not opposed the coming to power of a similarly leftist regime in Mozambique under the FRELIMO. In December 1975 William Colby, the Director of Central Intelligence, announced that there was little difference among the competing groups in Angola. They were all 'independents' and leftists. When asked why the USA had backed the FNLA he replied, "Because the Soviets are backing the MPLA is the simplest answer."

In essence, America's national interests in Angola were not threatened by Soviet and Cuban intervention, they were created by it. It was this reality that placed increasing strain on détente. Kissinger summed up the USA's perception of Soviet involvement in Angola when, at the end of 1975, he commented that the United States, "cannot be indifferent while an outside power embarks upon an interventionist policy – so distant from its homeland and so removed from traditional Russian interests." Ironically, the USA itself had been covertly supplying military assistance to the FNLA. The catalyst that triggered the USA response was the escalation of Cuban military aid and the connections the Soviet Union had with this. The USA could not continue its own covert aid for the FNLA because this would have aligned it with South Africa which was also aiding the FNLA campaign. This was at a point when black Africa was

Fig. 5 *Angolan child guerilla fighters*

challenging the last vestiges of white minority rule across the continent. In addition to this there was growing international condemnation of apartheid in South Africa. It was clear to the USA that South Africa was a political liability.

Kissinger's real concern was that the USA could offer no effective counter-action to stop the MPLA benefiting from Soviet and Cuban aid. In his words, "Angola represents the first time that the Soviets have moved militarily at long distance to impose a regime of their choice. It is the first time that the United States has failed to respond to Soviet military moves outside the immediate Soviet orbit." His concern focused on the international perception of the USA's apparent failure to take decisive and effective action in Angola. America's failure to respond could be regarded as an indication of a lack of determination to counter similar communist interventions in the future. This was the heart of the threat to détente. It could not survive if either side gained a unilateral advantage as had appeared to have happened over Angola. Kissinger was convinced that the Soviet Union was using Cuban forces as a proxy.

The Soviet Union's position

Significantly, the Soviet Union did not begin supporting the MPLA until after the USA had started its support for the FNLA in July 1974. The Soviet priority in 1974 was to ensure that China did not gain at their expense in Angola. The Soviets could not appear to be less able and less willing than the Chinese to support national liberation movements in developing nations. China was a clear rival for Soviet influence in southern Africa. The Soviet Union's compliance with détente had, in Neto's mind, forged a link between the USSR and the USA and that had weakened Soviet credibility in Angola.

For its part, the Soviet Union interpreted US and Chinese aid to the FNLA as part of a programme of Sino–American collaboration aimed at gaining influence in developing countries. Angola was simply a springboard from which to launch this collective influence. Furthermore, the Soviets were convinced that Sino–American actions were the outcome of the improved relations that had been developing since 1971. In December 1975 Kissinger acknowledged that China and the USA had "parallel views" on Angola but there was no "coordinated" joint action taking place there. The Soviet Union was convinced that its own actions in Angola were in line with the spirit underpinning détente. For the Soviet Union détente did not mean simply keeping things as they were. The Soviet Union had a legitimate right to aid 'peoples fighting for their liberation.' This was very much the position taken by Castro. He was committed to socialist international cooperation to support liberation and freedom. In July 1976 he announced that, "We have fulfilled our international duty with our brothers of Angola and we are proud of it."

Ultimately the Soviets wanted to avoid exposing themselves to the accusation that they would not support progressive and Marxist liberation movements, especially in developing countries. The Soviet Union sought to expand its own influence within the developing world and at the same time undermine the influence of both China and the USA. The problems in Angola highlighted the apparently differing perceptions of the USA and the Soviet Union as to what détente was. However it was significant that the USA had also provided aid during the Angolan crisis.

Activity

Group activity

Working in groups, assess the impact of the crisis in Angola. One group will argue that it was largely insignificant while the other will suggest it had a damaging, but not fatal impact on the future of détente.

Afghanistan, 1979

In April 1978 a coup led to the overthrow of Muhammad Daoud, a cousin of the former King of Afghanistan. Daoud had been in power since 1973, with the support of the leftist People's Democratic Party of Afghanistan (PDPA). It was that same group that had overthrown Daoud primarily because of his failure to implement the socialist principles to which he said he was committed. It was this April 1978 coup that ultimately led to the Soviet invasion of Afghanistan in December 1979, an event that had a profound effect on international politics during the 1980s.

Fig. 6 *Map of Afghanistan, 1979*

The Soviet Union and Afghanistan, 1978–9

The PDPA regime was an ally of the Soviet Union but it rapidly began to fragment and ultimately a faction within it, led by Hafizullah Amin, gained control. This dominant faction started a programme of radical, and disruptive, land reform. They began a campaign against the influence of Islam by rejecting the wearing of the Islamic veil and the use of Islamic green in the national flag. The Soviets were concerned that the regime was rapidly alienating many Afghans and this could lead to real instability. They also believed that Amin might realign Afghanistan with the United States, Pakistan and China. Essentially, Afghanistan would become a threat directly situated on the Soviet borders. To the Soviet Union Amin was unreliable as an ally and unable to control the growing Islamic opposition he was facing within Afghanistan. The Soviets were in danger of losing their strategic, ideological, political and economic influence in Afghanistan.

What were the Soviet interests in Afghanistan?

- There was a shared border stretching 2,500 kilometres adjoining the Muslim Central Asian republics of the USSR.
- Afghanistan was a socialist state and a regional ally of the USSR. If it aligned with the USA this would strengthen the USA's geo-strategic power in the region, at the expense of the USSR.

It appeared as if the Soviet Union was interested in aiding a threatened socialist state and protecting it from the misgovernment of Amin. The reality was that the USSR needed to protect its own security. Brezhnev believed that Afghanistan could be turned into "an imperialist bridgehead on our southern border" and as such it would be "a seat of serious danger to the security of the Soviet state." Afghanistan had to remain a buffer to protect Soviet security and the only effective way to ensure this was to undertake military intervention in Afghanistan in order to restore a stable and popular socialist state that was a loyal ally of the Soviet Union. Intervention was not viewed by the Soviet Union as part of a process of opportunist expansionism but rather as a security necessity. By late 1979 Soviet–American relations had already reached a low point. NATO was going to install new missiles in Europe, the SALT II Treaty was under strain and the USA was closely linked to China. Any further damage caused by military intervention in Afghanistan would be outweighed by the benefits of a pro-Soviet and stable Afghanistan.

Activity

Discussion activity

As a group, discuss the reasons why the Soviet Union entered Afghanistan. What do the reasons tell you about the Soviet Union's attitudes towards détente and SALT II?

As in Angola, the Soviets certainly viewed their actions in Afghanistan as being perfectly consistent with the Basic Principles of détente agreed in 1972. The military intervention was a defensive act designed to prevent Afghanistan plunging into chaos and becoming the victim of hostile external influences. For the Soviets it was intended to preserve, not destroy, the status quo. The Soviets saw the Basic Principles as an implicit acceptance that each of the superpowers' vital interests had to be guarded. Afghanistan had never been part of the US security system. The whole affair was, for the Soviets, within the Soviet sphere of influence and could not, therefore, be viewed as a Soviet challenge to the West and its vital interest.

The USA's reaction to Afghanistan, 1978–9

In the year following Daoud's removal, the USA hardly considered the possibility of Soviet military intervention in Afghanistan in order to change the new regime or to end the rising opposition to Amin among Afghans. The only question was over the extent of direct Soviet support for the regime. Events in Afghanistan assumed somewhat greater significance for the USA when the Shah's pro-American regime was overthrown in Iran by Islamic fundamentalists. The Americans feared that Ayatollah Khomeini's regime would collapse and leave Iran vulnerable to leftist and even communist influences. This could further reinforce the Soviet Union's regional influence. Soviet links with Afghanistan began to assume greater importance for the USA. At his summit meeting with Brezhnev, President Carter highlighted the USA's growing concerns when he said, "the United States has not interfered in the internal affairs of Afghanistan" and that "we expect the Soviet Union to do the same."

Key profile

Ayatollah Ruhollah Khomeini, 1900–89

Khomeini was the Iranian Shi'ite Muslim leader. From 1964 he was in exile because of his opposition to the Shah of Iran, only returning when the Shah's regime was overthrown in 1979. He turned Iran into an Islamic fundamentalist republic. For much of his rule Iran was involved in a bloody war with Iraq. He managed the ruthless oppression of all opposition within Iran and thousands of his opponents were executed.

Fig. 7 *Ayatollah Khomeini returns to Iran after the Shah's overthrow, 1 February 1979*

On 27 December 1979, the Soviets killed Amin and further increased the troop numbers which had begun on 24 December. For the USA the line between influencing events and directly intervening to determine them had been crossed. For détente it created a further crisis. Carter referred to the intervention as a "blatant violation of accepted international rules of behaviour" and "a grave threat to peace." A major turning point had been reached in US–Soviet relations. For all practical purposes détente was dead. This is best summed up through remarks Carter made in his memoirs: "The worst disappointment to me personally was the immediate and automatic loss of any chance of an early ratification of the SALT II Treaty." On 3 January 1980 Carter formally asked the US Senate to postpone indefinitely any further consideration of the SALT II Treaty because of the Soviet invasion of Afghanistan. The USA did not consider the range of possible Soviet motives. They did not consider whether the intervention was an attempt to maintain stability and an already pro-Soviet regime in Afghanistan or a direct act of aggression which was part of a planned process of regional expansionism. Many historians have taken the view that the Carter administration failed to fully assess Soviet motivation for the intervention. This narrowed Carter's thinking and ultimately his response has been perceived as a major factor in damaging the future of détente.

In an address to the nation on 4 January 1980 Carter set out a series of measures aimed at the Soviet Union. These included:

- a deferral of action on cultural and economic exchanges
- major restrictions on Soviet fishing privileges in American waters
- a ban on the sale of high technology and strategic items to the Soviets
- an embargo on sales of grain to the Soviet Union
- US military and economic assistance to Pakistan to enhance that state's security.

Other similar sanctions followed in the months to come. On 23 January 1980 the President unveiled the so-called Carter Doctrine for the defence of the Persian Gulf.

Fig. 8 *Muslim snipers overlooking an encampment of government troops in Kunar province, Afghanistan in September 1979*

The Carter Doctrine, 1980

On 8 January 1980, Carter made some significant remarks to members of the US Congress. He said:

> The Soviet invasion of Afghanistan is the greatest threat to peace since the Second World War. It's a sharp escalation in the aggressive history of the Soviet Union. We are the other superpower on earth, and it became my responsibility to take action. Our own nation's security was directly threatened. There is no doubt that the Soviet's move into Afghanistan, if done without adverse consequences, would have resulted in the temptation to move again and again until they reached warm water ports or until they acquired control over a major portion of the world's oil supplies.

2

One element of détente had always been about ensuring some degree of control over Soviet expansionism. By 1980 that element had become the dominant aim. The Carter Doctrine translated into an American commitment to prevent any further Soviet advance into the Persian Gulf area and south-west Asia. It emphasised the prospect of a military solution to any such expansionism and therefore focused on building up US strategic forces. Finally, it reinforced the need to expand relations with China.

Further to this, Carter also tried to persuade the NATO alliance and the West to suspend East–West détente. However, détente in Europe was working beneficially. While Europe deplored Soviet actions over

Activity

Revision chart

Make a revision chart to illustrate the various factors which helped to undermine détente in the 1970s. Underneath write a paragraph to support the factor – or country – you feel was most responsible for détente's deterioration.

Afghanistan they were not prepared to suspend détente in Europe. Europe's trade links with the Soviet Union not only continued but also expanded. Europe did not see its interests being served by allowing itself to become a pawn in the USA's global power strategy.

He went on to announce an increase in the defence budget for 1981. In effect Carter had linked America's relations with the Soviet Union and the future of détente to the Soviet Union's decision to maintain a military presence in Afghanistan. The Soviets would have to submit to America's demands for their withdrawal. This represented an ultimatum and shut down any possibility of a diplomatic solution. Also the question arises as to whether Soviet actions did threaten America's vital interest in the Persian Gulf and, therefore, whether the Carter Doctrine was a massive overreaction by the United States. The Soviets certainly took the view that the US leadership in 1980 had used the intervention in Afghanistan as a pretext that enabled them to dismantle détente, revive the nuclear arms race and build up a position of strength for the USA in the Persian Gulf. America's actions were not seen by the Soviet Union as a response to their intervention but as a classic piece of international opportunism. America was simply waiting for 'an Afghanistan' to happen in order to fulfil its real aim of bringing détente to an end.

The Soviet invasion of Afghanistan was the final blow in détente's existence. As far as the West was concerned, the invasion demanded international condemnation and a policy of containment to prevent further Soviet expansionism. The invasion did not represent a threat to world peace greater than any since the Second World War yet that was the view taken by the USA. Indeed the Carter administration determined that its entire relationship with the Soviet Union depended on a Soviet withdrawal from Afghanistan. Carter had made a fundamental shift in Soviet–American relations. The United States had moved away from the Nixon–Kissinger position of cooperation with, and the management of, the development of Soviet power and reverted to a position of containment more associated with the Truman–Eisenhower–Kennedy approach. This position became enshrined in the Carter Doctrine.

Learning outcomes

From studying this section, you should be able to understand the reasons why détente developed and the range of factors that contributed towards it. You have seen how the Cuban Missile Crisis was a turning point in the development of international relations, although it was to take several more years before that new relationship was established. You should be able to evaluate the differing motives among the superpowers and their differing perceptions of their new relationship, together with the positive outcomes of détente and its limitations.

Finally you have looked at the collapse of détente and the contribution that specific conflicts such as those in Angola, and particularly Afghanistan, made towards it.

'The Soviet Union was aggressively expansionist and showed little real enthusiasm for détente.' How valid is this assessment?

This question enables you to either agree or challenge the proposition. You may examine the idea that the Soviet Union was aggressively expansionist and question how such an approach was consistent with any form of détente. Indeed, you may suggest that there is little substantive evidence to support this view. Equally you may argue that détente was simply a means to an end for the Soviet Union and the end was to establish greater international influence. The Soviet Union never abandoned its commitment to supporting international revolution. The best case is one based on focused evidence and successfully challenges an alternative view.

3 The Final Years of the Cold War, 1981–91

7 The USSR Under Pressure

In this chapter you will learn about:

- the state of the Soviet economy by the early 1980s
- the economic policies and reforms introduced during the Gorbachev years
- the relationship between the economic condition of the USSR and the Cold War.

Key terms

GNP or Gross National Product: this is the annual value of the nation's productivity in terms of manufacturing and services. It acts as a measure of the economic growth or decline of a nation's wealth.

Brezhnev died in November 1982 and his successor, Yuri Andropov, confirmed in his first speech that the Soviet economy was in difficulties. He acknowledged that "there are many problems in our national economy that are overdue for solution. I do not have any ready receipts for their solution. But it is for all of us – the Central Committee of the Party – to find answers to them."

The condition of the Soviet economy

The Soviet economy had been slowing down during the 1970s. Between 1975 and 1980 the growth in **Gross National Product (GNP)** had been 2.7 per cent while during the second half of the 1960s it had reached 5.2 per cent. The foundations to the economic decline of the Soviet Union were laid during the 1970s. Even though the USSR produced 155 million tonnes of steel in 1977 compared to the 115 million tonnes produced by the USA, the USSR was still forced to import $2 billion worth of rolled steel, tin plate and large diameter steel piping. In terms of new technology the USSR was significantly behind western states. The USSR failed to integrate its technical advances from space and military research into the civilian economy.

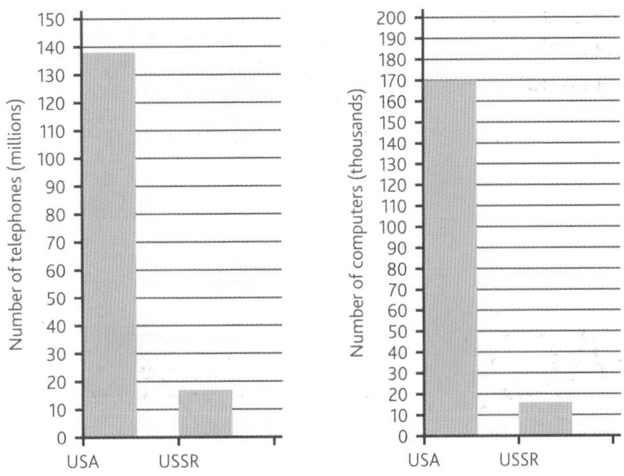

Fig. 1 *Technological gulf between USSR and USA, early 1980s*

The USSR simply did not keep pace with the West in these crucial areas of technology. Between 1979 and 1982 there was a world economic recession and it was during this period that crucial industrial sectors such as oil, coal, iron and steel began to plateau in terms of growth. The industrial decline was to have a significant impact on the economies of eastern European states and this in turn led to the weakening of communist control throughout the eastern bloc. The Soviet Union had been, for decades, the primary supplier of cheap fuel and raw materials to eastern Europe. As growth declined so did the Soviet Union's capacity to receive eastern European manufactured goods. This collapse in the flow of trade between the Soviet Union and eastern Europe in general fundamentally undermined popular confidence in the communist economic system.

By the early 1980s growth in agriculture had slowed down significantly. This was, in part, the result of continued droughts and poor harvests. In 1975 the Soviet Union entered a five-year agreement to buy up to 8 million tonnes of grain annually from the USA. This represented huge food price subsidies for the Soviet government. The unreformed Soviet system of collectivised agriculture only served to heighten the production problems facing the state.

These economic problems were made worse through the wider global context in which the Soviet Union functioned. By 1981 détente had drawn to a close and the USA placed embargoes on exports to the USSR, particularly the export of grain supplies. The end of détente triggered an escalation of the nuclear arms race, certainly up to 1984. In 1979 the USSR invaded Afghanistan. These factors added further to the increasing economic costs facing the state. Inevitably, these costs impacted on the Soviet people's quality of life. By 1981 the rate of growth in consumer goods had levelled at zero. In addition there had been a major decline in the provision of quality health care and a rise in the levels of infant mortality. The start of the 1980s heralded an ominous future for the Soviet economy and the growing realisation that the Soviet system, and indeed communism itself, was failing to deliver progressive improvements relative to the West. As Richard Crockatt notes, "No one would dare claim in 1980 what Khrushchev had claimed in 1960: that within a decade the Soviet Union would match and even overtake the United States."

Activity

Challenge your thinking

What would you consider to be the indicators of a strong or weak economy? Identify the main features of the Russian economy at the start of the 1980s and beside each indicate whether this was a strength or a weakness. What can you conclude about the state of the Russian economy at this time?

The economy under Gorbachev, 1985–90

Key profile

Mikhail Sergeyevich Gorbachev, 1931–present

Gorbachev was Soviet President between 1985 and 1991. He had been a member of the Politburo only since 1980. He held the role of General Secretary of the Communist Party between 1985 and 1991 and also President of the Supreme Soviet from 1988. In 1990 he was awarded the Nobel Peace Prize. He resigned his offices in December 1991.

Mikhail Gorbachev had presided over the Soviet Union's agricultural decline towards the end of the Brezhnev years. By 1985 he was the leader of the Soviet Union. Some historians take the view that when Gorbachev took the reigns of power the Soviet economy, although in a state of decline, was not on the brink of collapsing. However, many take the view that Gorbachev was the architect of the irreversible decline that the economy had reached by the beginning of the 1990s. This is not to say that Gorbachev in some way planned the collapse. His policies were activated within the highly controlled environment of the Soviet economy. Basic to this system was the concept of the command economy.

Fig. 2 *A bread queue in Moscow, 6 November 1991*

This was driven by an inflexible system of central planning. This central planning determined output targets and tended to reject innovation in management and the introduction of new ideas to maximise productivity. As Martin Goldman comments, "Soviet planners were simply unable to keep up with the speed with which one innovation superseded another." Central planning had been traditionally focused on the large scale production of industrial goods such as those related to coal, steel and machine tools. Relatively little focus was placed on the manufacture of consumer goods. The economic crisis faced by the Soviet Union did not in itself cause the collapse of communism, either in the Soviet Union or within the wider Soviet communist bloc of eastern Europe. However, in conjunction with ***glasnost*** (openness) and ***perestroika*** (restructuring) it performed a pivotal role. Such was the impact of the economic crisis on the Cold War. *Perestroika* was the key to Gorbachev's economic reforms, which were designed to improve the performance of the Soviet economy. Essentially, Gorbachev's approach was to maximise the potential of the existing economic and production systems rather than dismantle them. The problem was that the existing system was not working and therefore any retention of that failed system would not work either. Gorbachev made this statement to the 27th Congress of the Party in February 1986:

> Every readjustment of the economic mechanism begins with a rejection of old stereotypes of thought and actions, with a clear understanding of the new tasks. This refers primarily to the activity of our economic personnel, to the functionaries of the central links of administration. Most of them have a clear idea of the Party's initiatives and seek to find the best ways of carrying them out ...
>
> It is hard, however, to understand those who follow a 'wait and see' policy, or those who do not actually do anything or change anything. There will be no reconciliation with the stance taken by functionaries of that kind. All the more so do we have to part ways with those who hope that everything will settle down and return to the old lines. That will not happen, comrades!

1

Key terms

Glasnost* and *Perestroika: *Glasnost* literally means 'openness', and referred to a Soviet government policy of allowing more freedom to discuss social problems. *Perestroika* means 'restructuring' and referred to major social, political and economic reforms.

Cross-reference

For a further explanation of *glasnost* and *perestroika*, see Chapter 9.

Activity

Thinking point

Was Gorbachev naïve to think that *glasnost* and *perestroika* would restore economic stability to the Soviet Union?

Gorbachev linked mediocre economic growth to political, ideological and foreign policy problems. If the economy could be made to expand and become more efficient then these problems would be reduced. By implication, if Gorbachev's economic aims were not fulfilled then foreign policy problems would deepen as the economy failed to underpin foreign policy aims. It was clear that there was a direct link between the Soviet Union's economic performance and its ability to maintain its superpower position globally.

A closer look

The Anti-Alcohol Campaign, May 1985

Alcoholism was rife in the Soviet Union. It acted as a drain on the Soviet economy in a number of ways. Absenteeism from work and the inevitable cost to the Soviet health system were perhaps the most significant. Yegor Ligachev, a member of the Politburo, was given responsibility for this campaign and one of its focal points was to impose restrictions on the sale of vodka. The aim was to lower the production of vodka by 10 per cent over five years. Random breath tests were carried out by the police on ordinary citizens travelling on buses. Inevitably, the campaign was deeply unpopular. The immediate outcome from this Soviet version of prohibition was that many people simply produced their own home-made alcohol. This led to dramatic shortages of sugar, an essential ingredient in the manufacture of alcohol. Further to this, the government lost huge amounts of tax revenue as the sale of legal alcohol declined rapidly. By 1988 these restrictions were relaxed. Essentially, the campaign had achieved little towards addressing the fundamental problem of an increasingly distressed Soviet economy.

Industrial efficiency, 1985–7

Gorbachev wanted to increase production targets in light industry, machine building, food and meat and dairy products. Between 1985 and 1986 the people involved in these areas of production were made more responsible for their production targets. Any profits from over production could be ploughed back into the factories. Further control was devolved to the production factories as light industries were allowed to respond to the demands of market forces. Gorbachev wanted to improve the quality of manufactured goods. In May 1986 a system designed to act as a form of quality control was introduced. The organisation set up to implement this was the *Grospryomka*. This received a similar reception by most Soviet workers to the one the alcohol campaign had received. There was widespread opposition and by 1988 it was withdrawn.

The Law on Joint Ventures, January 1987

Gorbachev saw the value of foreign investment but for the Soviets it was crucial that communism was protected. At first the Law on Joint Ventures allowed foreign ownership on no more than 49 per cent of the business. Control remained in the hands of the state. This was extended to 100 per cent by 1990. The introduction of a McDonald's restaurant in Moscow is an example of such a venture. The Joint Ventures Law gradually ended the monopoly controlled by the state and this allowed foreign investment to develop. It also allowed flexibility between different enterprises and suggested that Soviet businesses could enter into competition with external states in the West. The problem was that even though these forward-looking practices were introduced they would never be truly effective, nor would the enterprises be truly independent while a communist controlled central planning system remained in place as the basis of the **command economy**. The effectiveness of the Joint Ventures scheme was further undermined by the state. Once a venture entered profitability it was heavily taxed. This not only drained the profits but it also reduced any incentive to grow.

Key terms

Command economy: an economic system that is centrally controlled by the government, and which often focuses on industrial output as its priority.

Inflation: the rising cost of living. As prices rise, workers demand pay rises in order to maintain their existing standard of living.

Did you know?

Some 27,000 Soviet citizens applied to work in the Moscow McDonalds in 1990. It took 14 years to negotiate permission for the fast-food chain to base its restaurants in the Soviet Union.

The Enterprise Law, January 1988

This focused on state-controlled enterprises and businesses. The aim was to decentralise authority and devolve decision making down to the businesses and enterprises themselves. There was to be a significant reduction in state subsidies for these enterprises and therefore they were to function as profit making organisations selling within wholesale markets. The enterprise would remain state owned and there was no suggestion that privatisation was being introduced. This was a clear example of restructuring rather than dismantling the economic system. The degree of independence that these enterprises achieved was limited. The state received around 85 per cent of production although the managers of the enterprises were able to sell the remaining 15 per cent to whoever they wished. An element of competition had vaguely emerged. One important reform in this system came with managers having more control over wage levels. The outcome was to increase the number of unemployed as workers were laid off for cost efficiency reasons. Enterprises were responsible for their own profitability. This inevitably meant that they made their workforces trimmer in order to cut costs. Overall the Enterprise Law was an attempt to operate a still largely command system within a market economy. The aim of providing some increased independence in order to promote initiatives and increase productivity was sound but the method represented a halfway house and could not, therefore, succeed.

Workers' discontent

Benefits for the mass of Soviet citizens were relatively few. **Inflation** and rising prices made the lives of ordinary citizens very strained. Gorbachev's administration faced serious problems in the late 1980s and into 1990. In July 1989 coal miners in the Kuzbass coalfield went on strike. This was part of the increasing dissatisfaction displayed by workers throughout the Soviet Union. The initial issue for the miners was one of low pay and poor working conditions. The discontent quickly spread to other regions. As the strikes spread to the Donbas mines and into Pechora and Karaganda, almost 200,000 miners were involved in industrial action. The miners called for an end to the control of the communist movement over the mines. This they saw as the best way to make the improvements that they were demanding. The political control was seen as a barrier to change. Miners even went as far as forming an unofficial trade union, an unheard-of development in the Soviet Union. In October 1989 the government accepted the basic right of workers to strike although strikes remained illegal in key economic areas.

Although an issue that underpinned the strikes had been low pay, the reality was that incomes were rising faster than levels of productivity. At the start of 1990 incomes rose by up to 15 per cent while productivity experienced zero growth. The Soviet Union's economy was in need of urgent reform.

Activity

Thinking point

Assess the effectiveness of Gorbachev's economic reforms up to 1989. How did life improve for the Soviet people?

Economic reform plans, 1990

By 1989 the economy was in a generally reasonable condition. Progress was slow but it was present.

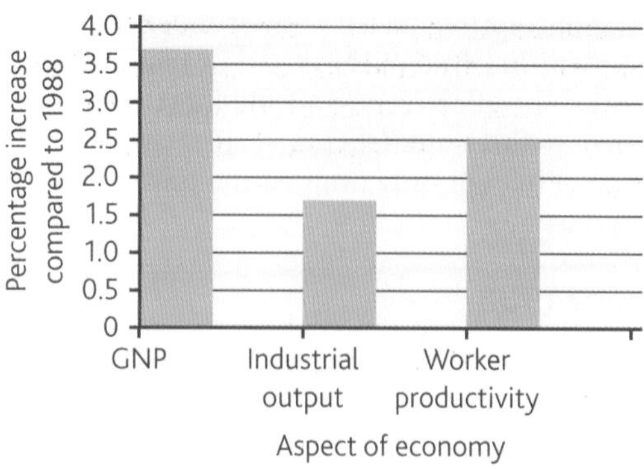

Fig. 3 *Soviet economic improvement, 1989*

Despite all this, it was clear that there had been a fall in living standards across the Soviet Union. As early as 1988 Gorbachev acknowledged that the economy was changing too slowly.

In March 1990 Gorbachev headed a Commission which had the responsibility for developing a reform package. Leading economists led by the Deputy Prime Minister, Dr Leonid Abalkin, acted as advisers to this commission. The aim was to produce a rapid programme of reforms which would be in place within a month. This ambitious target perhaps underlined not only the urgency of the problems but also the hurried approach that Gorbachev chose to adopt them.

The proposals were presented to the USSR Supreme Soviet in May. The initial move was to reduce state subsidies. This was to be the first tentative step towards a gradual shift to a market economy driven by supply and demand. The immediate cost of reducing subsidies was an anticipated increase in the price of consumer goods. The price of bread was expected to more than double. Increases in the costs of non-consumer goods were expected to be even higher. The prospects of high inflation and rising unemployment moved the Supreme Soviet to call for more restrained plans.

The position by 1991

The Soviet Union's economic position had become critical by the start of 1991. GNP had fallen by a further 8 per cent and the national income had reduced by 10 per cent. Industrial and agricultural output had both fallen dramatically. There was little help from external factors. Exports had toppled by a staggering 33 per cent and there had been a 45 per cent reduction in imports. The Soviet Union's trade with other countries appeared to be in a state of free fall. This economic crisis was further complicated by the growing moves towards political decentralisation and the rise of nationalism across the Union. A number of the republics within the Union were unwilling to cooperate with centrally planned change and they began to withhold revenue. This inevitably contributed to a significant shortfall in the national budget. It was clear that this situation meant that the planned spending on the military would be under threat. The Soviet Union was on the brink of disintegrating and the republics were increasingly determined not to cooperate with any centralising of the economy and centralised economic planning on a national level.

Exploring the detail

Comecon

Otherwise known as the Council of Mutual Economic Assistance (CMEA), Comecon was formed by the Soviet Union in 1949. Its aim was to integrate the economies of eastern Europe. The membership extended beyond Europe and included Cuba (1972) and Vietnam (1978). In effect, Comecon operated as a planning agency for the Soviet Union. Its economic objectives were directed from Moscow. As an organisation it was formally dissolved in 1991 with the collapse of the Soviet Union.

The Soviet economy and its impact on the Cold War

The communist bloc of eastern European states was an integral part of the Soviet Union's international power base. It was a crucial factor in the ability of the Soviet Union to function within the framework of the

Cold War. The internal economic problems within the Soviet Union undermined its ability to compete in this Cold War environment. These internal economic problems also undermined the economic strength of eastern European states. The organisation that held these diverse economies together was Comecon.

The collapse of Comecon

In June 1984 a Comecon economic summit was held in Moscow. Its aim was to promote 'intensive growth' through tighter coordination of national economic plans. The Soviet Union made it clear that cheap exports of fuel and raw materials to eastern Europe could not continue. This was a direct consequence of the deepening economic crisis in the Soviet Union. The unintended outcome of this move was to force eastern European states into stronger economic links with the West.

Fig. 4 *Boris Yeltsin and the coup of August 1991, which cut short Gorbachev's economic programme*

In December 1985 Comecon called for increased scientific and technical cooperation among the member states. The purpose of this was to accelerate productivity through rapid advances in technology and innovation. This plan failed because the communist system throughout eastern Europe was based on centrally planned economic development within each individual state. The system had isolated states from each other, therefore the idea of close cooperation simply could not work. There was no tradition, in such planned economies, of innovation and adaptability. Furthermore, eastern European states were increasingly reluctant to contribute to what they saw as schemes promoting Soviet economic interests.

The programme only succeeded in weakening the links between the Soviet Union and other Comecon members. The moves towards the collapse of Comecon were furthered by a development in 1985. The Secretary-General of Comecon, Vyacheslav Sychov, contacted the President of the EC Commission suggesting mutual diplomatic recognition between them. This meant that EC members could negotiate trade agreements with individual Comecon members. The whole process was concluded in June 1988. The EC was able to set up trade and cooperation agreements with Comecon members, starting with Hungary in December 1988.

During 1990–1 the final throes of Comecon's demise were enacted.

- In December 1989 the Soviet Union finally announced the end of the supply of cheap fuel to eastern European states. The Soviet economy simply could not take any further strain.
- As of 1 January 1991 all trade between Comecon members was to be driven by market prices rather than through unrealistic and crippling subsidies.
- Comecon as an organisation was formally ended on 28 September 1991.

Many argue that Comecon did little to create economic unity among eastern bloc states and that its end was the final chapter in the collapse of Soviet power and influence in eastern Europe.

Summary question

1 'Mikhail Gorbachev was entirely responsible for the failure to revive the Soviet Union's economy from 1985.' How valid is this assessment?

8 The Second Cold War

In this chapter you will learn about:

- the Presidency of Ronald Reagan from 1981
- East–West relations during the 1980s
- the development of US military power
- the relationship the USA had with Europe and Britain.

The 1980s brought a new era in the Cold War. After the era of détente, the Presidency of Ronald Reagan brought tension and suspicion, and the public once more began to fear the outright possibility of nuclear war. The 1980s saw the arms race accelerate, and the superpowers gained the capability to destroy the earth several times over.

Fig. 1 *Soviet SS-15 mobile short-range ICBM*

Reagan and US militarism during the 1980s

Ronald Reagan becomes President, 1981

> From Stettin on the Baltic to Varna on the Black Sea, the regimes planted by totalitarianism have had more than thirty years to establish their legitimacy. But none has been able to risk free elections. Regimes planted by bayonets do not take root. The objective of what I propose is quite simple to state: to foster the infrastructure of democracy. I have often wondered about the shyness of some of us in the West about standing for this ideal. This reluctance to use those vast resources at our command reminds me of the elderly lady whose home was bombed in the blitz. As the rescuers moved about they found a bottle of brandy she'd stored behind the staircase. One of the workers pulled out the cork to give her a taste of it. She came around and said, "Here now – put it back. That's for emergencies." Well, the emergency is upon us. Let us be shy no longer. Let us go to our strength. Let us offer hope. Let us tell the world that a new age is not only possible but probable.

1 *Extract from a speech Reagan delivered in 1982*

Key profile

Ronald Reagan, 1911–2004

Initially a Hollywood film actor, Reagan became governor of California in 1966 and President from 1981 until 1989. He was a right wing Republican and during his Presidency he cut taxes and spending on domestic social programmes while increasing military spending. He adopted an aggressive policy towards Central America and in 1983 invaded Granada in order to remove a Marxist regime there. He also backed the funding of anti-communist groups in Nicaragua.

President Reagan delivered these words as part of a speech he made before the British Parliament in June 1982. It clearly set the tone for his relationship with the Soviet Union. There was never the slightest chance that Reagan would contemplate war in order to remove the Soviet Union's ideological, political and economic strangle hold over eastern Europe. However, Reagan was determined to pursue aggressive policies which were designed to change Soviet behaviour.

Reagan was convinced that détente had resulted in the USA's trust in the Soviet Union being misplaced.

- He blamed previous administrations for allowing the USA to be taken advantage of and thereby allowing America's power globally to be eroded.
- In a speech in March 1983 he referred to Soviet leaders as "the focus of evil in the modern world," and that "the Soviet Union underlies all the unrest that is going on" in the world.
- He believed that the way to address the Soviet challenge was to abandon détente and the cooperative resolution of conflicts upon which it was founded. Reagan believed that the USA needed to return to unilateralism and restore its military strength.

Ronald Reagan wanted to revitalise America's pride in itself. He feared that communism was still expansionist and that it would spread unless the USA was able to contain it. This view effectively drew a line under détente and returned the USA to a position of containment and confrontation. This was the view of some historians on Reagan's contribution to the development of what has been inaccurately termed a Second Cold War.

Activity

Research activity

Research further detail about Ronald Reagan's thinking on relations with the communist world. Try to develop an assessment of his contribution to the end of détente and the start of the so-called Second Cold War.

Soviet reactions up to 1985

The USSR wanted a return to détente. There was an initial expectation that Reagan would support this although it was soon undermined by Reagan's confrontational rhetoric. Throughout 1981 and 1982 the Soviet leadership continued to promote the need for dialogue with the USA. Increasingly, the Soviet leadership came to believe that Reagan was interested in confrontation and cold war rather than the containment and competition which had characterised détente.

In November 1982 a change came in Soviet leadership with the death of Brezhnev. Yuri Andropov followed Brezhnev. He was committed to reviving détente but, like his predecessor, he realised that the USA was not. In June 1983, soon after Reagan's 'evil empire' speech, Andropov described the state of Soviet–American relations as being "marked by confrontation, unprecedented in the entire post-war period by its intensity and sharpness, of two diametrically opposite world outlooks, the two political courses, socialism and imperialism."

A closer look

KAL 007

On 1 September 1983 a major blow to Soviet–American relations came with the shooting down of a Korean civil airliner, KAL 007, by a Soviet interceptor. The Soviets claimed that the plane was on an intelligence gathering mission on behalf of the USA. The USA immediately denied this and accused the Soviet Union of wilfully destroying a civil aircraft and killing 269 people in the process. The incident clearly demonstrated the ever growing divide between the USA and the Soviet Union. The USA focused on Soviet barbarity while the USSR viewed the incident as being one of an act of US espionage.

On 28 September, in the wake of the KAL 007 incident, Andropov issued a statement from the Soviet leadership which evaluated the Reagan administration up to that point and clearly illustrated the attitudes of the Soviets. The Reagan administration was described as following "a militarist course that represents a serious threat to peace. Its essence is to try to ensure a dominating position in the world for the United States of America without regard for the interests of other states and peoples." Andropov went on to say, "If anyone had any illusions about the possibility of an evolution for the better in the policy of the present American administration, recent events have dispelled them once and for all." The Soviet leadership was not expecting to engage in serious negotiations with the US leadership at this point in time. For the Soviet Union the United States had abandoned détente and was moving towards a policy geared to military superiority over the USSR. There was also the view that the Reagan administration was seeking to undermine the Soviet Union and challenge national liberation movements globally.

Militarism and arms control up to 1985

Reagan's foreign policy was focused very heavily on a restoration of the USA's military power. Jimmy Carter's final defence budget had proposed $17.4 billion for military spending. By 1989 Reagan presented his military spending budget needs at $300 billion.

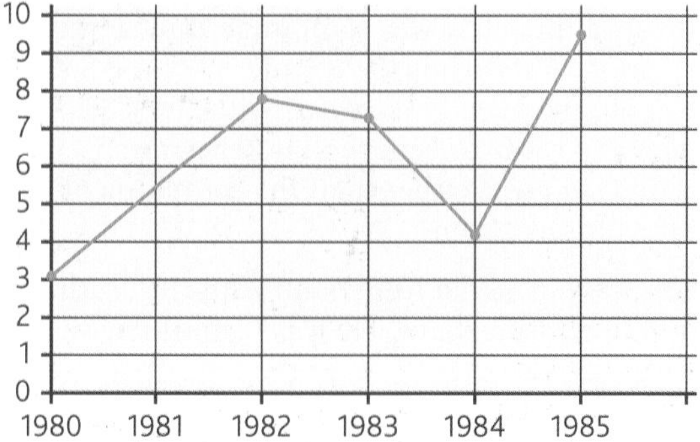

Fig. 2 *US growth in military spending, 1980, 1982–5 (N.B. No figure is given for 1981)*

This was at the heart of his aim to develop both nuclear and conventional forces in order to move the USA's military capacity from a defensive to an offensive level. Reagan oversaw the greatest expansion in US military power in the country's peacetime history. He approved the development of Stealth aircraft. These were designed to be invisible to enemy radar systems. He also restored development programmes that had been cancelled by Jimmy Carter. These included the B-1 bomber and neutron bomb programmes.

Early on in his administration Reagan had decided that the USA would not ratify the SALT II Treaty agreed by President Carter in June 1979. The administration showed no inclination towards resuming negotiations with the USSR. This reluctance was deepened through the after effects of the Soviet invasion of Afghanistan and the continuing state of martial law imposed by the communist regime in Poland in response to the Solidarity movement there. Throughout most of 1981 Soviet Ambassador Dobrynin repeatedly tried to restart the SALT II process but with no success. The administration did begin to accept the need for some limited cooperation by the end of 1981. This was very much in response to pressure from Europe and the increasingly popular nuclear 'freeze' movement that had developed in the USA. This expressed US public support for a freeze on the deployment of all nuclear weapons. The strategic arms talks were named as the Strategic Arms Reduction Talks (START).

Did you know?

Stealth aircraft have technology that enable them to avoid radar detection. The most notable examples are the F-117 Nighthawk fighter and the B-2 Spirit 'Stealth Bomber'. The Stealth programme was, and remains, immensely costly. Today a bomber costs about $2 billion to create and maintain. This Stealth technology has been used and developed since the 1980s and was deployed in the 2003 invasion of Iraq.

INF talks

A key element of the negotiations lay with establishing agreements over the intermediate-range nuclear forces (INF). The Reagan administration proposed the so-called 'zero option'. The basis of this US proposal was that the USA would not deploy Cruise and Pershing II missiles if the Soviet Union removed its SS-20 missiles from Europe. This was heavily, and deliberately, loaded against Soviet interests. Essentially the 'zero option' made an offer to the USSR that it could do nothing other than reject. While it would have ended the planned deployment of 572 US missiles to Europe it required the USSR to dismantle nearly 600 intermediate-range missiles deployed since the late 1950s. The option only dealt with land-based missiles and not all sea-based missiles and aircraft. This exemption would have enabled the USA to undertake unlimited expansion in these areas and thereby strengthen its strike capability against the Soviet Union. The plan restricted agreement to Soviet and US systems which meant that all British and French systems were excluded. Future expansion of their systems was not to be controlled. The final guarantee that the US plans would be rejected by the USSR came with the requirement that limitations be imposed on all Soviet intermediate-range land-based missiles wherever they were deployed, not simply those deployed in Europe. This would have eliminated such missiles in the Far East and therefore well beyond the range of western Europe.

Fig. 3 *Tomahawk Cruise Missile test*

START

The USA was only interested in deploying missiles in Europe and proceeded with this in November 1983. The deployment of the first Cruise and Pershing II missiles led to the USSR abandoning the talks. For the first time in over a decade the USA and the USSR were no longer engaged in any level of negotiation. This was illustrated through the failure of the START negotiations. START did not begin until mid-1982 and one year later the gap between the two sides remained as wide as ever. A proposed limit of 5,000 missile warheads would have meant a cut of about one third for each side. The problem lay with the proposal to set limits on ICBMs. These would have demanded a cut of more than half in Soviet ICBM warheads and more than two thirds in the Soviet SS-18 and SS-19 warheads. All other US strategic modernisation programmes would have continued, including the Pershing II European-based systems. Overall the proposals would have greatly increased the vulnerability of Soviet land-based missiles. The position was amply summed up in 1983 as a Soviet general commented, "You (the USA) want to solve your vulnerability problem by making our forces vulnerable."

Historians have suggested that the level of interest that the administration had in strategic arms limitation was unclear. The view of the administration was that only when US military power had been expanded would the Soviets have the necessary incentive to negotiate seriously. Just as the INF talks had stopped at the end of 1983, so did the START negotiations. The USSR clearly took the view that the USA was not seriously interested in negotiating a mutually beneficial and equitable agreement. The USSR also hoped that by them ending the negotiations the Western powers would apply pressure on the USA to adopt a more realistic and cooperative stance. Reagan's response was simply to blame the Soviet Union for the breakdown because it was the power that had abandoned the talks. In 1983 an important new factor appeared that would impact significantly on strategic arms negotiations.

SDI

In his 'National Security: Address to the Nation' on 23 March 1983 Reagan resurrected an additional element to the nuclear arms race.

Fig. 4 *President Reagan's address from the White House on the Strategic Defence Initiative, 23 March 1983*

The 1972 ABM Treaty had acknowledged that there could be no effective defence against offensive nuclear missiles. The ABM Treaty had effectively removed the issue of ballistic missile defence from the arms agenda. By the 1980s it was clear that 'missile vulnerability' was a reality. The belief was that if one side embarked on a first strike it could then effectively disarm any counterforce strike. In effect Reagan had moved from a position of assured defence as the basis of deterrence to one of assured retaliation. This concept was officially known as the Strategic Defence Initiative (SDI), but more popularly referred to as the 'Star Wars' programme. This term was coined by those who opposed SDI and, in order to discredit it among the public, the image of war being extended to outer space was created. This was a completely false association.

Reagan emphasised the alarming build-up of Soviet arms that had occurred during the 1970s. His plan was to address a means of eliminating the threat posed by strategic nuclear weapons. He believed in a system of defence against weapons of mass destruction rather than merely mass retaliatory action. Reagan believed that a defence system against ICBMs could act as an incentive for the Soviet Union to reduce its stocks of these weapons. If his strategic defence initiative made a first strike impossible to succeed there would be no need for heavy ICBMs with multiple warheads.

This approach was driven by Reagan himself. The USA launched a $26 billion five-year programme. Reagan believed that it was a way of ending the nuclear arms race. Mutual Assured Destruction (MAD) would be replaced by MAS (Mutual Assured Survival). However, SDI appeared to challenge the foundations of the concept of mutual deterrence. While each side had nuclear weapons of comparable destructive power there would be a clear deterrence in place. The SDI concept meant that the USA was interested in developing anti-ballistic missiles which ended that guarantee of mutual deterrence. Furthermore, SDI was incompatible with the ABM Treaty. The Treaty committed both sides 'not to deploy ABM systems for a defence of the territory of its country and not to provide a base for such a defence, and not to deploy ABM systems for defence of an individual region.' Article V of the Treaty was also clearly in conflict with the concept of SDI. It stated that, 'Each party undertakes not to develop, test, or deploy ABM systems or components which are sea-based, air-based, space-based or mobile land-based'.

Unsurprisingly, the Soviet response to the SDI scheme was negative. The Soviet leader, Yuri Andropov, reminded Reagan of mutual deterrence which formed the basis of the approach to nuclear weapons between the two powers. The Soviets, like many Americans, were convinced that the idea could not be delivered and that there was no real prospect of developing a truly effective defence system against an enemy first strike. However, the Soviets were equally convinced that such a defence system could be effective against a less deadly retaliatory strike. Thus, SDI was seen as part of an American plan to develop first strike capability. This was a massive shift from the existing order of nuclear relations. SDI was seen as a dangerous alternative to arms control. It fundamentally undermined the process of strategic arms limitation. The Soviet Union feared that SDI would trigger another arms race.

Activity

Thinking point

Why did Reagan adopt a positive approach to arms controls? How does this balance out with the massive American disarmament programme?

Key profile

Yuri Andropov, 1914–84

Andropov joined the Communist Union of Youth (the Komsomol) in 1930. Having been appointed Soviet Ambassador to Hungary in 1954 he supervised the Soviet invasion of that state in 1956. His experience broadened in 1967 with his appointment as Head of the KGB, the Soviet intelligence service. His career peaked when he became General Secretary of the Communist Party in the Soviet Union. He was known for his support for reductions in nuclear weapons levels although he achieved little in talks with President Reagan.

In reality there was no possibility of creating a means of developing an impenetrable missile defence system that could be reliably guaranteed to counter a massive nuclear attack. It was technically possible to develop a defence system that could eliminate a number of hostile missiles to the point where an enemy could not realistically plan a first strike attack with confidence of its success. In effect, SDI was an impossible dream but it had a significant impact on East–West relations and on American–European relations.

Relations between the USA and Europe, 1980–6

The relationship between the USA and Europe, known as the Western Alliance, had been in place since the end of the Second World War. The relationship had not been one of continuous harmony. By the start of the 1980s while American–Soviet détente had collapsed, European détente flourished. Europe did not abandon détente as the USA had done with the Soviet invasion of Afghanistan. There was simply a glaring lack of uniformity and coordination between the USA and Europe.

This lack of coordination had developed over decades and it had come to a head by the 1980s. America had supported the growth of an 'Atlantic community' but problems began to emerge as Europe became a major economic organisation and one that was becoming a threat to America's economic power globally. More significantly, the USA opposed the protectionism it associated with the EC. As Europe became increasingly more prosperous and economically integrated, the USA began to question the extent of its own economic commitment to the strategic defence of Europe.

The USA, Europe and arms control

The Reagan administration raised a number of basic problems in an already rather tense relationship between Europe and the USA. Europe doubted Reagan's commitment to arms control. It feared the development of the USA's apparent unilateral arms build-up under Reagan and particularly the move towards SDI which Europe viewed as a direct threat to the cherished ABM Treaty. Sir Geoffrey Howe, Britain's Foreign Secretary, referred to the ABM Treaty as the "keystone in the arch of security." It was felt that any threat to the ABM Treaty would risk an escalation in competition in offensive nuclear weapons. Also Europe saw SDI as part of an American plan aimed at isolationism and the possibility of the USA detaching itself from its long standing commitment to defend Europe. From the American perspective, Europe was too readily inclined to remain committed to détente and arms control – policies that went against the Reagan administration's understanding of how America's interests should be protected.

Despite this view the USA continued to remain closely tied to Europe through NATO. In May 1981 at a meeting of NATO foreign ministers, called to discuss alliance policy, the USA pushed to remove any references to détente. This was strongly opposed by the European allies. Eventually, the USA reluctantly accepted a commitment to a 'more constructive East–West relationship.' This agreement went on to accept that the NATO allies would 'maintain a dialogue with the Soviet Union and (would) work together for genuine détente and the development of East–West relations, whenever Soviet behaviour makes this possible.' In May 1982 the NATO allies not only reaffirmed these commitments but they also recognised as part of the Alliance security policy the need for 'arms control and disarmament, together with deterrence and defence.'

Fig. 5 *A US Air Force F-16 Fighter, 1980. The F-16 was a key aircraft in the air superiority role, guarding the USA and Europe against enemy aircraft*

America's apparent commitment to Europe's security also came through the INF debate. For the USA the INF deployment was viewed as a means of reinforcing the alliance. Europe's view came to be based on the belief that these deployments were driven by the USA's desire to influence European security and control European independence from the USA. To many Europeans the deployment appeared to be aimed at ensuring Europe was successfully manipulated by the USA. In November 1983 the USA confirmed its plan for the imminent deployment of Cruise and Pershing II missiles in Europe. As part of its protest the USSR withdrew from the INF talks.

Poland and the Solidarity Movement

The possibility of Soviet intervention in Poland in response to the emergence of the Solidarity Movement appeared to be receding by December 1980. The internal political crisis in Poland continued to intensify. In December 1981 General Jaruzelski and the Military Committee of National Salvation imposed martial law. Western states announced some limited economic controls in response to this action. The USA pursued a far more direct and wide-ranging set of proposals. All US government shipments of agricultural products were banned. Polish fishing rights in American waters were suspended as were landing rights to the Polish national airline in the USA. Later in 1981 the USA withdrew the most-favoured-nation (MFN) trade status it had previously granted Poland. The USA also blocked Poland from receiving assistance from the International Monetary Fund (IMF). The USA went much further than Western European states in the application of economic sanctions. The most significant response to the problems in Poland came when the USA suspended sales of oil and gas technology to the USSR. Hardliners in the Reagan administration had been, for some time, advocating policies that would place the Soviet economy under further pressure.

Activity

Group discussion

Split into two groups. One group prepares a list of the reasons why, based on the events of the 1980s, it was beneficial for Britain to maintain close relations with the United States. The other group's list focuses on reasons why the relationship was not necessarily in Britain's best interests. Once you have prepared the lists, take it in turns to read them out and then debate their content.

Exploring the detail

The Solidarity Movement

By 1980 there were major price rises in Poland. Workers at the *Lenin* shipyard at Gdansk, led by Lech Walesa, went on strike. The shipyard was occupied as he called for solidarity among the workers. They demanded independent unions, something banned in communist states. To restore some order the Polish communist government agreed to the demands. In December 1981 the government declared a state of martial law and brought Solidarity under control although many of its supporters continued to organise secretly. Its existence acted as an inspiration to others across eastern Europe who wanted reforms.

The Soviet gas pipeline, 1982

The US action against the Soviet Union intensified further in June 1982. Sales of equipment and technology for the construction of a Soviet gas pipeline into western Europe were banned. The ban also included the sale of US technology manufactured in western Europe under US licence. This was seen by European states as a restriction on trade. What further angered European states was the fact that the USA had signed a trade agreement with the USSR which enabled that state to buy US grain. This clumsy measure merely served to convince Europeans that they were paying for the economic assault on the USSR while the USA was benefiting.

The Soviet pipeline was intended to deliver about 20 per cent of the participating western European states' gas energy needs. The project generated employment at a time when unemployment was at a high point. It had reached 8 per cent in Germany alone. The USA attempted to justify its actions in terms of European security. The rationale was that Europe would become dependent on Soviet gas supplies and this would expose it to Soviet pressure in the form of threats to withhold the supply. Some Europeans came to the conclusion that US sanctions over the pipeline were not motivated by a desire to protect European security, or simply to put economic pressure on the Soviet Union, but rather as a means of undermining European détente. The pipeline represented a major economic link between East and West. The USA feared that its influence over western European policy towards the Soviet Union would be undermined if this link remained intact. This further fuelled Europe's growing doubts about the benefits of its relationship with the USA while such policies were in place.

European states strongly rejected what they regarded as American attempts to control them. The dispute came to a head when the USA announced that it would impose sanctions on any European firm defying its embargo against the Soviet Union. In the face of this European reaction the USA was forced to back down. In late 1982 the trade sanctions were withdrawn in return for an agreement that no further new gas contracts would be agreed with the Soviet Union.

Libya, 1986

In 1986 the USA took the decision to bomb military targets in Libya. The leader of Libya, Colonel Quaddafi, was also targeted in these bombing raids. Reagan stated early on in his administration that defeating terrorism would be a major objective of the USA. Evidence had been mounting since 1981 that Libya was a source of international terrorism. All political and economic ties between Libya and the USA had been severed in 1981. Libya had been linked to the 1985 bombings at airports in Rome and Vienna and it was the terrorist action against a Berlin nightclub in 1986 which triggered the US bombing of Libya.

This attack was facilitated by Britain. Air force bases in Britain were used by the USA to launch the attacks. There was widespread opposition to US actions across the rest of Europe. France and Spain refused to allow US military aircraft to fly through their airspace en route to Libya. There was a belief in Europe that the attacks would simply generate more terrorism and much of it would be inflicted on Europe, particularly against those states that had supported the USA. The USA and Europe had significantly different approaches towards the management of international terrorism. The Reagan administration favoured direct attacks such as those carried out against Libya. Many European states favoured other methods of reducing terrorism and a more united and coordinated approach to anti-terrorist actions within Europe.

The Reagan–Thatcher relationship

On 20 January 1981 Ronald Reagan was inaugurated as President of the USA. The British Prime Minister, Margaret Thatcher, sent him a letter of congratulation which stated:

> Dear Mr President,
>
> May I send you my congratulations, and those of my colleagues in the British government, on your inauguration as President of the United States. You face a formidable task of leadership at a dangerous time. But your inauguration is a symbol of hope for the (NATO) Alliance, and you can depend on our confidence and support as we work together to meet the challenges of the 1980s. I look forward to renewing our friendship and to consolidating the close relationship between our two countries. With best wishes. Warm personal regards,
>
> Yours sincerely,
>
> Margaret Thatcher

2

Key profile

Margaret Hilda Thatcher (1925–present)

Thatcher has been a British Conservative politician from 1959. She became the party leader in 1975 and Prime Minister between 1979 and 1990. She was commited to monetarism and the importance of market forces and free competition. She believed in the private sector having a greater role in traditional state-run activities such as health care. In 1982 she led Britain into a war with Argentina over control of the Falkland Islands. In international affairs she was an important link between Gorbachev and Presidents Reagan and Bush. Her lack of compromise led to her forced resignation as Prime Minster as the Conservative Party faced damaging internal divisions.

Margaret Thatcher visited Reagan in February 1981 and began what was seen as a honeymoon period in Anglo–American relations. There was no question that Britain would be anything other than a solid friend of the USA while Ronald Reagan and Margaret Thatcher were their leaders. In June 1982, Reagan visited Britain. In a speech he delivered to the combined Houses of Parliament he presented a devastating attack on the Soviet Union. He called for a 'crusade for freedom' and his target was the Soviet Union. Thatcher, like Reagan, was convinced that the Cold War had gone on too long and that the Soviet Union had been propped up

Fig. 6 *Ronald Reagan and Margaret Thatcher outside No.10 Downing Street*

by the effects of détente. For Thatcher, Reagan had put 'freedom on the offensive'.

There were some points of friction between Britain and the USA, particularly over Poland and then the Soviet gas pipeline, but for the most part Britain remained a staunch ally of the USA. Most significantly, Margaret Thatcher agreed to allow the USA to launch F-111 bombers against Libya in 1986. Britain certainly appeared to be a willing ally in support of American aggression. Thatcher's reward for this support came when the USA agreed to allow Britain to extradite for trial in Northern Ireland suspected IRA terrorists who were taking refuge in the USA. Although Britain deviated from the western European line on the USA's bombing of Libya, Margaret Thatcher was less willing to wholeheartedly back Reagan's SDI project.

Thatcher repeatedly voiced her concern that western Europe would be defenceless without the protective umbrella of the US nuclear force. In her view the SDI project threatened to bring this about. The cost of ridding the world of nuclear weapons would be the creation of a massive imbalance between the conventional forces of the West and the East. In a letter to Ronald Reagan, Thatcher commented:

> As regards the Strategic Defence Initiative I hope that I was able to explain to you clearly my preoccupation with the need not to weaken our efforts to consolidate support in Britain for the deployment of Cruise and for the modernisation of Trident by giving the impression that a future without nuclear weapons is near at hand. We must continue to make the case for deterrence based on nuclear weapons for several years to come.

3

Overview of American–European relations

The key issue by the mid-1980s was whether the Atlantic Alliance was still solid and firmly intact. Some historians have argued that it was, despite the strains it had faced since 1981. Many American commentators certainly believed that America still had a crucial role to play in Europe, both economically and strategically. In contrast to this was the view that the Alliance was slowly collapsing. Part of the rationale behind this conclusion was the recognition that through the EU Europe had become an increasingly powerful regional economy and one that was in direct competition with the USA. Although Europe's economy was not as powerful as that of the USA it did have the potential to expand. Similarly, Europe's defence systems were not fully developed, nor was there a common foreign policy among the member states of the EU. Despite these shortcomings Europe was developing into a more economically, politically and strategically integrated organisation. This inevitably led to the conclusion that the traditional relationship between the USA and Europe would change and there was a real possibility by the mid-1980s that Europe's dependency on the USA was diminishing.

Neither scenario fully developed. Although Europe was moving towards greater integration there was the ever present and continuing problem of incompatible national interests which undermined full integration. This was a factor in ensuring that some form of working relationship between Europe and the USA would remain in place throughout the 1980s.

Summary questions

1. How far was the development of a 'Second Cold War' the result of Ronald Reagan's policies in the years 1981 to 1985?
2. 'The relationship between Europe and the United States in the years 1981 to 1985 was as strong as it always had been.' How valid is this assessment?

9 The End of the Cold War, 1985–91

In this chapter you will learn about:

- the contribution made by Mikhail Gorbachev towards ending the Cold War
- the importance of the collapse of communism in eastern Europe
- factors leading towards the end of the Cold War.

Mikhail Sergeyevich Gorbachev was born into a Russian peasant family in 1931, and spent much of his youth driving combine harvesters on Soviet farms. In 1998, by contrast, *Time* magazine listed Gorbachev as one of the most influential people of the 20th century, a man who had finally brought the Cold War to an end.

Fig. 1 *A tank involved in the August 1991 coup*

Cross-reference

For more on Gorbachev's influence on the Soviet economy, see Chapter 7.

On 10 March 1985 the Soviet Union's leader, Konstantin Ustinovich Chernenko, died. His successor was Mikhail Gorbachev.

No previous General Secretary of the Soviet Communist Party had reached adulthood after the end of World War II. Gorbachev brought with him modernity and a new vitality to address the crises that the Soviet Union was facing by 1985. For Gorbachev, one key element of a solution to the crises lay in foreign policy and specifically in the Soviet Union's relations with the USA. Gorbachev offered a telling summary of his views through his memoirs published in 1996. He noted:

> We discussed the new role of Soviet diplomacy. I consider this meeting the starting point for the full scale implementation of our 'new thinking'. We realised that it was vitally necessary to correct the distorted ideas we had about other nations. These misconceptions had made us oppose the rest of the world for many decades, which had negative effects on our economy. We understand that in today's world of mutual interdependency, progress is unthinkable for any society which is fenced off from the world by impenetrable state frontiers and ideological barriers. We realised that in our nuclear age, you could not build a safe security system based solely on military means. This prompted us to propose an entirely new concept of global security.

1

The impact of Gorbachev, 1985–91

Key dates

US–Soviet Summits, 1985–91

Date	Place	Key players
November 1985	Geneva	Gorbachev and Reagan
October 1986	Reykjavik	Gorbachev and Reagan
December 1987	Washington	Gorbachev and Reagan
May–June 1988	Moscow	Gorbachev and Reagan
December 1989	Malta	Gorbachev and Bush
May 1990	Washington	Gorbachev and Bush
July 1991	Moscow	Gorbachev and Bush

In June 1985 Gorbachev replaced Andrei Gromyko as Soviet Foreign Minister with Edvard Shevardnadze, the Party boss in Tbilisi.

Key profile

Edvard Amvrosievich Shevardnadze, 1928–present

A Georgian with very limited diplomatic experience, Shevardnadze was appointed Soviet Foreign Minister by Gorbachev. He was a staunch supporter of Gorbachev's new thinking. He formed a sound working relationship with his American opposite number and this was instrumental in reinforcing the efforts of Gorbachev. He left the Politburo in July 1990 and resigned from the Communist Party in June 1991. He subsequently returned to his native state of Georgia and became its Head of State for a time.

Reagan's Secretary of State, George Shultz, later commented that, "The contrast between him and Gromyko was breathtaking . . . He could smile, engage, converse. He had the ability to persuade and be persuaded." It wasn't merely a new Foreign Minister that Gorbachev brought to the international relations arena. He also brought what became known as 'New Thinking' to Soviet foreign policy. Gorbachev accepted that the expansion of nuclear weapons was no guarantee of security for a state. There was no certain defence against nuclear attack. The achievement of security was a political rather than a military process and that necessitated an end to confrontation and competition between the superpowers. Another key element of the 'New Thinking' was interdependence. Gorbachev acknowledged that states had common interests and these could be best served by working together. He brought an end to the traditional Soviet notion of the inevitability of class war between the communist and capitalist states. Overall Gorbachev wanted to redefine the basis of superpower relations.

Associated with his 'New Thinking' in foreign policy was Gorbachev's notion of 'Europe is our common home.' He developed this from February 1986 during a visit to Paris. Gorbachev argued that there was a need to overcome the "artificiality and temporariness of the bloc-to-bloc confrontation and the archaic nature of the 'Iron Curtain'." This concept of a common European home envisaged an end to division in Europe. This idea did not signal the end of communism in the eastern European Soviet bloc but rather suggested a level of peaceful coexistence between all European states. There would be no need for offensive nuclear weapons in this environment of mutual cooperation. Greater economic links between East and West could be forged and the Soviet bloc could finally enter the global capitalist system so vital for its survival. This idea was clearly the first stage in Gorbachev's intention to abandon the Brezhnev Doctrine. In 1987 Gorbachev expanded on his notion of the route to European security when he said:

> We are firmly opposed to the division of the continent into military blocs facing each other, against the accumulation of military arsenals in Europe, against everything that is the source of the threat of war. In the spirit of the new thinking we advanced the idea of 'the common European home' (with) the recognition of a certain integrated whole, although the states in question belong to different social systems and are members of opposing military–political blocs ranged against each other.

2

In October 1985, on the eve of the planned Geneva Summit, Gorbachev introduced the concept of 'reasonable sufficiency'. This was based on an open rejection of aggression. The Soviets committed themselves to maintaining only those levels of conventional and nuclear forces that were deemed 'sufficient' and 'reasonable'. For the first time Soviet leaders were in a position to accept military cuts without demanding comparable cuts from the USA. This shift was of fundamental importance in enabling agreement to be made on intermediate nuclear forces (INF) in 1987.

The Geneva Summit, November 1985

Both Reagan and Gorbachev wanted this summit to look like a success. In many respects it was. Some historians have referred to the summit as 'a watershed in relations' between the Soviet Union and the USA. In the joint statement that followed the summit was the phrase, 'a nuclear war cannot be won and must never be fought.' The joint statement went on to refer to the 'importance of preventing any war between the US and USSR, whether nuclear or conventional.' These agreements underlined the fact that Gorbachev had removed the ideological split between East and West as a factor in international relations.

He later wrote that the period between March and December 1985 "was an extremely important period, marked by an intense search for new policy approaches leading to conclusions that became the core of the new thinking." For his part, Reagan wanted an indication that Gorbachev would materially change Soviet attitudes.

Complications before the next summit, 1986

Gorbachev wanted a spectacular initiative that would leave the clear impression that the Soviet Union was serious about ending the nuclear arms race, even though Reagan had shown considerable intransigence over SDI at Geneva. The 'initiative' amounted to a declaration that nuclear weapons would be abolished by the year 2000 and the first step in that process would be a 50 per cent cut in strategic nuclear weapons. The reaction of the Western powers

Activity

Talking point

How important was Gorbachev's thinking in terms of its contribution towards ending the Cold War?

Cross-reference

For more on the negotiations in relation to INF, see Chapter 8.

Did you know?

Reagan liked Gorbachev and he saw him as a man with whom he could reason. Gorbachev was less warm to Reagan. In his memoirs he noted, "Reagan appeared to me not simply a conservative, but a political 'dinosaur.'" Despite this, Gorbachev acknowledged that Reagan treated him with respect. The Geneva Summit marked the end of a period of fundamental transition for Gorbachev.

was mixed. The USA welcomed the initiative but was not prepared to suddenly abandon its SDI programme. Britain and France simply refused to even discuss the proposal and Margaret Thatcher called it 'pie in the sky'.

Did you know?

Gennady Zakharov was caught spying in a classic 'sting' operation. In 1986 he handed an envelope containing details of US Air Force jet engines to a student known as 'C. S.', in return for $1,000 in cash. 'C. S.' was actually working for the FBI, and Zakharov was arrested.

By August 1986 a new conflict suddenly drove a wedge between Reagan and Gorbachev. A Soviet employee of the United Nations, Gennady Zakharov, was arrested for organising spying activities against the USA. On 23 August Zakharov was arrested as he was about to pay a double agent for a package of classified information. The USSR responded by arresting Nicholas Daniloff, an American journalist based in Moscow. The problem was eventually resolved and Daniloff was released and Zakharov expelled from the USA. This then opened up the way for a further summit which was to take place in Reykjavik.

The Reykjavik Summit, October 1986

In 1990 Ronald Reagan wrote of the Reykjavik Summit, "I realised he had brought me to Iceland with one purpose: to kill the Strategic Defense Initiative . . . I was very disappointed – and very angry." In his remarks to the Politburo on October 14 Gorbachev commented, "With Reagan, we had to struggle in Reykjavik not only with a class enemy but with an extraordinarily primitive one, a feeble-minded cave man." At Reykjavik Reagan would not compromise on his determination to continue research and testing of nuclear defence systems. Western European leaders were largely behind Reagan's commitment to SDI mainly because it meant the USA would not accept an end to nuclear weapons. Margaret Thatcher and the French President, François Mitterand, simply could not understand Reagan's hatred of nuclear weapons.

Some commentators have taken the view that a historic chance to create the most sweeping and significant arms control agreement ever facing the superpowers was lost at Reykjavik. Despite this controversial view the summit did convince Gorbachev that Reagan really did want to bring the arms race to an end. He believed that Reagan undoubtedly regarded SDI as the means by which offensive nuclear weapons would be made irrelevant.

The Washington Summit, December 1987

In the build-up to this meeting some important changes in personnel took place on the American side. Strong supporters of the SDI policy left office. These included Defence Secretary, Casper Weinberger, and his Assistant Secretary, Richard Perle.

At this summit Reagan and Gorbachev signed the INF Treaty. Many historians regarded this agreement as the most significant step taken by the USA and the USSR to bring the arms race to an end. The framework for the treaty had already been designed by George Shultz, the US Secretary of State and the Soviet Foreign Minister, Edvard Shevardnadze in the weeks leading up to the summit. The Treaty removed all those nuclear weapons carried by intermediate-range ballistic missiles. The Soviets agreed to remove their SS-20 missiles while the USA would remove Cruise and Pershing II missiles. The Soviet Union removed far more nuclear weapons than did the United States. These included the SS-23 missiles which only had a range of 400 kilometres although the Treaty focused on eliminating missiles in the 500 to 2,000 kilometre range.

The importance of the INF Treaty lay not in the number of weapons it removed but in the precedent it set.

- It was the first time that both the Soviet Union and the USA had agreed to remove a whole class of nuclear weapons and to accept that each state had the right to verify the removal on each other's territory.
- It was also significant in that the Soviet Union made no demands that the Treaty was to be conditional on the USA withdrawing from SDI.
- The Soviet Union also made no demands that it should be able to retain one hundred SS-20 missiles as defence against China.
- Lastly, the Soviet Union accepted that British and French nuclear weapons need not be part of the overall deal.

This package meant that the Soviet Union had accepted all the key elements of the 'zero option' that Reagan had originally proposed in 1981. A further outcome of the summit came through Gorbachev's decision to withdraw from Afghanistan. He announced this in February 1988 and by May 1989 the last Soviet troops were withdrawn from Afghanistan.

Edvard Shevardnadze later commented on the decision to withdraw from Afghanistan. He said, "The decision to leave Afghanistan was the first and most difficult step (in reorientating Soviet foreign policy). Everything else flowed from that." The decision to withdraw was very much the result of America supplying the deadly Stinger missile system to the Afghan *mujaheddin* guerrilla fighters. In addition, it was clear to the Soviet Union that they would be indefinitely trapped in Afghanistan because the Afghan army was in no position to defeat the *mujaheddin*. By the late 1980s the Soviets had lost around 15,000 dead and there was an ever increasing economic cost which had domestic implications. Support for the Kabul regime finally ended with the collapse of the Soviet Union itself in December 1991.

Reagan later summed up his view of the Washington Summit. He referred to the celebrations in Moscow that followed the end of the Second World War. He spoke of the comment made by a Soviet Army major to an American diplomat, "Now it's time to live." He added, "I'm convinced that history will ultimately judge this summit, and its participants, not on missile counts but on how far we moved together for the fulfilment of that soldier's hopes." Gorbachev no longer referred to political dinosaurs and cavemen. For the first time ever it looked as if an end to the Cold War was finally in sight.

Fig. 3 *Reagan and Gorbachev in informal talks*

Exploring the detail

Weapons agreed to be removed by the INF Treaty:

- All missiles with ranges of 625–3,500 miles by 1991.
- All missiles with ranges of 300–625 miles by 1989.

Total = 2,692

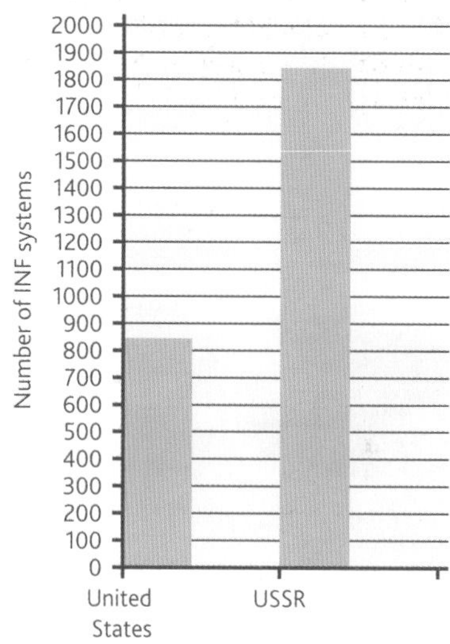

Fig. 2 *Intermediate-Range Nuclear Forces (INF) Systems, 1987*

The Moscow Summit, May–June 1988

In some ways the content of this summit was relatively unimportant. The old arguments on SDI and the ABM Treaty were rehearsed once more. When Reagan asked Gorbachev why he opposed strategic defences if both states had removed strategic offensive weapons, Gorbachev replied that the people of the Soviet Union believed that the SDI programme was designed to put offensive weapons into space. Most importantly, the Moscow Summit gave Reagan an opportunity to access the Russian people.

Cross-reference

For a discussion of the Brezhnev Doctrine, see Chapter 5.

The highpoint of Reagan's public appearances in Moscow came with his address to the students of Moscow State University. His theme was freedom and he struck a chord with his audience as he shared his vision of a Soviet Union free from the chains of totalitarian rule. As Reagan and Gorbachev strolled through Red Square in Moscow, a journalist asked of Reagan, "Do you still consider this an evil empire?" Reagan replied with the words, "No. That was another time, another era." This, among many other supportive comments, did much to reinforce Gorbachev's following within the Soviet Union itself. Reagan had been impressed by the Soviet people and they were certainly impressed with him.

On 7 December 1988 Gorbachev went on to deliver a major speech at the United Nations. In defining the principles of the 'new thinking', he emphasised the right of states to make their own choices. In effect Gorbachev formally announced the end of the Brezhnev Doctrine and therefore the end to the Soviet Union's commitment that socialist states must always remain socialist. Gorbachev had made an announcement of critical importance. Soviet foreign policy was no longer to be founded on the notion of international class struggle. This move was partly motivated by the fact that Gorbachev could hardly undertake internal reforms in the Soviet Union but prevent similar reforms in eastern Europe. This shift was translated into practical outcomes when Gorbachev went on to announce that the Soviet Union would unconditionally reduce its armed forces by half a million men. Anatoly Chernyaev commented on the speech and its impact:

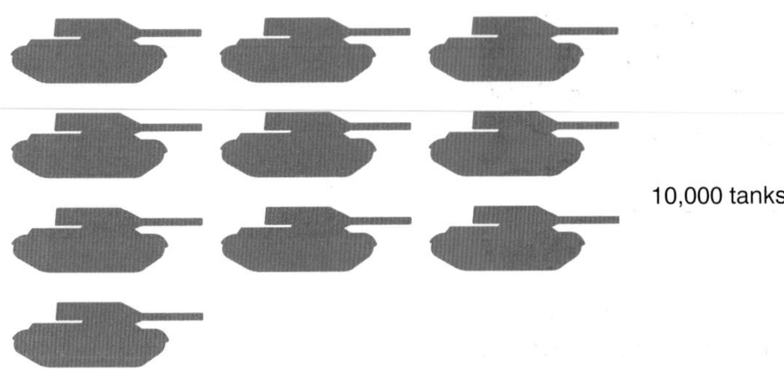

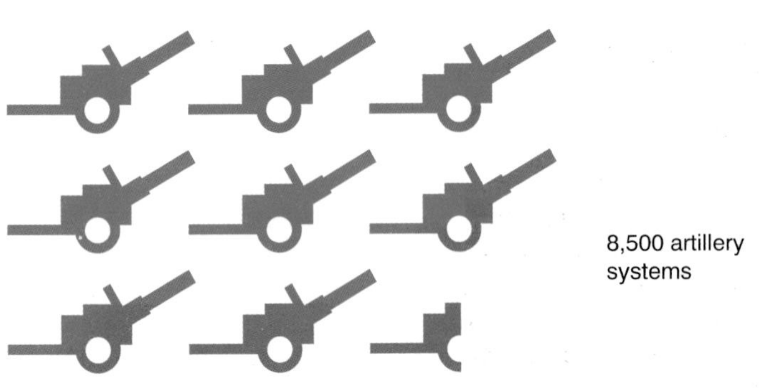

Fig. 4 *Weapons systems to be removed from eastern Europe by the Gorbachev reforms*

> Much has been written about the impression that Gorbachev made on the world in his UN speech. Having received such broad recognition and support, having been 'certified' a world class leader of great authority, he could be faster and surer in shaking off the fetters of the past in all aspects of foreign policy.

3

Gorbachev's speech to the UN suggested that the end of the Cold War ideological conflict was approaching.

The position at the end of Reagan's presidency

Both Ronald Reagan and Mikhail Gorbachev made fundamental contributions towards bringing the Cold War to an end. Some historians have argued that Ronald Reagan was the prime mover in this achievement. Reagan's commitment to rejecting détente and pursuing an apparently aggressive American arms build-up and particularly his focus on SDI has been seen as his strategy of forcing the Soviet Union into a position from where it could not compete with the USA. This view of Reagan's strategy was roundly rejected by George Kennan in 1992. He wrote:

> The suggestion that any Administration had the power to influence decisively the course of tremendous domestic political upheaval in another great country is simply childish. Nobody – no country, no party, no person – 'won' the Cold War. It was a long and costly political rivalry, fuelled on both sides by unreal and exaggerated estimates of the intentions and strength of the other party.

4

Certainly, by the end of 1988 it did seem that the end of the Cold War was imminent. However, the end came rather more slowly than expected.

A new president: George H. W. Bush, 1989

Key profile

George Herbert Walker Bush, 1924–present

Bush was US President between 1989 and 1993. Before entering politics in 1959 he had been in business in the Texas oil industry. He was elected into the House of Representatives in 1966 and was US Ambassador to the UN between 1971 and 1972. He ran the CIA between 1976 and 1977. As President he sanctioned the invasion of Panama in 1989 and was influential in organising the international response to Iraq's invasion of Kuwait in 1991.

Bush came into office and ordered a review of US policy towards the Soviet Union. He did not take the view that the Cold War was definitely over. Bush needed a way both to reassure the right wing of the Republican Party and to show that he had not simply inherited Reagan's approach and was unthinkingly continuing it. Arms control negotiations resumed by September 1989. The Soviet Union was facing meltdown in eastern Europe and Gorbachev's ability to negotiate with the USA from a position of strength was rapidly diminishing. Despite this more summits followed Bush's arrival.

At Malta in December 1989 moves were made towards a closer economic relationship between the Soviet Union and the USA. The Malta Summit marked the end of Cold War economic conflict. The Soviet Union was slowly moving towards a market-driven economy and away from the state-controlled centrally planned economy. Some informal agreements were

Activity

Group activity

Set up a number of small groups. Each group should take a summit and research the details further. Report back on the successes and failures of the summit and then consider as a whole how important the summit process was in arms control and the ending of the Cold War.

reached in terms of eastern Europe. Gorbachev made it clear that the Soviet Union would not use force to prevent eastern European states determining their own political futures. There was less consensus over the reunification of Germany. Few supported reunification, in the short term at least. Bush agreed not to intervene over Germany or the future of the Baltic states, some of whom were interested in independence from the Soviet Union. No formal agreements were signed. Six months later a further summit was held in Washington and this paved the way for major strategic arms reductions later in the year. By the time Bush and Gorbachev met at Malta, eastern Europe had changed beyond recognition as successive communist regimes fell from power. Gorbachev summed up his attitude towards East–West relations by this point when he said at Malta:

> The reliance on force, on military superiority and the arms race that stemmed from it, did not withstand the test. We reached a dangerous brink. It is good that we managed to stop. Therefore, we together – the USSR and the US – can do a lot to change radically our old approaches. We had already felt it in our contacts with the Reagan administration and this process continues today.

5

President Bush also expressed his views on the outcomes of the Malta Summit. He said:

> We stand at the threshold of a brand new era of US–Soviet relations. There is virtually no problem in the world – and certainly no problem in Europe – that improvement in the US–Soviet relationship will not help to ameliorate. A better US–Soviet relationship is to be valued in and of itself, but it also should be an instrument of positive change for the world.

6

In November 1990 the Conventional Forces in Europe Treaty (CFE) was signed by Gorbachev, Bush and other European leaders in Paris. Gorbachev agreed to end the superiority in military capability held by the Soviet Union in Europe. Limits were placed on the scale of military hardware any state could control. This was followed up in July 1991 with the final summit that Bush and Gorbachev would hold together. It took place in Moscow. The summit led to the conclusion of START I (Strategic Arms Reduction Treaty).

Table 1 *Main points of START I agreement*

	Missile launch	Warheads	Missile and bomb stocks
United States	Fixed at 1,600 launchers	Fixed at 6,000 warheads	Reduced from 12,000 to 9,000
Soviet Union	Fixed at 1,600 launchers	Fixed at 6,000 warheads (also agreed to cut SS-20 warheads by 50 per cent)	Reduced from 11,000 to 7,000

Finally it was agreed that nuclear technology was not to be passed on to third party states.

Gorbachev's influence in international relations finally came to an end in December 1991 when the Soviet Union was formally dissolved.

The end of the Cold War was not brought about simply through the outcomes of international summit agreements. Gorbachev's influence in ending the struggle extended beyond these and other factors had a profound influence on the nature of international relations.

The collapse of communism in the USSR

Gorbachev brought with him a reform programme which was to have a profound significance for the future of the Soviet Union and communism, and ultimately for the Cold War.

Cross-reference

The condition of the Soviet economy under Gorbachev has been considered in Chapter 7.

Glasnost (Openness)

This initiative lay in Gorbachev's commitment to promote the principle of the freedom to criticise far beyond that which had already existed in the Soviet Union for some time before his leadership. *Glasnost* also involved a relaxation of the controls the states had traditionally maintained over the media – the long-standing tradition of censorship. Many historians have taken the view that *glasnost* was not about suddenly injecting democracy into the Soviet Union. Gorbachev did not want to destroy the Soviet Union by gambling that the people would simply restate their support for the communist system through their opportunity to express themselves more openly. For Gorbachev, *glasnost* was the means by which the people could openly support the wider reforms he wanted and criticise those who stood in the way of their fulfilment. The openness was extended to the level of culture. In 1987 Pasternak's banned novel, *Dr Zhivago*, was published. A relaxation on oppression was undoubtedly one of the outcomes of *glasnost*. In 1986 the exiled scientist, Andrei Sakharov, was able to return to Moscow. The fundamental problem for *glasnost* was that it exposed the dominance of the Communist Party to challenge. Secondly, there was no certainty that the Soviet people would happily embrace and support Gorbachev's second initiative based on restructuring the Soviet system. What *glasnost* did was to undermine the dominance of the power of the Communist Party. In this way it began the unintended process of bringing communist rule in the Soviet Union to an end.

Did you know?

Dr Zhivago was a romantic story set during the Bolshevik revolution of 1917. Its main character came from a wealthy Russian background and was persecuted by the communists. The story presented the communists in a very negative way.

Fig. 5 *Demonstrations calling for limitations on* glasnost

Key profile

Andrei Sakharov, 1921–89

Sakharov was a leading Soviet physicist often regarded as the 'father of the Soviet atom bomb'. Between 1950 and 1968 he was a prominent figure in research on thermonuclear weapons but he increasingly called for an end to nuclear weapons development and the nuclear arms race during the Cold War. During the 1970s he became a vocal opponent of the Soviet Union's record on civil liberties and he called for greater political freedom throughout the communist world. As a result of this he was forced into internal exile in the small Russian city of Gorky until his return to Moscow in 1986.

Perestroika (Restructuring)

This initiative was designed primarily to reinforce the socialist system in the Soviet Union. In 1987 Gorbachev wrote in detail of his concept of *perestroika* and its purpose. In this work he commented:

> Of course, workers, farmers and intellectuals have always been represented in all bodies of authority and management, but they are not always drawn into the making and adoption of decisions to the extent required for the healthy development of socialist society.

7

The first step in the restructuring was that of reducing the power of the Communist Party. A new legislature, the Congress of People's Deputies, was to be created, two thirds of whose members were to be directly elected. The remaining third would remain in the hands of the Communist Party. Once again the Communist Party's power was undermined. One historian commented that there was "a whirlwind of free debate that scattered every known communist taboo." At the same time Gorbachev wanted to ensure he held on to the reins of power and was able to drive the reforms his way. He created an executive Presidency which he held and for which he was not subject to elections.

Activity

Talking point

What did Gorbachev hope to achieve by introducing *glasnost* and *perestroika*?

Fig. 6 *USSR postage stamp with pro-perestroika propaganda*

Nationalism within the Soviet Union

The Soviet Union was more accurately named the Soviet Empire. It was a multiethnic and multilingual state made up of 15 republics. It was largely held together by force and the power of the Communist Party. Under Gorbachev, as the power of the Party inevitably diminished, nationalist feelings that had been latent for decades began to emerge strongly.

Fig. 7 *Map of the Soviet Republics, 1989*

A number of nationalist problems erupted across the Soviet Union. In 1988 a crisis developed in Azerbaijan as Armenians in Nagorny Karabakh, an Armenian region administered by Azerbaijan, demanded separation from Azerbaijan and incorporation into Soviet Armenia. Gorbachev revealed his insensitivity to the Armenian nationalist movement when he sided with Azerbaijan. He was aware of the implications for the Soviet Union of backing separatist nationalist movements. Demands for Georgian independence flared in 1989. Twenty pro-independence marchers were killed. This merely heightened demands for independence.

The Soviet Union's Baltic states of Lithuania, Latvia and Estonia also had clear designs on independence. In May 1989 these three states held a Baltic Assembly in Tallinn and began talks on united action to promote economic and political sovereignty from the Soviet Union. In January Gorbachev sent troops into Vilnius, the capital city of Lithuania. Thirteen people were killed. Overall he failed to placate the nationalists by giving them more devolved power within the framework of the Soviet Union and he failed to use enough force to destroy them thereby retaining the support of the conservatives in the USSR who wanted firm action to prevent the break-up of the Soviet Union.

In August 1991 a coup to overthrow Gorbachev was set in place. This came largely as a response to the imminent introduction of a Union Treaty which would have given significant freedom to the 15 Soviet republics. In effect it would have marked the end of the Soviet Union.

Exploring the detail

The 1991 coup attempt

The 1991 coup attempt was led by communist hardliners who wanted to stop Gorbachev's reform programme. Gorbachev was held under house arrest at his holiday home in the Crimea, but the coup collapsed within three days and the coup leaders attemped to flee the country, but all were arrested and one committed suicide.

The coup failed but there was no return for Gorbachev. In December 1991 the leaders of Russia, Belarus and Ukraine met at Minsk and created the Commonwealth of Independent States (CIS). On 26 December the USSR Supreme Soviet voted to dissolve itself and formally end the existence of the Soviet Union. The next day Russia's President, Boris Yeltsin, seized Gorbachev's office in the Kremlin. At this point Gorbachev became yesterday's man. The final line had been drawn under the Cold War.

Key profile

Boris Nikolayevich Yeltsin, 1931–2007

Yeltsin became head of the Communist Party in Moscow in 1986 and president of the Russian Soviet Federative Socialist Republic between 1990 and 1991. From 1991 he was president of the newly formed Russian Federation. He was responsible for managing the Federation's secession from the USSR and the creation of the Commonwealth of Independent States. He supported nuclear disarmament and increased privatisation internally.

A closer look

Historical interpretations of the significance of Gorbachev

From the late 1980s, scholars of international relations argued over whether liberalism had emerged victorious in post-Cold War politics. The end of the Cold War was seen by observers as the positive sign of this development. With his policies of *glasnost* and *perestroika*, Soviet President Mikhail Gorbachev seemed to acknowledge the exhaustion of Marxist–Leninist theories and the discrediting of its practices. Gorbachev became the symbol of this change. Many scholars, including Francis Fukuyama, argued that with the fall of the Soviet Union, the Cold War was replaced by a world wide consensus based on the values of liberalism and sovereignty (each state governing its own affairs). The end of the standoff between the Soviet Union and the Western powers meant the close of a political climate in which the world had formed factions built around one of the two 'superpowers' in the so-called 'bipolar' opposition that had characterised international relations throughout the Cold War. Moreover, the notion of a 'Third World' that had lumped together extremely diverse states was no longer relevant: the end of the Cold War meant that these states no longer played the role that they previously had in the conflict of the superpowers to win allies abroad. Theorists of international relations also identified an ideological shift that occurred with the disintegration of the Soviet Union. From the mid-1980s, theorists and historians, including Robert Keohane in *After Hegemony* (1984) and Paul Kennedy in *The Rise and Fall of the Great Powers* (1987), had stressed the decline of the US as the primary post-war defender of the liberal creed. However, with the tearing down of the Berlin Wall in 1989, it appeared as though communism had ultimately lost in the Cold War. Soviet-era theories of planned government economies and nationalisation of industries were outpaced by theories that emphasised private initiative and the free market.

The collapse of communism in eastern Europe and the end of the Cold War

Fig. 8 *The fall of the Berlin Wall, 10 November 1989*

The impact of the events in eastern Europe have been amply summed up by Richard Crockatt when he noted, "Nothing can . . . undo one's sense of the enormity of the communist collapse in 1989. Its speed and comprehensiveness was a challenge to existing theories of political change. Its effects on East–West relations were such that virtually at a stroke Cold War notions became redundant."

Key dates

Chronology of change, 1989

January Independent political parties allowed in Hungary

April Poland ends its ban on the Solidarity Movement there

June Overwhelming election victory by Polish Solidarity candidates

July Poland's leader, General Jaruselski, invites Solidarity to form a coalition government

September Hungary permits East German refugees to enter Austria

October Multiparty democracy is built into a new constitution in Hungary

Erich Honecker, East Germany's communist leader, resigns and is replaced by Egon Krenz

November Czechoslovakia opens its borders to allow access to western European states

The Berlin Wall is brought down

Todor Zhivkov's regime in Bulgaria collapses

New governments in place in Hungary and Czechoslovakia

December Ceauşescu's regime in Romania is overthrown and he and his wife are executed

Did you know?

The Soviet Foreign Ministry referred to the end of the Brezhnev Doctrine in terms of the start of a new doctrine – the Sinatra Doctrine. This was based on Sinatra's song 'I did it my way'. It meant that eastern European states would now be free to 'do it their way'.

The key event which opened the flood gates for popular opposition to the communist regimes of eastern Europe was Gorbachev's rejection of the Brezhnev Doctrine. Many historians regarded Soviet control of eastern Europe and the preservation of socialist regimes there as being at the very heart of the Cold War. Containment and the Truman Doctrine, the keystones of the Cold War, had been introduced, according to the Americans, as a response to the real threat of Soviet ideological expansionism across Europe.

Gorbachev's move to liberalise eastern Europe and the consequent collapse of communist regimes there oversimplifies the events of 1989. The process of change stretched back to the 1956 Hungarian uprising and the 1968 Prague Spring. Perhaps the most significant part of the process was the emergence of East–West détente in Europe driven by Willy Brandt's Ostpolitik from 1969.

The background to 1989

From 1973 the West faced economic recession as a result of escalating oil prices. Trade between eastern Europe and the West began to decline and eastern Europe became increasingly dependent upon the Soviet Union. Although useful in the short term this shift led to long-term damage and a reduction in the ability of eastern Europe to export successfully to the West. Despite this trade issue Western technology and capital in the form of loans and investments did flow into eastern European economies. This all contributed to a 'Westernisation' of east European attitudes as more and more Western visitors, both tourists and businessmen, made contact with eastern Europe. A significant turning point came in the years 1979 to 1982 when another economic recession hit the West. The Soviet economy was also facing the Brezhnev 'years of stagnation' and the Soviet Union was unable to prop up eastern European economies as it had during the 1970s. In effect eastern Europe was trapped between a stagnating Soviet economy and a Western recession. Between 1979 and 1989 eastern European economies faced recession and zero growth. These factors, combined with the 'Gorbachev years', not only contributed to an end to communist rule in eastern Europe but also, ultimately, to an end to the Cold War. Added to this was Gorbachev's announcement that Soviet troops would be withdrawn from Afghanistan. This confirmed that the Soviet Union had renounced its use of military force in the affairs of neighbouring states.

Fig. 9 *Romania's communist leader, Ceauşescu, shortly before his overthrow, December 1989*

The era of revolution, 1989–91

By the 1980s it was clear that the ability of the communist regimes in eastern Europe to offer socialist solutions to meet the needs of the people had lost credibility. Half-hearted attempts to bring some limited capitalist economic policies into eastern Europe were not sufficient. Many historians argue that the collapse of communist regimes in eastern Europe was the outcome of a fundamental apathy within the communist leadership. There was a sense of hopelessness which the communist regimes could not address. Marxists have long argued that the ideal conditions for revolution come when the ruling group has lost confidence in its own ability to rule; when a significant section of the educated classes no longer backs the rulers and when there is growing popular disillusionment among the workers. All these conditions applied to eastern Europe by the late 1980s.

Once the Soviet Union finally abandoned the Brezhnev Doctrine the flood gates for change were flung open. In Poland, with the legalisation of Solidarity in April 1989, the way was paved for multiparty elections in June. In August 1989, a government dominated by Solidarity and led by Tadeusz Mazowiecki was formed. He was eastern Europe's first non-communist Prime Minister since the late 1940s. In May 1989 Hungary opened its border with Austria and in September made the decision officially to allow East German 'holiday makers' to escape to the West that way. During the summer months about 200,000 East Germans spent their holidays in Hungary. From September few returned. There was no public response from the Soviet Union.

In October 1989 Gorbachev visited East Germany and made it clear that no Soviet military aid would be available to reinforce the communist regime there. In September *Democracy Now* had been founded as part of the growing mood of dissatisfaction with the communist regime in East Germany. The country had experienced a disastrous collapse in its economy. In 1985 growth stood at 5.2 per cent but by 1989 it was only 2.8 per cent. In November 1989 East Germany's new Party leader Egon Krenz visited Gorbachev on an economic mission. The Soviet Union could offer no economic aid. On 9 November thousands of East Germans forced their way to the Berlin Wall and the border guards let them through. One American historian commented, "The taking of the Wall . . . transformed the world." Martin McCauley commented, "When the Berlin Wall came down on 9 November 1989, it marked the end of post-war politics. Revolution rolled over eastern Europe like an irresistible tide. It washed away four decades of communist rule as the people rejected Russian-style socialism." There is no evidence to suggest that Gorbachev had some kind of plan designed to dismantle communist control in eastern Europe. He did want to remove hardline communist leaders so they could be replaced by men of his own kind.

A peaceful transition away from communist rule was not achieved throughout eastern Europe. In Romania there was a bloody overthrow of the regime. Nikolae Ceauşescu and his wife, Elena, were executed by firing squad on Christmas Day 1989. His regime had been characterised by corruption, inefficiency and ethnic persecution. The popular response came in December when widespread clashes between ordinary citizens and the state secret police, the Securitate, began.

Fig. 10 *The border between East and West Germany is opened, November 1989*

Reunification of Germany

As eastern Europe entered 1990 the burning question was the future of East and West Germany now that the Berlin Wall had gone. West Germany's Chancellor Kohl was not merely interested in the reunification of the two Germanies. He also wanted a united Germany as a full member of NATO. The reunification of Germany was formally brought about in October 1990. In mid-July Kohl had met with Gorbachev. He was reluctant to see NATO and its military resources expand into East German territory. However, Gorbachev finally accepted what was almost an inevitability – the USSR was so in need of money that he was prepared to do a deal on this important issue. Many historians have taken the view that Gorbachev agreeing to German unification within NATO marked the end of the Cold War. Gorbachev agreed to remove the Soviet military presence from the GDR and insist on no restrictions of German sovereignty. This Soviet agreement was very much an initiative taken by Gorbachev and did not involve key individuals such as Shevardnadze or key institutions like the Soviet Politburo.

With the fall of the Berlin Wall, and the collapse of communism in the Soviet Union, the Cold War effectively ended. No longer were there communist and capitalist power blocs fighting for supremacy. The threat of nuclear war subsided and a new, although not necessarily peaceful, era in international relations began.

Activity

Revision activity

Look back over this chapter and pick out the key points that you think brought about the end of the Cold War. Make these points into a spider diagram that you then use to answer the AQA Examination-style question below.

Learning outcomes

In this section you have learned why the Cold War entered its final phase and ultimately came to an end. You have considered the relative importance of the contributing factors and acquired an understanding of how these factors are inter-related. You have also looked at the role of key individuals, particularly Ronald Reagan and Mikhail Gorbachev, in bringing the Cold War to a close.

'The Cold War came to an end because the Soviet Union was simply unable to continue with it.' How valid is this view?

This question raises the issue of the Soviet Union's commitment to ending the Cold War. The key words are 'How valid'. These are telling you to arrive at a balanced assessment rather than simply fully supporting one extreme or the other. It would be useful to consider the wider context. The USSR had been committed to détente and its economy was in decline. There were pragmatic and historical reasons why the Soviet Union should want to see an end to the Cold War. Does agreeing with the proposition suggest a fundamental weakness in Gorbachev? Is there any evidence to back this view? You should also consider wider events within your answer, in order to question the proposition. What international pressures – diplomatic, social or economic – were upon the Soviet Union at this time? How would the growth in US wealth and militarism alter the balance of power in the world? Could the Soviet Union have maintained the effort of the Cold War in the face of these pressures? There were plenty of hardline communists remaining in the Soviet system, so why did they fail to keep the standoff alive? In short, consider all the reasons that the Cold War came to an end, and not just focus on the declining Soviet economy.

4 Post-Cold War Relations, 1991–2004

10 Nationalism, Aggression and Superpower Responses, 1991–2004

In this chapter you will learn about:

- the context of the collapse of the Yugoslav state
- the growth of eastern European nationalism
- international involvement in the Yugoslav crisis
- the international response to Iraqi aggression in Kuwait, 1990–1
- the USA and Britain in Iraq and Afghanistan
- the West's response to terrorism after September 2001.

Fig. 1 *Map of Yugoslavia, 1991*

As the Berlin Wall came down, some thinkers predicted a new era of improved world relations. The American philosopher Francis Fukuyama even spoke of the 'End of History', meaning that Western liberal democracy would now become the universal system of government. Yet the period from 1991 to 2004 saw new levels of war, terrorism, religious fundamentalism and nationalism around the world. History, it seemed, was still very much being created and decided.

The collapse of Yugoslavia from 1991

A closer look

The pre-1991 context

Yugoslavia came into being after the First World War and was so named in 1929. By 1991 it consisted of a collection of loosely confederated Republics which had to be held together from the end of the Second World War by the efforts of the national leader, Josip Broz Tito, and a degree of ideological unity through communism. By 1990 the state comprised Bosnia-Herzegovina, Croatia, Kosovo, Macedonia, Montenegro, Serbia, Slovenia and Vojvodina. The state was a mix of scattered national groups and diverse religions based on Catholicism, Orthodoxy and Islam. The Second World War exposed Yugoslavia to a wave of nationalism and ethnic divisions but these were subdued when the war ended.

Yugoslavia was a communist state but not under the influence of the Soviet Union as other eastern European states became after 1945. This proved to be another factor promoting unity. The reality was that if the state degenerated into any form of disorder or civil war the Soviet Union would step in to restore 'order'. Also, Tito ensured that any emergence of aggressive nationalism within the confederation would be dealt with effectively. He used repressive measures to stamp out Croatian nationalism in the 1970s. In 1974 Yugoslavia introduced the practice of a 'rotating Presidency'. This meant that all the component states had their time to lead the federation. In 1980 Tito died but this did not mark the immediate start of the collapse of Yugoslavia. Economic problems deepened during the 1980s and there was a significant growth in nationalism and ethnic conflict. This was the backdrop to the events in the collapse of Yugoslavia from 1991.

The communist regimes of eastern Europe were in a state of collapse by 1991. By 1991, communist power was not eradicated across Yugoslavia, but it was certainly undermined. The multiparty elections of 1991 weakened the former communist domination. By late 1990 each of the republics which made up the country of Yugoslavia was ruled by non-communist national elites. The communist party had shared a common ideology, common political interests and common loyalties across the republics. The new political masters had none of the sense of a common ideology, political interests and loyalties which the communists had imposed and this became a primary factor in the violent disintegration of the Yugoslavian state.

Wars of independence and the international response

In June 1991, Slovenia and Croatia declared their independence. This triggered a civil war. The Serbian minority in Croatia were determined not to relinquish their links with Serbia. The conflict rapidly spread into Bosnia-Herzegovina which also declared independence in March 1992. Serbia emphatically rejected an independent Bosnian state. The whole conflict was further deepened through the wide ethnic mix that existed across the region. The break-up of Yugoslavia would produce one of the cruellest civil wars of the post-war world, with each state attempting to achieve its own ethnic and political agendas. Over the next ten years, more than 100,000 people would die in the conflict.

Activity

Research activity

Create a fact file focused on examples of atrocities and military conflict across Yugoslavia between 1991 and 1995. Use this to draw some conclusions about the scale of the crisis in Yugoslavia and the motives that drove the actions of different groups.

Slovenia

The nationalist leaders of Slovenia, who had come to power in mid-1990, demanded independence from Yugoslavia by mid-June 1991. This inevitably led to a confrontation with the Yugoslav national army. Slovenia's leadership hoped that this conflict would lead to European intervention and international recognition of Slovenia's independence. Slovenia was convinced that the European Community (EC) would act as a mediator in order to preserve the peace in Europe. The conflict was a media and propaganda coup for Slovenia. The Yugoslav army was presented as an invading force against the brave Slovene defenders.

An EC-negotiated cease-fire was brought into effect on 7 July 1991. To many Europeans the conflict in Slovenia and the wider Yugoslavia offered a chance to the EC to assert itself as an international force. The EC sent three state representatives to Yugoslavia. Its head was Luxembourg's Foreign Minister Jacques Poos. He declared, "This is the hour of Europe." All sides agreed to the Brioni Accord. This ended the fighting and included a three-month moratorium on independence for Slovenia. This hardly appeared as a triumph for the EC. The Accord was simply a means of buying time in order to enable Yugoslavia's leaders to find a lasting solution to the crisis. Many Slovenes felt that they were being forced by the EC to remain within Yugoslavia. Equally by agreeing to the Brioni Accord the Yugoslav government in effect gave up its control of Slovenia. On 18 July the Yugoslav army withdrew.

When the EC-negotiated **moratorium** ended in October 1991 Slovenia simply restated its declaration of independence. One historian commented on the impact of international intervention, "The principal achievement of the war in Slovenia – independence and the removal of the opposing military forces – appeared to have been a direct result of the EC intervention in the war: by securing the withdrawal of the Yugoslav army . . . the EC **troika** effectively neutralised the opposing military force."

Key terms

Moratorium: an agreed period of delay in a meeting or other proceedings.

Troika: a committee of three members.

Croatia

Croatia also wanted independence. A complication in Croatia came in the form of Serb militia groups demanding to hold on to ethnic Serb dominated areas within Croatia, particularly Krajina. On 2 May 1991 a group of Croatian police were ambushed by Serb militia at Borovo Selo in eastern Slavonia. Allegations of torture and mutilation followed. Serbian Krajina leaders went beyond seeking to retain control of the Serb areas in Croatia. As the Yugoslav army tried to stand between the Croats and the Serbs this was seen by the Croats as aiding the Serbs. By August 1991 Croatia had come to regard the Yugoslav federal army as an army of occupation. Croatia had formed the Croatian National Guard (the Zbor narodne garde or ZNG) in May 1991. By November 1991 the fighting seemed to have reached a stalemate.

Fig. 2 *Dubrovnik burns in 1991 during the fighting as Yugoslavia broke apart*

As in Slovenia, the EC moved to establish cease-fire. In August 1991 the EC announced a Peace Conference on Yugoslavia, the ambitious aim of which was to establish a settlement for the whole country. EC ministers also gave the Yugoslav army and the Serb militia forces an ultimatum requiring them to observe the cease-fire. Failure to comply would lead to 'international action'. One historian commented that, "The declaration inaugurated the model of international conflict management in former Yugoslavia in which an international mediator threatens one or, more rarely, all parties to the conflict with military action unless it (or they) cease military action, while at the same time it invites all sides, without any particular threat or incentive, to accept what it deems a compromise solution." The chief EC negotiator was Lord Carrington. His UN counterpart was the American statesman, Cyrus Vance.

Key profiles

Lord Carrington, 1919–present

Lord Carrington was a British Conservative politican who served as the Foreign Secretary between 1979 and 1982 and the Secretary-General of NATO from 1984 to 1988, among other offices. In 1991 Lord Carrington acted as chief EC negotiator in diplomatic talks over the Yugoslavian crisis.

Cyrus Vance, 1917–2002

Vance trained as a lawyer, entered politics and became Deputy Secretary for Defence during the Johnson administration. He represented the USA at the failed 1968 Paris Peace talks in an attempt to get the USA out of Vietnam. He was a committed supporter of the SALT II negotiations with the Soviet Union and during the Carter administration he was, between 1977 and 1980, the US Secretary of State. He resigned over the USA's involvement in the arms for hostages scandel in 1980.

The EC tried to broker a reconstructed constitution for Yugoslavia based on an alliance of states. The EC plan proposed a special status for national minorities in areas where they were in the majority. This included separate legislatures and judiciaries. The problem was that Slovenia had already achieved independence and the Serb militias had established their control over the Serb majority areas in Croatia. The EC plan was, therefore, doomed to fail. In January 1992 the EC recognised the independence of both Slovenia and Croatia although Britain and France remained deeply sceptical about this action. This shift towards recognition came largely as a result of pressure from the German Foreign Minister Hans Dietrich Genscher and the EC's recognition of its own impotence in Yugoslavia. In effect, this EC recognition of independence legitimised the territorial claims of the largest national groups in each republic and therefore appeared to ignore the aspirations of the minorities. The EC also failed to address the militant opposition from minority groups such as the Serbs in Croatia. To this extent the EC enabled the violence to continue. The international response appeared to be a negative and counter-productive one.

The UN assumed the role of peacemaker from October 1991, with the following effects:

- Cyrus Vance was appointed as the UN Secretary-General's personal envoy to Yugoslavia.
- The Croatian government agreed to UN mediation.
- Vance negotiated the deployment of 14,000 UN troops in Croatia.
- Vance also organised the creation of UNPAs (United Nations Protected Areas). These would be demilitarised.

Babic, the leader of Serb Krajina, argued that the withdrawal of the military forces of the Yugoslav army would leave the Serbs unprotected. He had little faith in the protection of the UN. An uneasy standoff developed in Croatia. A turning point came in 1995 when America offered its support to integrate the four UNPAs into Croatia. The USA hoped to use Croatia in its settlement of yet another Yugoslav conflict, the one that had erupted in Bosnia-Herzegovina. It was America's backing that gave Croatia the confidence to take over the UNPAs without the need to reach a political compromise with the Krajina Serbs.

This process started in May 1995 when the Croatian army occupied western Slavonia (UNPS – Sector West). During August and September similar actions followed in the Krajina region of western Bosnia. This international support for Croatia meant that by 1998 the last UNPA, in eastern Slavonia, had been brought under Croat control. Ethnic cleansing was complete by this point as 94 per cent of Croatia was declared to be Croat.

Bosnia-Herzegovina

The republic was run by a coalition of three national groups:

- (Muslim) Party of Democratic Action (SDA)
- Serb Democratic Party (SDS)
- Croat Democratic Union (HDZ).

The SDA wanted a united and centralised Bosnia-Herzegovina, independent from other Yugoslav republics. The Serbs rejected this and demanded a divided Bosnia-Herzegovina and the creation of a Serb state. The Croat group initially backed the SDA but later called for a Bosnian Croat state to be created. In March 1992 the Muslim leader, President Alija Izetbegovic, called a **referendum** to decide upon the issue of independence. This referendum had been suggested in December 1991 by the EC Arbitration Commission as

Key terms

Referendum: an opportunity for the people to vote on a proposal made by government rather than the elected government making the decision in the normal consistutional manner. It acts as a free vote and is sometimes referred to as a plebiscite.

a condition for recognition of Bosnia-Herzegovina by the EC. 63.4 per cent of registered voters voted and, of these, 99.8 voted for independence. The Serbs declared it invalid. The leader of the SDS, Radovan Karadzic, warned of the outbreak of war in Bosnia-Herzegovina. He told Muslim party leaders:

> Do not think that you will not lead Bosnia-Herzegovina into hell, and do not think that you will not perhaps lead the Muslim people into annihilation, because the Muslim people cannot defend themselves if there is a war.

Key profiles

Alija Izetbegovic, 1925–2003

Izetbegovic was seen as a Muslim nationalist and accused of seeking to establish an Islamic state in Bosnia-Herzegovina. He finally became President of the newly created independent Bosnia-Herzegovina in 1990 and remained in that office until 1996.

Radovan Karadzic, 1945–present

Karadzic established the Serbian Democratc Party in 1989. Its declared aim was to create an independent Greater Serb state. This was established soon after when he declared the existence of an independent republic of Bosnia and Herzegovina. This was called Republika Srpska and Karadzic was established as its head of state. He was later accused of war crimes and was linked especially to the shelling of Sarajevo and the massacre of 7,500 muslims in Srebrenica in 1995. An international arrest warrant was issued, and rather than face the charges, Karadzic went into hiding. He was eventually arrested in 2008 and faces trial.

Fig. 3 *In Bosnia-Herzegovina a Muslim prays at the grave of his murdered son*

Karadzic insisted that Bosnian Serbs were opposed to withdrawing from Yugoslavia. The Muslim declaration triggered a Bosnian Serb response of seceding from Bosnia-Herzegovina. This extended to a determination to win areas of control where the Serbs were not in the majority. On 7 April 1992 the EC and the USA recognised Bosnia-Herzegovina's independence. The battlelines were now drawn between the Serbs and the Muslims and their Croat allies. From 1993 the Muslims became known as **Bosniacs**. The conflict in Bosnia-Herzegovina lasted until the end of 1995. The war aims of those involved shifted during this period. Historians have suggested that the conflict may be defined in three different phases:

- the war between the Muslim–Croat coalition and the Serb forces (1992–3)
- the Muslim–Croat war and the Muslim–Muslim war (1993–4)
- the establishment of joint NATO, Muslim, Croatian offensives against the Serbs (March–October 1995).

The Bosniacs lacked both the military personnel and the industrial resources necessary to compete effectively against the Serbs. Unlike the Serbs, the Muslim forces had no access to the sea through which they could receive military supplies from outside. To make matters worse, the Muslims controlled less than half of the territory of the country. Serb determination to resist was heightened by propaganda which claimed the Muslims were aiming to establish an Islamic fundamentalist state. Ultimately, the Bosniacs became convinced that only with external military intervention would they be able to shift the balance of military power in their favour.

Key terms

Bosniac: people culturally and historically identified with Bosnia and Herzegovina, sharing a common language and a traditional practice of the Muslim religion.

Activity

Group activity

Split into three groups, each group representing one of the Yugoslav states described here. After 10 minutes of preparation, each group should present a summary of their situation at the beginning of the break-up of Yugoslavia.

The international response to the crisis in Bosnia-Herzegovina

The UN, the EC and NATO

The EC was not willing to support the newly recognised government of Bosnia-Herzegovina with military aid, nor indeed was the USA. Therefore the main source of international aid for the Muslim government came from Saudi Arabia, Pakistan, Iran and Turkey. As a result of the bombing of civilians in Sarajevo in May 1992 the UN imposed economic sanctions on the Federal Republic of Yugoslavia, but to little effect. In April 1993 the UN responded to the Bosnian Serb artillery attacks on the eastern Bosnian town of Srebrenica by declaring it a 'safe area free from armed attack or other hostile act.' This status was extended in May 1993 to other towns and cities deemed vulnerable to Bosnian Serb artillery. These included Bihac, Zepa, Tuzla and Sarajevo. This UN action served to protect the Muslim military as well as Muslim civilians. The UN's role initially was one of establishing protection areas in order to deliver humanitarian relief. The UN revealed evidence of serious human rights abuses against Muslims in Bosnia-Herzegovina. These included evidence of massacres, torture and the ill-treatment of prisoners. In May 1994 the UN Security Council established an International Tribunal whose role was to prosecute those responsible for these crimes against humanity. It was July 1995 when the President of the Serb Republic, Radovan Karadzic and the Chief of Staff of the Serb armed forces, Ratko Mladic, were indicted for war crimes.

Table 1 *Purpose of the main international bodies*

United Nations	European Community	NATO
Dedicated 'to maintaining international peace and security, developing friendly relations among nations and promoting social progress, better living standards and human rights.' (From UN website.)	To promote economic, social, legal, cultural, and environmental cooperation between the European nations.	A military defence alliance currently consisting of 28 member states, with each state agreeing to mutual defence if one of the other states is attacked.

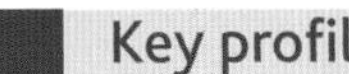

Activity

Challenge your thinking

Look at the purpose of the three international organisations in the table. In what ways might their interests overlap (e.g. defence)? Can you see situations in which their interests might clash?

Key profile

Ratko Mladic, 1942–present

Mladic was the Chief of Staff of the Bosnian Serb Army and directly linked to the massacres at Srebrenica and the bombing of Sarajevo. He was a close ally and confidant of Karadzic. He was traced and arrested for his war crimes in 2006.

Joint UN and EC action in Bosnia-Herzegovina was a characteristic of the conflict. In late 1992 Cyrus Vance and the EC representative, Lord David Owen, presented their proposals. This was known as the Vance–Owen Peace Plan.

The plan called for the country to be divided into ten provinces, each with a high level of independence. It failed to recognise the Serb demand for a united Serb state. Despite this others felt that the plan rewarded Serb aggression. The plan was simply rejected by both the Serbs and the Bosniacs. A further plan was put forward. The Owen–Stoltenberg plan attempted to recognise Serb demands for a separate Serb controlled territory by dividing Bosnia-Herzegovina into three discrete republics. The Muslims rejected this idea because it offered them insufficient territory. The USA then proposed a plan of its own based on the creation of a Muslim–Croat federation in Bosnia-Herzegovina. In February 1994 it was agreed that a federation should be established. Negotiations widened to include Russia, France, Germany and Britain by April 1994. This group effectively took over from the UN and EC. The outcome was a plan to divide Bosnia-Herzegovina giving the Muslim–Croat federation 51 per cent of the republic with the rest being given to the Bosnian Serbs; the latter immediately refused to accept it. International opinion was that the Serbs must be made to accept the plan, by force if necessary. In August 1995 NATO launched Operation Deliberate Force. NATO began air strikes and bombarded Serb positions. The pretext for the action was the massacre at the Markala market in Sarajevo, a UN 'safe area' where 30 civilians were killed by Serb artillery fire.

Exploring the detail

The massacre at Ahmici

A number of Bosniac civilians were massacred in the village of Ahmici in April 1993 by Croatian troops. This was a deliberate and calculated murder carried out by dragging people from their homes and attempting to shoot everyone, including women and children. Croatian snipers were deployed to ensure that no one escaped. 104 bodies were found by British troops. It has been described as one of the most gruesome examples of ethnic cleansing.

Activity

Talking point

How effective was external intervention in the Yugoslav crisis? Make a timeline of events and by each event record its signficance in the conflict.

The Dayton Agreement, November 1995

The USA was determined to broker a settlement in Bosnia-Herzegovina. America was convinced that UN and European intervention would not succeed given the performance to date. The chief US negotiator, Richard Holbrooke, began the process of bringing the key players together as early as August 1995. He realised that the problems in Bosnia-Herzegovina may not only create divisions among Europeans but may also alienate them from the USA. A settlement driven by the USA would minimise these outcomes. The European representatives were merely observers at the talks that were to follow.

On 26 October Izetbegovic, Tudjman and Milosevic met at a US Air Force base in Dayton, Ohio. This meeting resulted in the 'General Framework Agreement for Peace in Bosnia and Herzegovina' and this was formally signed in Paris on 14 December. A constitution for the newly created state of Bosnia-Herzegovina was drawn up. This defined the structure of the legislature and the scale of representation from among the three principal groups, the Bosniacs, the Croats and the Serbs. To make the agreement work a supervision force was set up. This was called the 'Implementation Force' (IFOR) and it was under NATO command. Its mandate to implement the Paris agreement was to last for one year when it was replaced by the 'Stabilisation Force' (SFOR).

In many respects the US-brokered Dayton Agreement had only limited success. The military conflict and the accompanying slaughter were stopped. However, none of the parties achieved its main objectives. The unified state that the Bosniacs wanted, which would have enabled them to assert their political dominance, was not achieved. Both the Serbs and the Croats failed in their efforts to break away from Bosnia-Herzegovina.

Exploring the detail

Kosovo

Kosovo sits at the southern edge of the former Yugoslavia, on the Albanian border. About 90 per cent of the population of Kosovo was made up of ethnic Albanians. Nationalist feelings were gaining strength and there was opposition to the Serb dominance of politics. The Serbs regarded Kosovo as having symbolic importance to their own national identity. The problem also assumed religious significance as the Serbs were Christians while the Kosovo Albanians were Muslims.

Kosovo

The issue of nationalism came to a head in Kosovo in early 1996. There were outbreaks of violence. Throughout March and April the Kosovo Liberation Army (KLA) carried out a series of attack against Serbs. In September of that year, there followed attacks against the Yugoslav military in Kosovo. At the funeral of a Kosovo Albanian, killed by the Serb police in December 1997, masked KLA fighters announced, "Serbia is massacring Albanians. The Kosovo Liberation Army is the only force fighting for the freedom of Kosovo." Within a few months the KLA had transformed itself into a mass guerrilla force leading an armed uprising against Serb control. The Yugoslav army's response was firm. By August 1998 thousands of Kosovo Albanians were turned into refugees.

In September 1998 the UN Security Council passed Resolution 1119 calling for a cease-fire. In October NATO established an 'activation order' for air strikes against Serbia and Montenegro. Under this pressure, Milosevic agreed to withdraw military forces. This cease-fire was overseen by US observers and the Organisation for Security and Cooperation in Europe (OSCE). The KLA were happy with the arrangement because it allowed them to recover territory lost to the Yugoslav military. International intervention had enabled the KLA to ready itself for any future military operations.

In January 1999 international observers were made aware of the massacre of 45 Kosovo Albanians in the village of Racak in western Kosovo. This event triggered the USA, with the backing of the threat of NATO air strikes, to summon a meeting at Rambouillet, near Paris, in February 1999. An important element of this plan was to enable a NATO force to replace the Yugoslav army in Kosovo. Milosevic refused to accept this proposal. Once again it appeared as if international intervention had facilitated national liberation. NATO would intervene by force to implement the proposals and this would make the KLA's liberation of Kosovo a *fait accompli* (an accomplished fact). That was the KLA's perception.

Fig. 4 *Serbian President Slobodan Milosevic, 1991*

The NATO bombing began in March 1999. Its aim was to protect civilians and to minimise Yugoslavia's military power in Kosovo. NATO also dropped anti-Milosevic propaganda, the aim of which was to push for the removal of Milosevic from power. In May 1999 Milosevic was indicted for crimes against humanity by The Hague International Tribunal. He was charged with organising the mass expulsion and murder of Kosovo Albanians. NATO's bombing failed to undermine the Yugoslav army's military power.

In June 1999 a peace agreement was established. This was negotiated by the Russian envoy, Victor Cheromydin and the EU envoy, Martti Arthisaari. All military forces were to withdraw from Kosovo. A NATO force would support a civilian administration which would manage substantial autonomy for Kosovo within the Federal Republic of Yugoslavia. Both sides could claim this as a victory, as indeed could NATO and the international community.

Cross-reference

For more on the UN's relationship with Kosovo in the late 1990s, see Chapter 12.

Activity

Thinking point

Is there any link between the end of the Cold War and the crisis in Yugoslavia?

Growing eastern European nationalism

From 1989 most eastern European states began the following transitions:

Table 2

From	To
Communist dictatorship	Democracy
Centrally controlled economy	Free market capitalism
Direct and indirect Soviet control	Full national independence

In some respects the collapse of the communist system in eastern Europe could be compared to the decolonisation process that many developing countries had experienced after World War II. When communism collapsed there was an explosion of national euphoria. The emphasis on national identity was also fostered by greater openness in education and the media. The classic example of post-communist nationalism came in Czechoslovakia. In 1993 the independent state of Slovakia was formed. Its ex-communist Prime Minister, Vladimir Merciar commented, "We have waited 1000 years for this opportunity."

The nationalist euphoria that followed the end of communist control also generated much xenophobia and intolerant nationalist thinking across eastern Europe. To some extent it became apparent that one form of intolerance and extremism displayed by the communist system was replaced with a new form of intolerance and extremism. This development was heightened by the failure to deliver rapid improvements in living standards and consumerism.

In 1994 the Czech President, Vaclav Havel commented:

> The birth of a new and genuinely stable European order is taking place more slowly and with greater difficulty and pain than most of us had expected five years ago. Many countries that shook off their totalitarian regimes still feel insufficiently anchored in the community of democratic states.

2

The post-communist era led to a very slow and uncertain transition to a new democratic system and this allowed some degree of aggressive nationalism to develop across many eastern European states.

Superpower responses to international aggression

Kuwait and the Gulf War, 1991

Context

Between 1980 and 1988 Iraq had been engaged in a bloody and expensive war with Iran. By the end of the war Iraq owed nearly

$100 billion to foreign creditors. To compound the economic crisis Iraq's main source of foreign revenue came from oil sales. Oil prices had fallen due to a glut of oil on the international markets. By 1988 Iraq's annual income stood at an inadequate $10 billion. The economic crisis threatened the political survival of Iraq's dictator, President Saddam Hussein as unemployment and poverty escalated in the country.

Fig. 5 *US attack aircraft fly over burning oil wells in Kuwait during Operation Desert Storm, 1991*

Key profile

Saddam Hussein, 1937–2006

Saddam Hussein joined the Ba'ath party in 1957 and took part in the unsuccessful attempt to overthrow Iraq's Prime Minister, Abd a-Karm Qsim, in 1959. In 1968 the Ba'ath movement took power in Iraq and when President Amad asan al-Bakr resigned, Saddam Hussein took absolute control. He rapidly established a dictatorship and created a police state in order to guard his own power from any internal threats. Regionally, he wanted to take Egypt's role as leader of the Arab world and to establish Iraq's control over the Persian Gulf. His end started when the USA demanded his removal from office in 2003. He was executed in December 2006.

Cross-reference

For more on the Ba'ath Party, see Exploring the detail, page 143.

Iraq had reasonable relations with the non-Middle Eastern powers. The USA was keen to have an ally in the Middle East after the fall of the pro-American Shah of Iran in 1979. By 1990 the USA provided in excess of $3 billion worth of trade. Despite this Western states were reluctant to provide financial aid to Saddam in view of his scandalous human rights record in Iraq. France was willing to sell weapons to Iraq and while this heightened Saddam's military strength it also increased Iraq's debts. There was little hope of help from the USSR as its own economy was under severe pressure. Regionally, Iraq's principal allies were Jordan and the PLO. Saddam had borrowed heavily from Gulf States in order to fund his war with Iran but by 1990 it was clear that these debts could not be repaid. As OPEC (Organisation of the Petroleum Exporting Companies) oil production increased the price of oil dropped to $18 a barrel by early 1990. This deepened Iraq's economic crisis even further. The only device Saddam Hussein had was his powerful military machine. That appeared to be the means by which a survival route for Saddam Hussein could be created and that was what he used it for.

Exploring the detail

The Iran–Iraq War, 1980–8

Each side in this war claimed the other was responsible for starting the conflict. The real cause lay with the leader of Iraq, Saddam Hussein. He feared that his power in Iraq was under threat through Iran's encouragement of the Shi'ite majority in Iraq to turn against him and overthrow him and the Sunni government. The war led to about 1 million casualties and it had a profoundly damaging impact on the economies of both states.

The invasion of Kuwait

In July 1990 Saddam accused neighbouring Kuwait of stealing oil from Iraq's Rumaila oilfield and he demanded immediate repayment of $2 billion. He blamed Kuwait's overproduction of oil for the depressed international price. The solution was to reduce production and increase oil prices and for Kuwait to suspend all war debts owed by Iraq. These diplomatic moves were supported by massive Iraqi troop movements towards the Kuwait–Iraq border. Initially, Kuwait refused to be threatened by Iraq and simply ignored the demands. The US Ambassador to Iraq, April Glaspie, met with Saddam Hussein in July and failed to emphasise any potential military response by the USA should Iraq invade Kuwait. Even by the end of July, when 100,000 Iraqi troops were stationed on the Kuwait–Iraq border, George Bush took no further action to prevent an invasion. In the early hours of 2 August 1990 Iraqi forces launched an attack on Kuwait. Within hours any effective resistance in Kuwait was over. It also appeared as if Saddam Hussein's economic problems were over as he now controlled all of Kuwait's oil production.

The international response

The immediate collective response was to impose economic sanctions on Iraq through the United Nations and the demand for an immediate withdrawal from Kuwait. It appeared as if, in the rapidly emerging post-Cold War environment, the United Nations was united and would lead a collective security response to the invasion. However, the real force behind the international response was the United States. Iraq held 20 per cent of the world's oil production and was in a position to threaten a further 20 per cent in the neighbouring state of Saudi Arabia. The United States received a large percentage of its oil imports from Saudi Arabia. There was also the problem of the free passage of oil through the Persian Gulf. This was the route for oil that supported the economies of Europe and Japan.

On 6 August 1990 Saudi Arabia agreed to allow the USA to establish what was known as Operation Desert Shield. This meant moving up to 250,000 troops into Saudi Arabia. A deadline for Iraq's withdrawal from Kuwait was set for 15 January 1991. If that withdrawal deadline was not met, then Operation Desert Shield would become Operation Desert Storm. Kuwait would be forcibly liberated. America assembled a coalition of powers that could be used to implement Operation Desert Storm. Egypt's military debt to the USA, amounting to around $6 billion, was written off. Egypt joined the coalition. Syria's President Assad joined the coalition because he believed that the removal of Saddam Hussein could only strengthen his own position as the head of the Ba'ath Movement. Jordan opted to remain neutral. Israel, the most obvious ally for the USA, agreed to remain out of the coalition. Bush was convinced that Israel's participation would alienate the Arab states and undermine the coalition.

Despite some opposition in Parliament, Britain was fully behind the USA. One of Margaret Thatcher's last major political acts was to commit Britain to the anti-Iraq coalition. Operation Granby committed almost 45,000 British troops. The French were a little less enthusiastic because they had long been a close supporter of Iraq. All military decisions made by the French commander, Lieutenant-General Michel Roquejeoffre, had to be referred back to the Defence Minister. Although offering no military contribution, the German Chancellor, Helmut Kohl, did provide financial aid and accepted the redeployment of US troops from their NATO commitment in Europe. Other European states such as Greece, Denmark, Italy and the Netherlands gave some naval and air support.

Cross-reference

For more on the role of the UN in the 1991 Gulf War, see Chapter 12.

Exploring the detail

The Ba'ath Movement

Essentially the Ba'ath Party presented itself as the party of Arab nationalism in the Middle East. However, its aims and policies have tended to be rather vague and there has been no real unity among its members regionally. It was the ruling party in Iraq from 1968.

Fig. 6 *The devastation left by Coalition air attacks on Kuwait highway in 1991*

During this period the USA and its allies built up their military presence in Saudi Arabia. In November the United Nations passed Resolution 678 which authorised the use of force unless Iraq withdrew by 15 January. A final diplomatic move came at the end of November when US Secretary of State Baker met with Iraq's Foreign Minister, Tariq Aziz in Geneva. Aziz demanded that any negotiations be linked to the Palestinian–Israeli Crisis. The USA refused. On 16 January 1991 the Americans and their coalition partners launched the military assault against Iraq and thereby engaged in Operation Desert Storm and the Gulf War. Not only were Iraqi forces pushed from Kuwait but coalition forces struck deep into Iraq itself.

The Safwan Surrender Talks, March 1991

The US military commander, General Norman Schwarzkopf met with Iraq's Deputy Chief of Staff, General Sultan Hashim Ahmed. Among the surrender terms the Americans made no attempt to remove Saddam Hussein from power, nor did they prevent Iraqi forces from using military helicopters over Iraqi soil. These weapons were used to crush Shia rebels in southern Iraq and defeat a Kurdish uprising in the north. The USA believed that the overthrow of Saddam Hussein would come from within Iraq itself. It also held the view that 'Better the devil you know than the one you don't'.

President Bush insisted that the Gulf War had not been about defending the sovereignty of one small country, Kuwait. It was, in his words, about a "big idea; a new world order." This new order was "peaceful settlement of disputes, solidarity against aggression, reduced and controlled arsenals, and just treatment of all peoples." Relatively soon this optimistic view of international relations within this new order was faced with the growing menace of international terrorism.

Although the Gulf War was brought to an end it was not the end of international monitoring of Iraq. Drastic economic sanctions followed and the United Nations established inspection teams to identify Saddam Hussein's possession of weapons of mass destruction (WMS) in April 1991. Iraq refused to cooperate and expelled all the American members of the inspection team. In December 1998 Britain and America launched Operation Desert Fox. This was a bombing campaign aimed at suspected biological, chemical and nuclear production points. The operation was a failure and in October 1999 the UN finally abandoned its weapons inspection efforts.

Exploring the detail

Internal opposition to Saddam Hussein

There were numerous groups who threatened Hussein's power in Iraq. In the north of the country there was a strong nationalist movement among the Kurdish population. This region wanted independence from Iraq. Saddam Hussein unleashed violence against Iraq's Kurdish population in order to quell opposition. In the south there was opposition from the Shia community. This group was controlled by slightly less extreme methods.

Activity

Talking point

Examine the motives underpinning the international response to the issues in Iraq. Split into three groups. One group will argue in favour of international intervention against Iraq in 1991; the other group will argue against. The third group will discuss the issues and consider questions to ask. When the third group has heard both arguments and posed their questions, they should declare which of the groups it thinks made the strongest case and why.

The USA and Britain in Iraq and Afganistan

9/11

On 11 September 2001 Islamic terrorists hijacked two airliners and flew them into the Twin Towers of the World Trade Centre in lower Manhattan, New York. Over 3,000 people were killed. A third airliner partially damaged the Pentagon and a fourth crash-landed in a field in Pennsylvania. This supreme act of terrorism finally confirmed a shift in international relations that had existed for some time. In February 1998 the World Islamic Front had declared Jihad against the USA. It stated:

> First, for over seven years the United States has been occupying the lands of Islam in the holiest of places, the Arabian peninsula . . . Second, despite the great devastations inflicted on the Iraqi people by the crusader-Zionist alliance, the Americans are once again trying to repeat the horrific massacres. Third, if the Americans' aims are religious and economic, the aim is also to serve the Jews' petty state and divert attention from its occupation of Jerusalem and murder of Muslims there.

3

Activity

Research activity

Using the internet and other sources, find out exactly what occurred on 11 September 2001. Can you explain why the terrorists launched their attack, and how the attack changed America's relationship with the world?

Cross-reference

For more on the role of the UN in Iraq, see Chapter 12.

Terrorism was not new but America's response to it was. A war on terror was declared. Not only were the terrorists themselves and the regimes that supported them targeted, but also any state which had backed terrorism in any form. In his State of the Union address in January 2002 President George W. Bush made this new era of international security absolutely clear. He said:

> Our . . . goal is to prevent regimes that sponsor terror from threatening America or our friends and allies with weapons of mass destruction. Some of these regimes have been pretty quiet since September 11. But we know their true nature . . . Iraq continues to flaunt its hostility toward America and to support terror. States like these, and their terrorist allies, constitute an axis of evil, arming to threaten the peace of the world.

4

Included in Bush's 'axis of evil' were Iran, Iraq and North Korea. From this point, terrorism, dictatorships that backed it and weapons of mass destruction which could be made available to it were all linked together as part of this 'axis of evil.' The war against terrorism was transformed from one waged against a particular enemy into a sustained worldwide struggle against those states that supported terrorism. This new approach almost legitimised the USA to take whatever action it wanted, whenever and wherever it deemed necessary in the battle against terrorism. Any notion of post-Cold War collective security emerging as the basis for a new order of international relations had ended as of 11 September 2001.

Activity

Talking point

Has the end of the Cold War increased the USA's global power?

Afghanistan, 2001

The driving force of Islamic terrorism was Osama bin Laden and his al-Qaeda organisation. From May 1996 he had been organising terrorist training camps in Afghanistan, a state dominated by the Taliban regime. In October 2001 George W. Bush declared Osama bin Laden to be the prime suspect responsible for 9/11. America demanded that the Taliban regime in Afghanistan hand over al-Qaeda leaders to the US and enable the US to ensure that all al-Qaeda training camps had been closed. The Taliban denied any links between bin Laden and 9/11. On 7 October 2001 the USA and Britain launched Operation Enduring

Fig. 7 *US troops in Afghanistan, 2001*

Freedom in a bid to capture bin Laden, destroy al-Qaeda and remove the Taliban regime. There was no United Nations authorisation for this American-led military action. America insisted that it was an act of self-defence rather than one of aggression and therefore consistent with Article 51 of the UN Charter. The operation was a success in that the Taliban regime was removed from power but bin Laden was not captured. In December 2001 the UN Security Council set up the International Security Assistance Force which had the authority to help the Afghan Interim Authority to maintain security. Command of this force passed to NATO in August 2003. Despite this, by 2003 the Taliban were regaining strength and it was clear that the coalition had not succeeded in removing militants. The military action in Afghanistan had not ended by 2004.

A closer look

al-Qaeda and Osama bin Laden

This organisation was formed in 1993 by Osama bin Laden, a Saudi Arabian-born Islamic fundamentalist. In Arabic al-Qaeda means 'the base'. It was created from bin Laden's disillusionment with Saudi Arabia's cooperation with the USA during the Gulf War. The organisation was committed to conducting a 'Holy War' against the USA whom it accused of looting the resources of the Muslim world and aiding the enemies of Islam. Osama bin Laden's aim was to estabish a terrorist organisation that could destabilise the USA and its Western allies as much as possible. The training ground for this preparation for terrorism was Afghanistan. There Osama bin Laden had originally fought with the fundamentalist Taliban movement against Soviet occupation during the 1980s. The Taliban practise an extreme version of Sharia law, a code that governs every aspect of daily life, government and business according to Islamic religious codes. The Taliban offered al-Qaeda the means to train terrorist groups that could operate across the world in order to fulfil Osama bin Laden's anti-American aims.

Iraq, 2003

In March 2003 US and British forces invaded Iraq and by December Saddam Hussein was captured. It appeared as if the USA had taken the view that any action was legitimate if the US believed that it was under threat. Many commentators argued that by adopting this stance against Iraq the USA had fallen into bin Laden's trap and alienated Muslims throughout the world and committed itself and its allies to a conflict from which they could not easily withdraw. It appeared as if the errors begun in Afghanistan were destined to continue. The struggle against international terrorism began to create instability rather than security and the USA, as the dominant superpower, began to emerge as a new imperialist state in the post-Cold War world.

In its war against terrorism the USA not only linked Iraq with supporting terrorist organisations but also with having the capacity to develop weapons of mass destruction. These could be available to al-Qaeda and therefore pose a huge threat to the USA. In February 2003 Secretary of State Colin Powell had announced at the UN that:

> Iraq's behaviour shows that Saddam Hussein and his regime are concealing their efforts to produce weapons of mass destruction . . . (but) our concern is not just about these illicit weapons. It's the way these weapons can be connected to terrorism and terrorist organisations.

Some commentators suggested that America had a hidden agenda underpinning its invasion of Iraq. A Saudi journalist, Saleh al-Namla noted that through the invasion America "would not only become a major mover in the international oil market, but a principal player in it. This would mean not only control of the quantity and price of oil but also the ability to exercise arbitrariness by striking at petroleum countries causing their bankruptcy." Saudi Arabia was convinced that the USA saw its opportunity in Iraq to establish Western control over Arab oil and its supply and prices. By 2004 the UN lifted its sanctions on the export of oil from Iraq and these could begin once production exceeded domestic demand. In 2004 the possible US hidden agenda remained. Who will allocate the spending of oil revenue and what will determine these decisions?

A key factor in the USA's rationale for invading Iraq was Saddam Hussein's support for international terrorism. Hussein had shown support for Palestinian terrorist groups and he had declared a commitment to the destruction of Israel. Groups such as the Palestine Liberation Front and Abu Nidal were supported by Iraq. Osama bin Laden's survivors from Afghanistan were able to set up the Ansar al-Islam (the Supporters of Islam) base. The US government was keen to establish in the minds of Americans the link between the 9/11 attacks, al-Qaeda who carried out the attacks and the war in Iraq.

On the issue of weapons of mass destruction the evidence produced for their existence has been meagre. In his speech to the two Houses of Congress on 17 July 2003, Britain's Prime Minister, Tony Blair, conceded that both himself and President Bush would be forgiven by history if no weapons of mass destruction were found in Iraq. Much of the evidence for the invasion of Iraq was based on Saddam Hussein's boasts in the 1980s that his scientists were developing such weapons. Similarly there was some evidence that Iraq had developed biological and chemical weapons before the invasion but little that any such weapons existed at the time of the invasion. In March 2003, due to the lack of any concrete evidence of the existence of such weapons, the Americans resorted to using the fact that a number of German companies had traded in chemical substances with Iraq, and that these chemicals could have been used to create the weapons.

Despite this, Iraq systematically impeded UN inspection efforts. Evidence was found of biological weapon production and Iraq eventually declared its possession of 8,500 litres of anthrax. Chemical weapons were used by Iraq in its war against Iran. Mustard gas and VX nerve gas was used against the Iranians and against the Kurdish population of Iraq itself. Whether weapons of mass destruction actually existed or whether they were destroyed immediately prior to the invasion will remain something of a mystery. Opponents of the war challenged the international response as a lie. As the *Daily Telegraph* reported, "Tony Blair stands charged in effect of committing British troops on the basis of a lie." The USA took the view that to allow Saddam Hussein to remain in power would have destabilised the Middle East further and would have enabled terrorism to flourish.

Activity

Research activity

Using the internet and text sources, research the arguments made for and against the invasion of Iraq. Debate the various arguments in small groups. Then research what has happened since the invasion. Which argument do you find the most convincing and why?

Fig. 8 *Playing cards depicting the USA's most wanted Iraqi leaders, 2003*

These priorities outweighed all other considerations, particularly when international relations had entered America's concept of a new world order in the post-Cold War world.

Summary questions

1. 'The international response to the crisis in Yugoslavia during the 1990s proved to be totally inadequate.' How valid is this assessment?
2. To what extent did the terrorist attack on the USA in September 2001 change international relations?

11 The Expansion of the European Union after 1991

In this chapter you will learn about:

- the enlargement of the European Union (EU) from 1991 to 2004
- the strengths and weaknesses of the enlarged EU
- the effect of EU enlargement on international relations
- the impact of the expansion of NATO.

Fig. 1 *1 May celebrations in Warsaw*

The idea of a unified Europe was very appealing to many in the aftermath of World War II, when Europe had been split apart by nationalist and ethnic divisions. The European Union (EU), established in 1993 out of earlier European organisations, was the boldest attempt to create a united Europe, and it included powerful new bodies and a single European currency for many member states. Yet the greatest challenge for the EU was, and remains, the holding together of such different national identities.

The further enlargement of the EU

A closer look

The background to the EU

At the end of World War II, many European countries looked for ways in which the old nationalist divisions could be replaced by a more united Europe. One of the first attempts to achieve this aim was the European Coal and Steel Community (ECSC). Its members were Belgium, France, Italy, Luxembourg, the Netherlands and West Germany, and it aimed to centralise control of national coal and steel industries. These six countries eventually created in 1957, via the Treaties of Rome, a European body with broader powers known as the European Economic Community (EEC), which sat alongside the ECSC and also a new organisation, the European Atomic Energy Community (Euratom). In 1967 these three agencies were brought under a single organisation, the European Community (EC), which underwent a period of steady enlargement as more and more countries bought into the advantages of membership. In 1991, what is known as the Maastricht Treaty was negotiated between the EC member states, and in 1993 this created the European Union (EU).

The original members of the EEC in 1957 were Belgium, France, Federal Republic of Germany, Italy, Luxembourg and The Netherlands.

A phase of continued expansion then followed:

Table 1

State	Application	Accession
Denmark	May 1967	January 1973
Ireland	May 1967	January 1973
United Kingdom	May 1967	January 1973
Greece	June 1975	January 1981
Portugal	March 1977	January 1986
Spain	March 1977	January 1986
Sweden	July 1991	January 1995
Finland	March 1992	January 1995
Austria	July 1989	January 1995
Cyprus	July 1990	May 2004
Malta	July 1990	May 2004
Hungary	March 1994	May 2004
Poland	April 1994	May 2004
Slovakia	June 1995	May 2004
Latvia	October 1995	May 2004
Estonia	November 1995	May 2004
Lithuania	December 1995	May 2004
Czech Republic	January 1996	May 2004
Slovenia	June 1996	May 2004

By May 2004 the total number of member states was 25.

Western European states had traditionally suggested that once communism had withered in central and eastern Europe these former communist states would be welcomed into the prosperity and security enjoyed by the rest of Europe. In effect this meant membership of the EU and NATO. The high hopes of central and eastern European states were not rapidly met by EU members. However, a gradual pre-accession strategy was established and this involved technical and financial aid for the former communist states.

A significant enlargement of the EU began with the signing of the European Agreements in 1992. This began the process of enlarging the EU by admitting former eastern bloc states. This was a radically new departure for the EU. The European Agreements created **free trade agreements** on industrial goods but excluding agricultural goods. These agreements were aimed at contributing to stability and economic growth among those states that wished to enter the EU. The Copenhagen Summit of 1993 formally ratified the European Agreements as the first step towards full membership of the EU. The EU also defined criteria for entry. These included:

- the creation of democratic institutions
- a commitment to protect human rights

Key terms

Free Trade Agreement: this is the idea that international trade will develop most effciently if there are few restrictions on it. The most significant restriction is taxation imposed by the importing state. Free trade agreements ensure that reciprocal low tax arrangements are implemented by states trading with each other. Such agreements are seen as a way of generating trade and all the consequent benefits from it without the constraint of higher cost goods because of taxation policies.

- a market economy
- recognition of minorities and their protection
- the ability to adopt economic and monetary union.

In 1993 six countries were guaranteed eventual membership of the EU. These were Bulgaria, the Czech Republic, Hungary, Poland, Romania and Slovakia. Four others, Estonia, Latvia, Lithuania and Slovenia, eventually received the same assurances. The decision to expand the EU was rooted in the certainty that it was the most effective way to bring to an end the divisions within Europe as a whole. Membership of the organisation was the most effective way to manage the transition of central and eastern European states from what were one-party dictatorships with centrally planned and state-controlled economies to democracies with free market status.

Some historians have argued that expansion of the EU was vital in a post-Cold War Europe. The collapse of communism in central and eastern Europe presented a potential threat to the security of the rest of Europe. The states that had been controlled by the communist system since the end of the Second World War were suddenly faced with the freedom to establish new political systems and new economic structures. Those in favour of expansion argued that expansion of the EU through the membership of these former communist states would ensure they became effective democracies which could operate market economies. Membership would enable these states to make the transition easily and could only benefit the existing members because it would massively reduce the possibility of instability across central and eastern Europe.

The potential gains from enlargement for the member states, and for potential new members, were defined as follows:

- The EU's internal market would be enlarged to consist of over 100 million more consumers with the potential to spend and trade.
- Economic growth would be stimulated throughout the Union.
- States from central and eastern Europe would become integrated into western European political and economic systems and this would inevitably strengthen security and stability for the Union as a whole. Both the USA and Russia supported an expansion of the EU for this reason.
- It would improve environmental standards in central and eastern Europe as new members were required to conform to EU standards. These improvements would also apply to issues linked to social rights and social stability across the EU but particularly among the new member states.

Enlargement of EU membership had clear political and economic costs as well as potential gains for the existing members. The addition of further members increased EU market competition and the need to redistribute resources across the EU. The richer member states were faced with a potentially high financial contribution to the EU budget. A further issue which acted as a form of brake on eastward enlargement lay in the increasing diversity of ethnic and cultural contributions being made to the EU. There was a growing fear that the EU would become the victim of an East–West divide. There was the clear issue of European identity and the development of a common sense of purpose

Activity

Group activity

As a group, examine the reasons why the EU expanded. Try to prioritise these into some order of importance.

among an increasingly heterogeneous collection of member states. Many of these concerns were addressed through what was known as Agenda 2000. This was defined immediately after the Treaty of Amsterdam in 1997.

Agenda 2000

The official title of this EU action programme was 'Agenda 2000: For a Stronger and Wider Union'. Its focus was on three inter-related issues: budgets, policies and enlargements. Agenda 2000 laid out an overview for the enlargement when it identified the principal questions which would emerge for all applicant states:

> Enlargement to some 25 countries and 475 million inhabitants will bring considerable political and economic advantages, and will further Union policies if certain conditions are met.
>
> Enlargement will, however, bring greater heterogeneity to the Union. This could limit the benefits of enlargement and make more difficult further development unless adequate preparations are made.
>
> It is vital to use the preaccession period to ensure that applicants make adequate preparations for membership. This will require substantial investment in sectors such as the environment, transport, energy, industrial restructuring, agriculture and rural society.

Agenda 2000 recognised the significant price gaps that existed in agricultural produce between the current EU members and the applicants. It was accepted that restructuring and modernisation was necessary to prepare for entry. A transition period was planned in order to cushion the shock of price adjustment to applicant states and gradually prepare them for full integration into the common agricultural market. Agenda 2000 reaffirmed that it was essential that applicant states were ready and able to conform to EU standards in order to prevent divisions within the EU. This was apparent in terms of environmental standards. Given the scale of the environmental problems in most applicant states a plan was devised which attempted to prioritise environmental reform. The first step was to address the issues of water and air pollution. A similar priority was given to transport development. Applicant states were required to comply with the existing EU Common Transport Policy.

Many of the applicant states were using nuclear power to generate energy. Agenda 2000 required all applicants to bring their levels of nuclear safety up to international standards. It was anticipated that modernisation programmes would be fully implemented over a period of seven to ten years. This requirement was particularly relevant in Bulgaria, Slovakia, Hungary and the Czech Republic. Essentially Agenda 2000 was about preparing an applicant for membership and ensuring that the existing members were not disadvantaged by the change. It underlined the aim of making the EU stronger rather than an enlargement undermining EU strength and unity.

Did you know?

The EU was keen to deal with disputes of one kind or another that existed between applicant states. An example of such a problem was the dispute that existed between Hungary and Slovakia over a dam on the River Danube. Agenda 2000 required applicants to settle their disputes and submit themselves to the jurisdiction of the International Court of Justice.

Reactions to Agenda 2000

The recommendation was to open negotiations immediately with five countries of central and eastern Europe. This inevitably meant that five others would be considered later. In a sense, this created a two-tier entry and the five who were not in the first wave of enlargement were largely dissatisfied with the outcome. The 'successful' five included Poland, Hungary, Estonia and Slovenia. The five whose entry into negotiations was delayed were Latvia, Lithuania, Romania, Bulgaria and Slovakia.

The applicant states

Latvia and Lithuania felt that the other Baltic state applicant, Estonia, had been assessed more favourably than they had in the Agenda 2000. Latvia's Prime Minister Krasts warned of divisions among the Baltic states unless they were all treated in the same way. There must be simultaneous negotiations with all three rather than merely Estonia. A Latvian diplomat had commented, "What we want is to be on the train from the beginning; if we are not, it would give an indication that the EU still regards us as within the Russian sphere of influence." Lithuania's Prime Minister Vagnorius also reiterated this concern over Estonia being considered in the first wave of enlargement.

Prime Minister Ciorbea of Romania commented that, "expansion by waves is justified in the case of NATO, but is not justified for EU enlargement, which is a process of continuous integration; we will continue our political and diplomatic fight right through until December for the adoption of a political decision on EU expansion." Romania argued that to separate the applicant countries into two groups for the opening of negotiations for EU entry was divisive and counter-productive. The point was well made by Romania that the two-tier approach would lead to greater direct foreign investment in those countries selected for the first wave.

To some extent Bulgaria accepted the decision, but certainly did not fully support it. Slovakia's response was equally restrained. Slovakia accepted some of its limitations but also argued that it was not fundamentally different from other applicant states. There was a reluctance on the part of some political groups to carry through the political reforms envisaged for EU membership. Most incredibly the Slovakian Prime Minister, Merciar, even suggested a population exchange between Hungarians in Slovakia and Slovaks in Hungary. The responses of the other five applicants were predictably positive.

The EU Commission itself replied to the idea that there should be a common start for all ten states through an article published in September 1997. Hans van den Broek wrote through the *Financial Times*:

> The idea that the EU is drawing new dividing lines across Europe is a red herring. There are no 'ins and outs' but rather 'ins and pre-ins'. As with economic and monetary union, proper preparation is crucial. Agenda 2000 confirms that we will work with each country to help it prepare for membership. The EU will monitor progress in overcoming problems. As soon as a candidate has fulfilled conditions set out by our heads of government, the Commission will recommend that enlargement negotiations start. This is not merely 'leaving the door open' but a firm commitment.

2

The response of the Commission was practical and reassuring. There was little convincing evidence that the procedure had acted in a divisive way among applicant states. The concern was directed against the EU rather than other applicants.

EU members

The reaction among existing member states towards enlargement was positive. One factor influencing the reaction came through the geographic location of applicant states in relation to existing members. Most states were interested in their immediate neighbours. Austria, for example, was particularly interested in Slovenia, Hungary, Slovakia and the Czech Republic. Germany was alert to the applications of Poland, the Czech Republic, Slovakia and Hungary. These states lay on its eastern frontiers and acted as a buffer between itself and the former Soviet Union. As one commentator noted, "One can predict which candidates for EU membership will be the object of interest for a given country by taking a look at the map of Europe and seeing which candidates lie on a direct line between it and Moscow." Commissioner Has van den Broek summed up the response of the member states when he reported to the European Parliament in October 1997, "One firm conclusion has been reached, namely that where differentiation is applied, it should never mean discrimination."

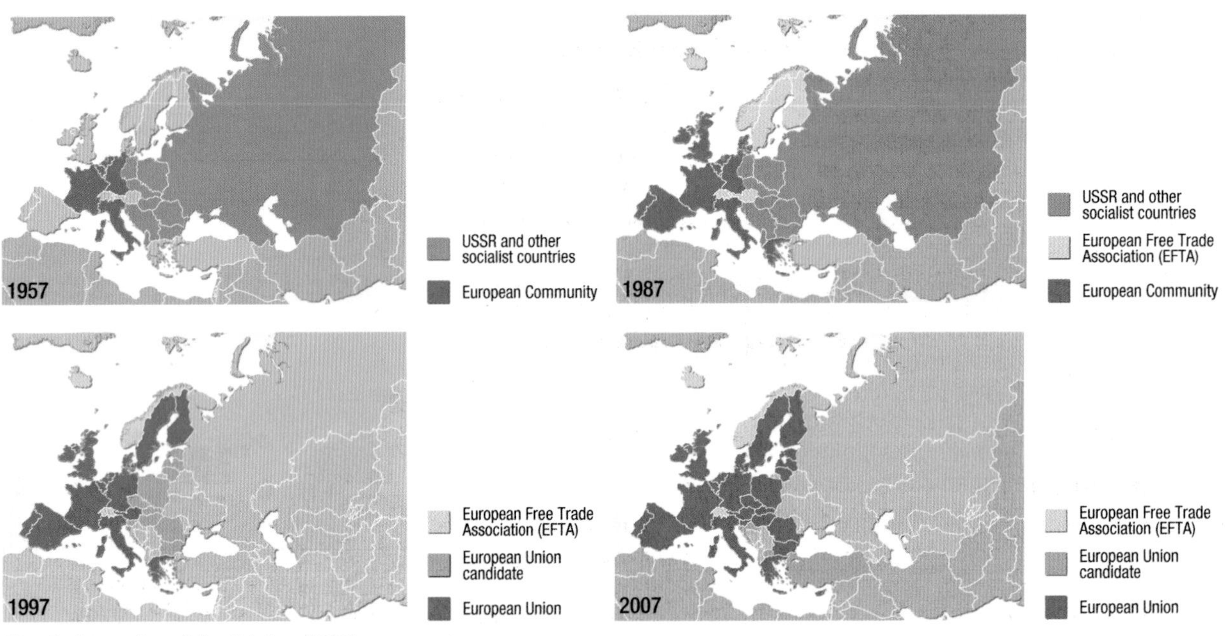

Fig. 2 *Expansion of the EU since 1957*

The recommendation of the Commission in Agenda 2000 was accepted by the European Council in December 1997. The Council declared that 'enlargement is a comprehensive, inclusive and ongoing process, which will take place in stages; each of the applicant states will proceed at its own rate, depending on its degree of preparedness.' The Council accepted the need to offer preaccession aid in order to enable applicant states to be at the height of readiness to enter the EU. A comprehensive package of aid and support for applicant states was agreed by the Council and the European Council President, Jean-Claude Juncker, and considered the outcomes to be 'monumental'. Commission President Santer announced that the European Council's support "had opened the path to the peaceful unification of our continent."

Political and economic integration and its impact on international relations

A basic issue to consider when examining the role of the EU in terms of international relations is whether an organisation with so many members can function collectively and maintain a consensus of policy. Attempts to establish a common foreign policy date back to the 1970s when membership of the EEC totalled nine. The policy was known as European Political Cooperation (ECP) but its range was very limited and by the 1990s it was clear that a united and coordinated foreign policy shared by the member states was not working. There was no common approach towards either the 1991 Gulf War or the collapse of Yugoslavia. A turning point came in 1991 with the Maastricht Treaty and the creation of the Common Foreign and Security Policy (CFSP).

The development of a common foreign and security policy

The Maastricht Treaty established some basic provisions for foreign and security policy among EU members:

- There was to be a common foreign and security policy. There would be an agreed common policy rather than simply attempts to coordinate individual national policies as had been the case up to 1992.
- Defence as well as security was to be part of the role of the CFSP.

At Maastricht it was agreed that the CFSP included 'all questions related to security of the Union, including the eventual framing of a common defence policy, which might in time lead to a common defence policy.' In 1997 the Amsterdam Treaty moved the EU closer to a definite policy formulation structure when it referred to 'the progressive framing of a common defence policy.' Part of the CFSP is the European Security and Defence Policy (ESDP). Despite the desire to establish a common policy on foreign relations and security the EU remains at the mercy of member states being unwilling to relinquish their national control of these policy areas.

An overview of EU relations with the superpowers

Relations with Russia

Many of the newer members of the EU are states that have either been part of the former Soviet Union or have had long-standing relations with the USSR during the era of the Cold War and the dominance of communism in central and eastern Europe. For the EU a stable and prosperous Russia is an advantage. Russia is perceived as an essential partner in political and security issues affecting the EU and positive relations between the EU and Russia are vital. Moves towards setting this relationship in place had already been made before the 2004 expansion of member states. In 1994 the EU signed the Partnership and Cooperation Agreement (PAC) with Russia. This focused on providing a framework for cooperation in such diverse areas as foreign and security policy, transport, energy policy, and financial and technical aid issues. It was not until the end of 1997 that the PAC was implemented because of Russian military action in Chechnya.

The EU's recognition of a degree of dependency upon Russia was further illustrated in 1999 through efforts to strengthen relations in terms of foreign and security issues. However, Russia's continued aggression in Chechnya hampered these moves. The terrorism carried out in the USA in September 2001 went some way to neutralise Russia's actions

Activity

Thinking point

Assess the significance of Agenda 2000. What did it mean for a) applicant states and b) EU members?

Activity

Challenge your thinking

Is the expansion of the EU into a politically integrated organisation a step too far? What are the potential problems with trying to ensure a large regional grouping will work together to achieve some common objective?

Exploring the detail

Chechnya

This region of the former Soviet Union declared its independence in 1991. It was not until 1994 that Boris Yeltsin sent in Russian troops to restore control and return Chechnya into the Russian fold. A bloody war followed and by 1996 this had resulted in the defeat of Russian forces. In 1997 the rebel leader, Aslan Maskhadov was elected President and he was formally recognised by Russia. The conflict in Chechnya temporarily ended until 1999.

in Chechnya because they could be presented as part of the war against international terrorism. The potential problem in terms of relations with Russia lies in the extent to which the EU develops a strong collective defence capability. This becomes particularly significant given the number of former Soviet Baltic states that were members of the EU by 2004, in addition to the membership of Poland. The development of a stronger collective defence capability could alarm Russia and raise fears about its own security. The EU's defence and security cannot be established purely in terms of conventional defence forces.

Relations with the United States

The enlarged EU has been keen to maintain a close relationship with the USA, certainly as far as security matters are concerned. The USA has been a consistently strong supporter of EU enlargement and this process has served to reinforce the USA's links with the EU. The central and eastern European states who presented themselves for membership regard the best guarantee for their security as coming from the USA rather than the EU. Should the security situation in central and eastern Europe become fragile, it is the USA who would offer the most effective military protection.

Some EU states have been less than enthusiastic about the influence of the USA. France, Germany and Belgium were particularly critical of the USA's decision to embark on a war with Iraq in 2003. The newly arriving central and eastern European states were clearly pro-USA and thereby expanded the Atlanticist arm of the EU membership. Although there was a danger that this could drive a wedge between the members of the EU it also served to reinforce the importance of the USA; the EU could not afford to develop a security policy which excluded US concerns. The key to preserving this link with the USA was seen to be through NATO rather than an expanding and independent European Security and Defence Policy (ESDP).

European security and NATO

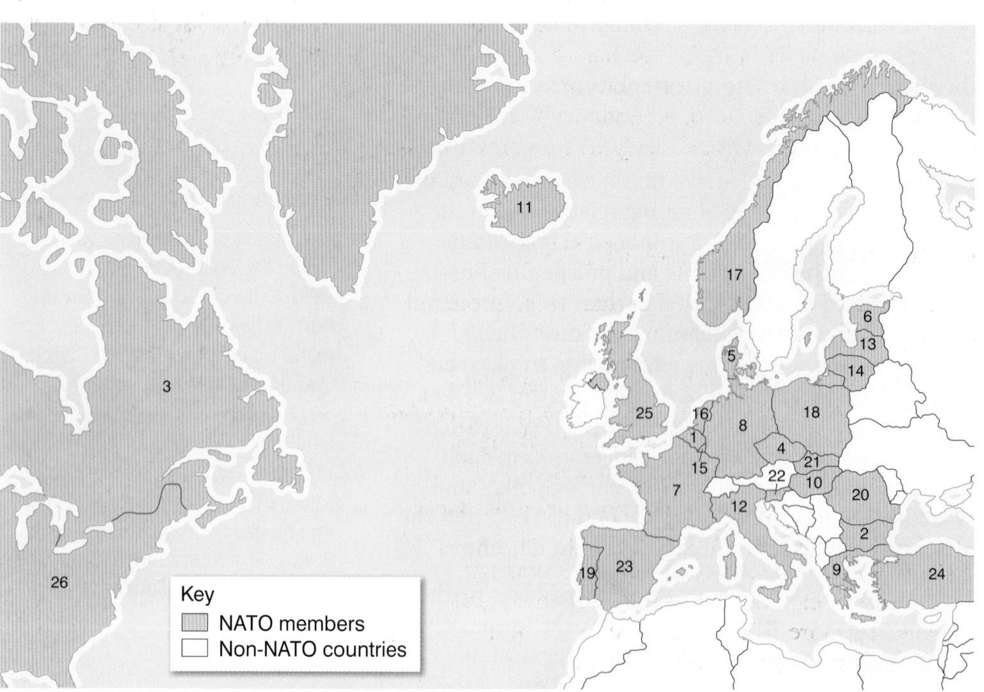

1 Belgium
2 Bulgaria
3 Canada
4 Czech Republic
5 Denmark
6 Estonia
7 France
8 Germany
9 Greece
10 Hungary
11 Iceland
12 Italy
13 Latvia
14 Lithuania
15 Luxembourg
16 Netherlands
17 Norway
18 Poland
19 Portugal
20 Romania
21 Slovakia
22 Slovenia
23 Spain
24 Turkey
25 United Kingdom
26 United States

Fig. 3 *NATO membership by the end of 2004*

NATO had been a crucial part of the western defence system during the Cold War. The end of the Cold War brought a re-evaluation of NATO's role and the relationship that one of the founding fathers of NATO – the USA – would have with Europe. In May 1990 NATO announced that it no longer regarded the Warsaw Pact states as a threat to the security of Europe. By July 1990 there were moves towards establishing military cooperation between the two.

At Maastricht in 1991, the EU set out its plans to create a CFSP, the details of which have been outlined earlier. Clear divisions began to appear between the British and the French. Britain regarded NATO as the foundation of European security while the French were backing a separate defence strategy for the EU members which was not dominated by the USA. It was increasingly clear through the 1990s that any structured form of EU defence system would not develop. The USA was the clear leader of NATO but there was no united European leadership of an EU defence force. The British and French positions form the extremes, with other member states adopting some middle-of-the-road compromise position.

NATO enlargement has moved faster that EU enlargement. European states accept that such enlargement has provided greater security and regional stability. Poland, the Czech Republic and Hungary have all accepted the benefits of NATO membership. These states are more committed to NATO than any purely EU security organisation. All three were convinced that NATO membership would bring with it a security guarantee endorsed by the USA. NATO represented the means by which disputes could be resolved and not degenerate as they had done in Bosnia. During that conflict the USA's leadership role within NATO was vital to the process of halting aggression. The 1990s showed that NATO was still the heart of European security even after the end of the Cold War and that the USA's role within NATO was still vital to European security. Linkage with the USA gives NATO a global status and resources it beyond any level any other European state could aspire to. This close relationship between Europe and the USA has continued since NATO's foundation in 1949 and for the most part post-Cold War Europe has recognised this relationship as a positive and necessary one. European security, despite some moves to develop a degree of independence through ESDP, remains firmly attached to NATO and the USA's leading role within it.

Activity

Thinking point

In what ways did the expansion of the EU affect international relations? Write down as many ideas as you can think of and then discuss these with a partner. When you have prepared a full list, make a chart in which you place your ideas in order of importance. Review your list after you have read the next section.

Contemporary debate on the enlargement of NATO

Despite the final acceptance of an expanded NATO there were some significant objections. These may be summarised as follows:

- Enlargement would reduce the security of Europe. This view was based on the belief that it would strengthen nationalism within Russia and make it less likely, therefore, that Russia would be willing to cooperate with Europe over arms reduction agreements.
- Linked to this was the belief that Russia would move towards closer ties with China in order to offset what it saw as growing links between Europe and the USA. The view was that any expansion of NATO would be seen as an expansion of American power and influence in Europe and therefore this would have to be counter-balanced by Russia through stronger ties with China.

- There was real concern that an enlarged NATO would be able to function coherently. As the membership grew then so would the geographic area that NATO would be responsible for defending. A geographic increase would also bring an increase in national interests which could be in conflict with each other. In effect enlargement would compromise NATO's unity and therefore its effectiveness.
- Membership of NATO was regarded by some objectors as irrelevant to the more central issue of successfully transforming central and eastern European states into democracies in order for them to integrate into an enlarged EU. NATO enlargement was seen as a distraction from the more important need to expand the EU successfully.

Fig. 4 *EU national flags*

However, the objections have not been shown to have real substance. There was no evidence to suggest that development of Russian foreign policy was affected by the NATO enlargement since July 1997. In addition to this, NATO is not purely a European defence organisation. It fulfilled the role of deterrence and it increased Europe's strategic security. There has been no evidence to suggest that its effectiveness was undermined by its expansion. NATO's enlargement with candidates for membership of an expanding EU was a positive step, rather than a negative or irrelevant one. Membership of NATO increased stability within these states and improved civil-military relations. Historians have argued that membership of NATO was a necessary and complementary factor in preparing states as members of the EU. NATO reinforced European security and this was consistent with the EU seeking to develop a defence identity.

Enlargement and post-Cold War challenges

There were concerns in Europe that any expansion of NATO would deter the USA from retaining its commitment to Europe, particularly in a post-Cold War environment. Others in Europe feared that NATO would increasingly become a tool to manage American interests. This latter point assumed even greater credibility as NATO membership expanded eastwards. The French were particularly vocal on this issue. The USA criticised what it saw as unwarranted involvement in NATO affairs by Russia. Russia was given the right to be consulted in Council. President Yeltsin's Foreign Minister Yevgeny showed an enthusiasm to interfere with NATO plans when they protested about the arrest of Serbian war criminals by NATO forces in Bosnia and supported the French in their rejection of NATO pressure being placed on Iran and Iraq.

NATO's initial post-Cold War expansion by three additional members represented more than merely a growth in numbers and an expansion in geographic control. It also underlined NATO's transformation from what had been a system of collective defence into what became a political system providing collective security for a newly expanding and increasingly united Europe. NATO's expansion was not conceived as a means of adding further military strength to the organisation. The expansion took place at a time when there was no immediate military threat to Europe. This reinforced the view that its purpose was aimed at a system of collective security rather than at a purely defensive alliance designed to resist an external threat.

The fact that Russia was granted a special consultative role in NATO represented another major move towards the perception of NATO as an organisation that had become focused on collective security. Political analysts and historians Gale Mattox and Daniel Whiteneck sum this transformation up through their observation that:

> Perhaps such change was inevitable from that evening in late 1991 when the Soviet flag was lowered from atop Kremlin spires one last time. A collective defence alliance seemed to have little purpose in a Europe where the democratic West faced no real foe.

3

The economic impact of enlargement

The new member states that were accepted into the EU in 2004 had income levels of between one third and two thirds those of the EU average. The differences were not significantly great towards the bottom end of the original 15 members. The top end of the new members was fairly close to the bottom end of the original 15. The issue was how to ensure that the weaker new members were able to develop economically in order to move towards equal economic status within the EU.

Fig. 5 *Valga on the Latvian–Estonian border displays the EU flag in 2008*

Table 2 *Key data on the original 15 members, new members and other applicants*

State *EU-15*	Population (millions)	GDP* (billion euro)	GDP (per capita**)	Per cent employed in agriculture
Austria	8.1	210	26.7	5.8
Belgium	10.3	257	25.1	1.4
Denmark	5.4	180	28.3	3.5
Finland	5.2	135	24.6	5.8
France	59.3	1456	23.9	4.1
Germany	82.4	2063	24.8	2.6
Greece	10.6	130	16.5	16.0
Ireland	3.9	116	28.4	7.0
Italy	58.0	1217	25.0	5.2
Luxembourg	0.4	22	45.0	1.5
Netherlands	16.1	427	26.6	3.1
Portugal	10.3	123	17.3	12.9
Spain	40.4	650	19.9	6.5
Sweden	8.9	234	24.9	2.6
UK	60.1	1591	24.2	1.4
New members				
Cyprus	0.8	10	18.5	4.9
Czech Rep.	10.3	63	14.6	4.9
Estonia	1.4	6	10.9	6.9
Hungary	10.2	58	12.6	6.1
Latvia	2.4	8	7.9	15.1
Lithuania	3.5	13	8.8	16.5
Malta	0.4	4	13.3	1.9
Poland	38.6	197	9.0	19.2
Slovakia	5.4	23	12.0	6.3
Slovenia	2.0	21	17.0	9.9
Other Applicants				
Bulgaria	7.9	15	7.7	26.7
Romania	22.4	44	6.2	44.4
Turkey	66.3	165	6.2	37.0

* GDP – Gross Domestic Product: the market value of all final goods and services made within the borders of a nation in a year
** per capita: literally 'for each head' (for each person)

New members already had established trading partners and this raised the issue of integrating the new members into the EU trade policy priorities. The established trading partners of most of the new members who were to enter in 2004 were predominantly focused in the east, particularly with the former Soviet states. Hungary was especially keen to retain its ties with these trading partners. Slovenia had a free trade agreement with Croatia and the former Yugoslav Republic of Macedonia. This was not accepted under the terms of Slovenia's entry into the EU. Despite this, as with previous enlargements, the EU shifted its trade relations with its new neighbours. The reality was that the economies of the new member states would have been undermined if they had been forced to divert their trading away from their traditional trade partners immediately. This redirection of trade by the EU was seen as an essential part of enlargement in order to prevent the EU becoming protectionist and damaging the economies of other non-EU neighbours.

Membership brought with it trade diversion. In time the new members shifted away from their traditional trading partners. Significantly, about 70 per cent of the trade of the 2004 group of members was already with EU states and the new members only contributed about three per cent of world trade. Hence, rather than damaging world trade through joining the EU, the impact of this move was minimal. In addition to this, membership of the EU led to a reduction in the level of tariffs used by the new members. EU trade tariffs were lower than those in place in new member states.

Table 3 *Average tariff levels (per cent) in 2001*

Product	Poland	Hungary	Czech Rep.	Estonia	Slovenia	EU-15
Agriculture	34	31	13.4	15.2	13.7	16.2
Fisheries	18.3	15.1	0.1	3.2	5.9	12.4
Industrial	9.9	7.1	4.6	0	8.1	3.6

Membership of the EU meant that trade policies adopted by the prospective members had to be in line with current EU trade policy. It was clear that this requirement was not always easy to enforce. The EU's attempts to carry through this requirement did have some impact on world trade. An example of this came when Poland set up a bilateral trading agreement with the USA in 2001 without any prior consultation with the EU.

Fig. 6 *A Polish migrant worker on a British farm*

The economic impact of the enlargement of the EU has been focused on the transition from socialism to capitalism with which new member states have been faced. This necessitated a financial transformation. The process of transition, although underway by the point of admission to the EU, is still being undertaken to this day. On a wider geographic scale, enlargement changed EU trade policy by shifting its geographic focus eastwards through trade agreements with states on the EU's eastern border. Significantly, previous enlargements pre-1991 did not result in the EU becoming more protectionist and more committed to trading within its own expanding membership. The post-1991 enlargements have shown no indication that this non-protectionist outcome has changed. The enlarged EU remained committed to trade liberalisation. In effect the economic impact on international relations was minimal.

Outcome of enlargement

The conclusion reported in Agenda 2000 sums up the outcome of enlargement. It said that:

> When the cost of enlargement is assessed political benefits such as promotion of regional stability should be taken into account, not least because of their direct economic implications. Enlargement is an investment in peace, stability and prosperity for the people of Europe.

4

An enlarged EU created greater unity and stability despite the potential problems it inevitably generated.

The other key development in Europe after the end of the Cold War was the expansion of NATO and the need to review the role of the Atlantic alliance between Europe and the USA. The eastward movement of NATO raised implications about the relationship NATO and Europe would have with the non-EU states and particularly Russia.

Summary questions

1 'The advantages of enlarging the EU after the end of the Cold War were significant for its member states.' How valid is this assessment?

2 To what extent did the expansion of NATO membership ensure the security of Europe?

12 The Role of the United Nations in the post-Cold War Environment

In this chapter you will learn about:

- an overview of UN intervention during the Cold War
- the impact of the ending of the Cold War from 1991
- the position of the UN by 2004.

Fig. 1 *The UN Security Council*

The United Nations has been one of the most controversial post-war international agencies. Some view it as an essential tool for peacekeeping and diplomacy, useful for putting pressure on aggressive states and for managing international crises. Others, however, see it as a weak organisation that puts the self-interest of its member states above humanitarian concerns, and a body that has been unable to prevent some of the world's worst violations of human rights.

The UN up to 1988

The United Nations was established in October 1945, and was originally comprised of 51 member states. Emerging from the horrors of World War II, the global community sought a new international organisation that could work to prevent war and genocide occurring again. The UN Charter document laid out the organisation's key objectives:

> 1 To maintain international peace and security, and to that end: to take effective collective measures for the prevention and removal of threats to peace, and for the suppression of acts of aggression or other breaches of the peace, and to bring about by peaceful means, and in conformity with the principles of justice and international law, adjustment or settlement of international disputes or situations which might lead to a breach of the peace.
>
> 2 To develop friendly relations among nations based on respect for the principle of equal rights and self-determination of peoples, and to take other appropriate measures to strengthen universal peace.
>
> 3 To achieve international cooperation in solving international problems of an economic, social, cultural, or humanitarian character, and in promoting and encouraging respect for human rights and for fundamental freedoms for all without distinction as to race, sex, language, or religion.
>
> 4 To be a centre for harmonising the actions of nations in the attainment of these common ends.
>
> **1**

Although World War II was over, the world was still faced with numerous local conflicts. Consequently the UN, which could command international military forces, found itself called upon for numerous peacekeeping operations over the next three decades.

Table 1 *UN peacekeeping operations, 1948–78*

Year	UN Operation
1948–present	United Nations Truce Supervision Organisation (UNTSO)
1949–present	United Nations Military Observer Group in India and Pakistan (UNMOGIP)
1956–67	United Nations Emergency Force (UNEF)
1958	United Nations Observation Group in Lebanon (UNOGIL)
1960–4	United Nations Operation in the Congo (ONUC)
1962–3	United Nations Security Force in West New Guinea (UNSF)
1963–4	United Nations Yemen Observation Mission (UNYOM)
1964–present	United Nations Peacekeeping Force in Cyprus (UNFICYP)
1965–6	United Nations India–Pakistan Observation Mission (UNIPOM)
1973–9	Second United Nations Emergency Force (UNEF II)
1974–present	United Nations Disengagement Observation Force (UNDOF)
1978–present	United Nations Force in Lebanon (UNIFL)

Activity

Research activity

Separate into several groups. In your group, research one example of UN intervention before 1989 and explore how successful that intervention was, and why.

Key terms

Veto: the permanent member states of the Security Council had the power to vote against any action or intervention by the UN. This power was built into the Charter of the UN to ensure that the powerful states would be willing to participate in collective action. A simple majority system would have deterred many states from joining, particularly the communist eastern bloc powers who were convinced that the UN was a tool of western policy.

The Cold War greatly constrained the effectiveness of the UN as a peacekeeping organisation. Security Council members had the power to **veto** UN intervention and this power was used frequently because of superpower Cold War interests. As Table 1 illustrates, there were only twelve UN interventions between 1948 and 1978. The use of the veto was a primary factor in this relative inaction. Table 3 illustrates the profound shift in UN interventionism once the Cold War had ended. The dramatic shift in the use of the veto is also strongly indicative of the new attitudes adopted towards international peacekeeping as Table 2 illustrates:

Table 2 *Security Council Vetoes, 1946–2004*

Period	China	France	Britain	USA	USSR/ Russia	Total
1946–1955	1	2	0	0	80	83
1956–1965	0	2	3	0	26	31
1966–1975	2	2	10	12	7	33
1976–1985	0	9	11	34	6	60
1986–1995	0	3	8	24	2	37
1996–1999	2	0	0	2	0	4
2000–2004	0	0	0	8	1	9
Total	5	18	32	80	122	257

The Cold War largely paralysed UN interventionism. Peacekeeping operations could only be undertaken with the unanimous agreement of the Security Council. It became an accepted tradition that such operations also depended on the consent of the conflicting parties. The UN's role was to be based on strict impartiality. Its peacekeeping forces could not take sides in a conflict.

Fig. 2 *The UN General Assembly*

Table 3 *Selected UN Peace and Security Operations, 1988–2004*

Year	Operation
1988–90	United Nations Good Offices Mission in Afghanistan and Pakistan (UNGOMAP)
1988–91	United Nations Iran–Iraq Military Observer Group (UNIIMOG)
1991–5	United Nations Observer Mission in El Salvador (ONUSAL)
1991–5	United Nations Angola Verification Mission II (UNAVEM)
1991–present	United Nations Mission for the Referendum in Western Sahara (MINURSO)
1991–present	United Nations Iraq–Kuwait Observer Mission (UNIKOM)
1992–3	United Nations Operation in Somalia (UNOSOM)
1993–6	United Nations Assistance Mission for Rwanda (UNAMIR)
1993–7	United Nations Mission in Liberia (UNOMIL)
1993–present	United Nations Mission in Georgia (UNOMIG) United Nations Mission in Bosnia and Herzegovina (UNMIBH)
1996–7	United Nations Support Mission in Haiti (UNSMIH)
1999–2002	United Nations Mission in East Timor (UNTAET)
1999–present	United Nation Organisation Mission in the Democratic Republic of the Congo (MONUC)
1999–present	United Nations Mission in Sierra Leone (UNAMSIL)
2000–present	United Nations Mission in Ethiopia and Eritrea (UNMEE)
2002–present	United Nations Mission of Support in East Timor (UNMISET)
2002–present	United Nations Mission in Afghanistan (UNAMA)

The UN and the end of the Cold War

In 1988 Mikhail Gorbachev announced a new Soviet relationship with the UN. He was committed to cooperation in the management of international conflicts. UN peacekeeping offered the Soviet Union a way out of the 'bleeding wound' of Afghanistan. This triggered a shift in US policy as Ronald Reagan publicly praised the UN's role as an international peacekeeper. He announced through the General Assembly that "the United Nations has the opportunity to live and breathe and work as never before." Both the Soviet Union and the USA agreed to pay their financial debts to the UN in order to enable it to function effectively. In effect superpower cooperation was expanding and the UN appeared to be one of the first beneficiaries of this post-Cold War cooperation. Britain and France also recognised that they could maintain their own international status and influence through the UN's revival as an international peacekeeper. Similarly the USA accepted that it was more productive to use the UN as the basis of international cooperation rather than to use force to achieve its objectives.

Cross-reference

For in-depth coverage of Gorbachev and his reforms, see Chapters 7 and 9.

What became increasingly clear in the post-Cold War era was that the challenges facing the UN were significantly different from those it had faced since its inception in 1945. The Soviet Union and Yugoslavia have themselves given birth to almost twenty new states. Somalia and Haiti effectively ceased to have any form of coordinated and organised government by 1993. The new world order that emerged was further complicated by international terrorism led by al-Qaeda.

The true rebirth of the post-Cold War UN began with the 1991 Gulf War.

The UN in action during the 1990s

UN involvement in the 1991 Gulf War

When Iraq invaded its oil-rich neighbour, Kuwait, in August 1991 the UN Security Council passed twelve resolutions aimed at forcing Iraq to withdraw. Resolution 678 enabled member states to use 'all necessary means' to remove Iraq from Kuwait. Iraq's failure to withdraw by 15 January 1991 led to a twenty-eight power UN coalition force being formed. This removed Iraqi forces from Kuwait. In doing so the coalition forces not only attacked Iraqi troops in Kuwait, it also bombed Iraq itself.

The UN action raised a number of concerns. The most significant was that the coalition was dominated by US forces. Many critics argued that the USA created an anti-Iraq coalition in order to serve US interests. The UN was presented as a tool used to promote US influence. The USA used its political and economic power in the Security Council to ensure its own Persian Gulf agenda was fulfilled. The USA promised financial packages to a number of developing countries. It offered political concessions to both the USSR and to China. Significantly, it was the USA that led the coalition forces in Kuwait and thereby determined what the strategic aims and methods of that force would be in terms of Iraq. The UN Security Council was left to assume the role of merely that of a bystander. This UN enforcement action in the Persian Gulf was the first in the new post-Cold War era and it revealed the limited powers of the Security Council in the face of US determination to implement its own regional agenda. The UN's role in the Persian Gulf in 1991 was more than merely a peacekeeping one. Under the direction of a US-driven intervention, the UN moved towards enforcement and away from peacekeeping.

Activity

Thinking point

Examine each of the following interventions listed in this section of the book. Define exactly why the United Nations became involved on each occasion, and the level of success it achieved. Do you see any particular patterns, or problems, emerging about the way the UN was used?

Cross-reference

For more about the UN involvement in the 1991 Gulf War, see Chapter 10.

Exploring the detail

UN Resolutions

UN Resolutions are typically issued by the General Assembly or the Security Council. They are statements of action or intent to which some or all of the member states are committed.

In addition to this, another shift in the UN's role began to emerge in the post-Cold War context of international relations and international peacekeeping. From the end of the Cold War it became increasingly clear that the UN faced greater challenges than could be met through the traditional peacekeeping role of the organisation. This became clear through a series of UN interventions during the 1990s.

Cambodia, 1992–3

The first significant involvement came in Cambodia. In February 1992 the Security Council established the United Nations Transition Authority in Cambodia (UNTAC). Its role was to produce a 'just and durable settlement to the Cambodian conflict' based on free elections. It was to achieve this within 18 months. Part of this process necessitated simultaneously disarming the Khmer Rouge guerrillas and the government forces. The UN entered the crisis in Cambodia in a traditional peacekeeping role. By May 1993 the UN had succeeded in managing national elections. Once the elections had been held the UN began to withdraw its personnel. The elections had been an apparent triumph for the UN, if for no other reason than the beginnings of democracy had been established in Cambodia. In the 10 years after the UN's withdrawal Cambodia developed only slowly as a mature liberal democracy. Despite this gradual change the UN did succeed in moving the state away from its repressive political system. Greater openness came into Cambodia and debate and criticism came to be tolerated. As Berdal and Leifer commented, "Cambodia is much more usefully seen as an example of the possibilities as well as the limitations of the UN's role in transplanting democracy and political stability to countries that are emerging, in what is necessarily a traumatised, weakened and divided condition from protracted periods of instability, violence and war."

Exploring the detail

The Khmer Rouge

Established in the 1960s, the Khmer Rouge was the communist movement in Cambodia. Its leader, Pol Pot, controlled the country between 1974 and 1978. Pol Pot believed in returning society to its most basic level; part of this plan was to murder intellectuals and academics. The organisation was overthrown but continued to conduct a guerrilla war until 1991 when it won a voice in the governing body of Cambodia. From 1985 its leader was Khieu Samphan.

Despite the apparent successes enjoyed by the UN in its intervention in Cambodia there were some significant shortcomings. Cambodia remained a fundamentally unstable state after UNTAC had left. The Cambodian problem illustrates the limitations faced by the UN in post-Cold War peacekeeping. The end of the Cold War meant that there was an end to the constraints imposed by the Cold War on UN peacekeeping. Theoretically, the UN could carry out its role without superpower interference. The problem was that because the superpowers no longer had specific interests, they no longer influenced their former client states. In effect, the role of the superpowers had been as positive as it had been negative during the Cold War. The end of the Cold War had also brought to an end the very positive impact of superpower involvement in the work of the UN. In terms of Cambodia, the UN was effective in establishing the administrative framework for democracy and stability but the absence of superpower influence undermined the chances of that process being translated into a long-term and lasting one.

Somalia, 1992–5

With the end of the Cold War, superpower interest in Somalia faded. Prior to this there had been considerable interest in Somalia, primarily from the USA. Somalia's strategic position on the Horn of Africa became significant when the USSR backed the revolutionary regime established in neighbouring Ethiopia during the 1970s and 1980s. The USA in turn supported the Somali regime of Siyad Barre. By 1991 this regime had collapsed and all form of government in Somalia ceased to exist; internal chaos had become endemic. It had become a country ruled by warlords. About a third of its population faced death from starvation.

Key terms

Developing states: a general term for some states in Central and South America, Africa, and Asia. The term denotes those states that are economically underdeveloped and often have problems managing their national security. The Cold War context in which many of these states had to conduct their foreign policies often actually worsened their problems. However, the end of the Cold War has tended to reduce the importance of developing states as far as the superpowers are concerned.

Exploring the detail

'Black Hawk Down'

On 3 October 1993 an attempt was made by US forces to capture key leaders linked to the Somali warlord Mohamed Farrah Aidid. In the process of this action two army helicopters were brought down in Mogadishu, the heartland of Aidid's territory. This led to a desperate rescue mission undertaken by US forces. What should have been a simple 45 minute rescue lasted 15 hours and left 18 Americans dead and about 1000 Somali casualties. The incident is recorded in US military annals as one displaying supreme acts of bravery.

Cross-reference

For a detailed account of the break-up of Yugoslavia, see Chapter 10.

In August 1992 the Security Council established United Nations Operation in Somalia (UNOSOM). The aim of UNOSOM was to provide humanitarian aid. The violence could not be contained by the small UN force in Somalia and by December 1992 the USA offered 27,000 troops in order to provide security for UN aid to Somalia. The Security Council set up a Unified Task Force (UNITAF) to be under American operational control. The Americans labelled the action Operation Restore Hope. This force succeeded in opening a door for humanitarian aid but the basic problem remained. Somalia still did not have any form of central government or authority. Even the presence of America failed to curb the chaos. There were considerable anti-American feelings among many **developing states** and Somalia was different in this respect.

In May 1993 the Security Council authorised UNOSOM II. This was to be under UN rather than US control. A period of bloody violence followed as UN forces clashed with one of the principal warlords, Mohammed Aidid. Part of the conflict was known as the Battle of Mogadishu or 'Black Hawk Down'. The UN operation in Somalia faced two basic problems. The objectives of the operation shifted from delivering humanitarian relief to nation- and state-building. A more fundamental problem lay in the reluctance of the USA to continue its role in the action. By May 1994 President Clinton's administration decided to reverse America's attitude towards assertive multilateralism. America's participation in multilateral military action in Somalia was crucial, as was its withdrawal from it.

The last UN forces vacated Somalia in March 1995. The operation had turned into one of enforcement rather than peacekeeping. Somalia had not been a consenting state to UN intervention. The UN faced continuous military opposition from the many warring factions. This made a peacekeeping role almost impossible. The worst of the humanitarian crisis had been resolved but by 2003 Somalia still remained without a viable central government.

Activity

Thinking point

What does the case of Somalia tell us about the limits of UN peacekeeping? In a small group, imagine you are leaders of a UN peacekeeping force heading to a war-torn and failed state. Try to think of your priorities for the mission (e.g. establish utilities, protect vulnerable minorities). What does this exercise tell you about the difficulties of peacekeeping?

The former Yugoslavia, 1992–5

The UN experienced failure in its intervention in the former Yugoslavia. The international community faced a fundamental contradiction. It was committed both to the sanctity of state frontiers and the right of self-determination and the protection of the rights of ethnic minorities.

The traditional peacekeeping entry point for the UN was the existence of a responsive host state. The most effective peacekeeping interventions during the Cold War had been those in which the conflicting sides were organised and wanted a solution. This was not the case in the former Yugoslavia. A basic question facing the international community was whether intervention should aim to lessen humanitarian suffering or whether it should be based on the principle of the sanctity of frontiers. In the case of Yugoslavia the frontier issue was an enforcement issue. For the UN there was also the question of whether the problems in

Yugoslavia could be dealt with through the EU and NATO as European agencies. Despite these issues, in February 1992 the UN established the United Nations Protection Force (UNPROFOR). Its immediate mandate was to 'create the conditions of peace and security required for the overall settlement of the … crisis.' Its role was based on a traditional interpositionary one. By August the mandate was extended to deliver humanitarian aid and the force was empowered to use 'all measures necessary' to achieve this aim.

The UNPROFOR mandate was widened to include the creation of safe areas for refugees in Bosnia and using NATO to enforce sanctions. The UN's role expanded from a fairly traditional peacekeeping presence to a much more complex and demanding one. The cooperation with NATO as a regional organisation was the first of its kind for the UN. There were some spectacular failures for the UN which underlined the changed and more complex role it faced in post-Cold War Yugoslavia. In July 1995, 7,500 Bosnian Muslim men and boys were massacred in Srebrenica by Bosnian Serbs. There was little evidence of much political will on the part of UN members to set up enforcement action against this group and their supporters. The Dayton Peace Accords were established in November 1995 through the good offices of the USA. This effectively ended the UN's peacekeeping role in Bosnia and Croatia. These Accords introduced the NATO Implementation Force (IFOR). Among this force of 60,000 troops were 20,000 Americans.

It was clear that the UN's role was made all the more difficult by the fact that it did not enjoy the consent of those in conflict. The enforcement role of the UN became more prominent and more urgent in the former Yugoslavia than in any other previous involvement. Once again the post-Cold War international environment was generating far more complex problems than the UN had previously encountered.

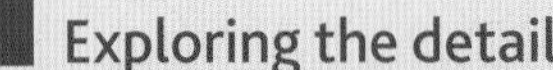

Exploring the detail

The Srebrenica Massacre

This was an ethnic cleansing action carried out by the Army Republika Srpska led by Ratko Mladic. The aim was to eliminate Bosnian Muslims (Bosniacs). Those in Srebrenica were seen as being representative of Muslims in general. The action was a purely ethnic one in that the victims were selected entirely because of their religious and cultural identity. The victims had no military role.

Activity

Talking point

Write two newspaper articles on the Srebrenica Massacre, one from the Serbian side and one from the Bosnian Muslim side. How would both sides justify their viewpoints?

Rwanda, 1993–6

Between April and June 1994, some 800,000 citizens of the African state of Rwanda were murdered. The victims were mainly members of the minority Tutsi tribe, turned on by the majority Hutus after the death of the Hutu Rwandan President Juvenal Habyarimana, whose plane was shot down over Kigali airport on 6 April 1994. A further 2 million people were displaced and 2 million others fled as refugees into neighbouring states. A UN force (UNAMIR) had been in Rwanda for eight months by May 1994. Its role had been to facilitate the Arusha Peace Accords between the Rwanda Hutus and the Tutsis. It was widely believed that this UN Mission was poorly prepared for the challenges that awaited it.

The UN's response to the Rwanda crisis was indecisive and inadequate. There was no swift response from a substantial force deployed by a strong military power. There was no significant concerted international pressure, particularly from the USA. The Security Council actually reduced UN military forces after attacks against a small number of Belgian peacekeepers. Between June and August 1994 there was the French-led Operation Turquoise. This was designed to stabilise the south western part of the country. The French actually used their presence to protect some of their Hutu allies in the region. During July and August the USA set up Operation Support Hope. This provided some humanitarian relief.

Fig. 3 *The UN International Court of Justice*

The UN failed to establish a secure environment in Rwanda. There was a fear among many in the international community that involvement in Rwanda could lead to a hopeless long-term commitment. Considerable humanitarian aid reached Rwanda but only after the genocide had been completed. The UN's role in response to the crisis in Rwanda has been judged by many as one of its greatest failures. This was very much the UN's own self-assessment by 1997. The incoming Secretary General, Kofi Annan admitted during a visit to Kigali, "We must and we do acknowledge that the world failed Rwanda at that time of evil. The international community and the United Nations could not muster the political will to confront it." He went on to say, "There was a United Nations force in the country at the time, but it was neither mandated nor equipped for the kind of forceful action which would have been needed to prevent or halt the genocide. On behalf of the United Nations, I acknowledge this failure and express my deep remorse." Annan's remorse may also have been linked to his own failings. He had been in charge of the UN's peacekeeping department in New York at the time of the crisis and he had ignored the calls in April 1994 from the Force Commander, Romeo Dallaire, for a more proactive role for his force in order to stem the growing genocide.

Key profile

Kofi Annan, 1938–present

Annan was born in Ghana and joined the UN in 1962 as a worker for the World Health Organisation. He held a number of senior positions and became Under Secretary-General for Peacekeeping. In 1995 he was appointed as the Secretary-General's Special Representative in Yugoslavia.

Kosovo, 1999

The 1990s made it increasingly clear that the UN's traditional approaches were becoming irrelevant. The problems in Kosovo illustrate this problem. The UN did not intervene in Kosovo until a cease-fire had been established. Many commentators argue that the UN Security Council was largely ignored by the major Western powers that used NATO as the means of fulfilling their own interventionist aims. It follows from this that the authority and credibility of the Security Council, and the UN as a whole, was undermined.

Serbia had begun a programme of ethnic cleansing directed against Kosovar Albanians in 1999. This ethnic cleansing was conducted with ruthlessness by the Serbian and Yugoslav military. International attempts at diplomacy which were designed to change Serb policy towards ethnic Albanians prior to the 'cleansing' action had failed. The Yugoslav President, Slobodan Milosevic had consistently shown an absolute disregard for international opinion over Kosovo. By late January 1999 the USA was increasingly moving away from diplomacy and towards a military solution. Kofi Annan had reached a similar position. In a speech given before NATO leaders he concluded:

> The bloody wars of the last decade have left us with no illusions about the difficulty of halting internal conflicts by reason or by force particularly against the wishes of the government of a sovereign state. But nor have they left us with any illusions about the need to use force, when all other means have failed. We may be reaching that limit, once again, in the former Yugoslavia.

Key profile

Slobodan Milosevic, 1941–2006

Milosovic studied law and developed a career in business. In 1978 he became president of a Belgrade bank. Always committed to politics, he became Chief of the Communist Party Organisation in Belgrade in 1984 and went on to become President of Serbia in 1987, a post he held until 1997 when he became President of Yugoslavia. During the collapse of the unified Yugoslavia he was responsible for promoting ethnic crimes and he went on trial in 2001 at the International War Crimes Tribunal held in The Hague. He died of a heart attack in 2006.

Diplomacy was not immediately abandoned. A further attempt was made in February 1999 at Rambouillet. The international community, represented by Britain, France, the United States, Germany, Italy and Russia attempted to broker a settlement between Yugoslavia and an Albanian Kosovar delegation. Milosevic's unwillingness to reach a compromise caused the talks to collapse. It made any further diplomatic efforts appear pointless. This became obvious in March when NATO forces began what was to be a 77-day bombardment of Serbian targets. This has been interpreted as a breach of international law as it did not have the explicit approval of the UN Security Council. NATO's Secretary-General, Javier Solana, took the view that it was justified in human terms and therefore a legitimate action. The international response was less understanding. Both China and Russia viewed NATO's actions as illegal. Generally the UN's response was ambivalent. The Secretary-General acknowledged that NATO had not received Security Council approval but he emphasised that the Serbs should not be simply allowed to get away with the humanitarian crisis which was unfolding in Kosovo.

In response to the NATO bombings the Serbs stepped up their programme of ethnic cleansing in Kosovo. About 1.8 million ethnic Albanians were displaced in this action. Due to the intensification of NATO bombing Milosevic finally agreed on 3 June to end the violence in Kosovo and withdraw all Serbian forces. It was on 10 June that the Security Council adopted Resolution 1244 as the UN Mission in Kosovo (UNMIK). This was to undertake a largely administrative role in conjunction with NATO. Until this point the UN had taken a very marginal role in Kosovo. The role the UN assumed from June was new. 49,000 NATO troops were to maintain security but it was UNMIK that was to have authority over the people and territory of Kosovo and all aspects of its civil administration. UNMIK was charged with establishing self-government in the region.

Key profile

Javier Solana, 1942–present

Solana is an eminent physicist. He entered Spanish politics in 1977 and became a Cabinet Minister in 1982. By 1992 he had reached the position of Minister of Foreign Affairs. In December 1995 he left Spanish politics and was appointed Secretary-General of NATO where he remained until his appointment in October 1999 as Secretary-General for the Council of the European Union. In this post his primary aim has been to promote unity among the member states on foreign and security policy ideas.

A number of crucial problems were associated with the Resolution. It placed a vast task on the UN administration. Upwards of 800,000 refugees had to be repatriated. The Serbian action had devastated housing and public buildings like schools and hospitals. In effect, the UNMIK was responsible for returning a devastated Kosovo to some degree of normality. A further problem lay in the fact that security appeared to be the responsibility of NATO but there was no clear division of responsibility between NATO and the UN. UN policies such as privatisation were poorly organised and implemented. Significantly, the ethnic Albanians wanted independence but the UN mandate required respect for Yugoslavia's sovereignty and for the protection of Serbs living in Kosovo. The UN was simply out of its depth in Kosovo and its tasks were too great to ensure success.

Activity

Thinking point

In what ways did the end of the Cold War change the role of the UN?

Key terms

Autonomous: having the power of self-government, sometimes within another organisation. Essentially it suggests a degree of independence.

East Timor, 1999–2002

In 1975 Indonesia had invaded the former Portuguese colony of East Timor. After a long period of struggle for East Timor, the Indonesians agreed to hold a plebiscite on the future of the territory. It was agreed that this 'popular consultation' was to take place in August 1999 and that the UN Secretary-General would be responsible for organising it. The issue was whether the people of East Timor would accept or reject a special **autonomous** status within the Republic of Indonesia. In June 1999 the UN established UNAMET, the UN Mission in East Timor with the mandate to conduct the consultation. The vote was held on 30 August and it resulted in 78.5 per cent of the people opting for independence.

The result was followed by extensive violence in which nearly half a million East Timorese were forced from their homes. In September, Indonesia accepted a UN force that was to be authorised to 'take all necessary measures' to achieve three specific tasks: 'to restore peace and security in East Timor; to protect and support UNAMET in carrying out its tasks; and, within force capabilities, to facilitate humanitarian assistance operations.' With the violence subdued the UN was able to establish a Transitional Administration in East Timor (UNTAET) in October 1999. Its primary role was to establish and maintain law and order and to prepare the state for self-government and sustainable development. The process developed numerous problems as the UN's special representative, Vieira de Mello acknowledged in 2000:

UNTAET consulted on major policy issues, but in the end it retained all the responsibility for the design and execution of policy. What is more, the National Consultative Council came under increasing scrutiny for not being representative enough of East Timor Society and not transparent enough in its deliberations. Faced as we were with our own difficulties in the establishment of this mission, we did not, we could not involve the Timorese at large as much as they were entitled to.

Essentially, the UN was offering only limited and somewhat confused consultation to the Timorese people about their future. The East Timorese Cabinet complained that they were "caricatures of ministers in a government of a banana republic" and that they had "no power, no duties, no resources to function adequately." Despite these problems UNTAET succeeded in organising elections and paved the way for full independence. On 20 May 2002 East Timor was declared independent and UNTAET was replaced by the UN Mission of Support in East Timor (UNMISET). This remained with a scaled-down peacekeeping force until 2004.

The elections were a success and they were carried out peacefully. UNTAET had appeared to have fulfilled its stated role. The UN's role was that of exercising almost sovereign powers in East Timor, albeit on a temporary basis. Not only did UNTAET administer East Timor; it also created laws and negotiated treaties. The UN's involvement in East Timor represented a steep learning curve and one that may be repeated in other future UN operations which involve a transition to independence.

A closer look

Interpretations of the UN's role

The UN was founded upon the principle of collective security. This is the idea that states work together to maintain international peace because it is in all their interests to do so. The reality became different. The UN operated in a Cold War environment. This meant that it tended to be effective as a peacekeeper when the superpowers cooperated with its work. That cooperation was dependent on whether it was in the interests of individual powers to do so or not. Throughout the Cold War the UN's effectiveness as a peacekeeper was constrained by the ever-present impact of the Cold War. The end of the Cold War should have brought these constraints to an end. However, historians still debate the effectiveness of the UN in the post-Cold War world.

There is general agreement that international society consists of sovereign and independent states and that these states, although primarily concerned with defending their own national interests, are willing to support the role of the UN as an agent of international peacekeeping. The issue that divides historians is based on the importance of national sovereignty. On the one hand there are those who argue that the UN cannot be effective, even in the post-Cold War world, because national self-interest still drives the actions of most states. Such states will not accept interference by the UN in their own domestic affairs or the domestic affairs of any state. This school of interpretation explains the failings of the UN in Rwanda, for example. The logical outcome of this view is that the UN will never be effective as a peacekeeper because its power to intervene, for example in civil wars, will always be restricted by the dominance of state sovereignty.

The alternative view is that as globalisation progresses and international society becomes more integrated, it is almost inevitable that the sovereign status of states will decline and the UN will assume a more effective role as a global peacekeeping agency. The evidence of the 1990s suggests that there is an ever-increasing need for wider UN intervention and limitations on the non-interventionist thinking linked to sovereignty. However, the ruse of international terrorism has reinforced the views of those historians who argue the realist, national self-interest position. 9/11 revived the quest for US global power and undermined its commitment to international cooperation that extended beyond its own self-interest.

Sierra Leone, 1999–present

Fig. 4 *UN peacekeeping on the border between North and South Korea*

A civil war erupted in Sierra Leone in March 1991. By 1998 the war had intensified and showed no signs of coming to a peaceful conclusion. In July of that year the Security Council finally established the UN Observer Mission in Sierra Leone (UNOMSIL). Its role was to monitor the military and economic situation in the country. As rebel forces approached the capital, Freetown, in January 1999 the UN Observer Mission began to evacuate.

In October 1999 the UN implemented a more sizeable and effective peacekeeping force in Sierra Leone, known as the UN Mission in Sierra Leone (UNAMSIL). The UNAMSIL deployment became a huge operation – up to 17,500 UN soldiers – and included many Nigerian and British troops. The deployment saw UN forces being much more militarily forceful against warring parties. For example, in 2000, after a local group of insurgents kidnapped six British and one local soldier, British soldiers launched a major rescue operation, freeing the hostages and killing 17 insurgents. The mission in Sierra Leone was declared complete and successful in 2005.

The impact of the 11 September 2001 attacks: Iraq

Secretary-General Kofi Annan commented in response to the events of 11 September 2001, "Terrorism is a global menace. It calls for a united, global response. To defeat it all nations must take counsel together and act in unison. That is why we have the United Nations." The Security Council recognised 'the inherent right of individual or collective self-defence' in response to terrorism when it introduced Resolution 1368. The USA invoked this self-defence approach against terrorism. It declared a military campaign in Afghanistan and focused on Iraq's so-called weapons of mass destruction. The USA sought legitimacy for its actions through the UN.

Cross-reference

For more about the effects of the 9/11 attacks, see Chapter 10.

One thing became increasingly clear. By late 2002, George W. Bush's administration was anxious to get the Security Council to accept that only a military rather than a diplomatic solution was appropriate to address the issue of Iraq's links with international terrorism and the country's failure to comply with UN disarmament resolutions. The USA faced a growing lack of support within the UN memberships. Only Britain and Spain were willing to back the US demands for military action against Iraq. Ironically, the Security Council had endorsed US military attacks against the Taliban government in Afghanistan. Over Iraq both France and Russia were not convinced that the USA had shown a sufficient link between Iraq and terrorist attacks against the USA. The end of the Cold War had not brought a guaranteed end to fundamental disagreements in the Security Council.

The Bush administration merely argued that Saddam Hussein's regime might cooperate with anti-American terrorists. The opponents of the UN were not willing to accept what they referred to as the Bush Doctrine. This promoted the notion that the USA must carry out pre-emptive or anticipatory self-defence. This meant that the basis of US international relations in this new age of aggressive anti-American terrorism was to be founded upon the idea that Washington would decide what government, through its perceived links with terrorism, would be targeted. Furthermore, the Security Council had already created a weapons inspection system. This was the United Nations Monitoring, Verification and Inspection Commission (UNMOVIC) and its role was to monitor and, if necessary, verify the existence of chemical and biological weapons. A similar agency existed for nuclear weapons.

The USA was reluctant to place any faith in these inspection agencies. This was partly because it believed that lengthy diplomacy would only undermine US military pressure on Iraq. Some observers took the view that national self-interest determined the responses of some states that opposed the USA in the UN over Iraq. France was seen as a state wishing to play the role of a global superpower despite its economic and military limitations. The Russians held the view that the USA had not backed them in their quest for a major post-Cold War role in international relations. The Russians also had economic interests in Iraq. Domestic politics appeared to dominate the German stance against America. Domestic German public opinion was against a war with Iraq. There was a popularly held view that the USA was never really interested in multilateral diplomacy. Washington wanted to operate from an unfettered unilateral position and be free to use its superior power against any 'rogue state' that it felt threatened US interests. Perception of a threat was sufficient and there was little need to prove a substantial link with al-Qaeda for example. The USA could not turn to NATO to legitimise its intentions in Iraq because NATO was also divided over its response.

The issue of Iraq in 2003 raised the fundamental problem that continued to face the UN as a peacekeeping organisation. There had to be a collective authorisation for force to be used. The USA's commitment to the so-called Bush Doctrine in 2003 was profoundly inconsistent with the UN's commitment to regulate force through international agreement. The USA's policy of conducting a war against terrorism did great damage to the UN and it caused significant divisions among the international community. It was clear that the Security Council in 2003 was not prepared to endorse decisive preventive action. Substantial links between Iraq and al-Qaeda were not established, nor did Iraq have large amounts of chemical or biological weapons that were operational. There was no active nuclear weapons programme in place. In effect, Iraq did not present a danger to US security nor did it appear to be closely linked to those who did.

As always, the USA was always the most important state in the UN. This was as true after the Cold War had ended as it had been at the height of the Cold War. Militarily and economically the USA was the dominant world power. By the start of the 21st century there was increasing opposition within the UN towards US unilateralism.

Activity

Group discussion

In small groups, discuss why terrorism is such a hard phenomenon for even large organisations like NATO and the UN to fight. Think about the strengths and weaknesses of terrorist activity, including factors such as whether you think terrorists can really shape international relations.

The US invasion of Iraq led to an intensification of this opposition to unilateralism. This issue currently is, and will undoubtedly remain for the immediate future, a major problem for the UN and the consensus upon which it depends.

Darfur, 2003–4

At the start of 2003 a humanitarian crisis began to unfold in the western region of Darfur in the Sudan. Fighting between government forces and rebels from the Sudanese Liberation Army made thousands of people refugees. By 2004 there were 100,000 refugees and a million others displaced. In May 2004, the Security Council finally called upon the Sudanese government to disarm its feared Arab militia groups (the Janjaweed). This proved to be a futile request and went unheeded by the Sudanese authorities. More robust Security Council action was prevented when China and Russia abstained in a Security Council vote.

Exploring the detail

The Janjaweed

In Arabic Janjaweed means 'a man with a gun on a horse'. The Janjaweed were drawn from nomadic Arab tribes often in conflict with Darfur's settled African farmers. In 2003 the non-Arab Sudan Liberation Army and the Justice and Equality Movement embarked on a civil war with the Arab Sudanese government. At this point, the Janjaweed started to attack non-Arab settlements but focused on the ethnic conflict with the non-Arab population.

This outcome illustrated a particular problem that faced the UN. Both Russia and China had economic interests in the Sudan and therefore opposed any UN enforcement measures there. Even the USA displayed its clear self-interest and did nothing significant to push for more substantial UN intervention. The USA did not want to undermine the cooperation it needed from the Sudanese in its own struggle against international terrorism. Equally, Islamic states were not willing to put pressure on other Islamic states. The view was that the Islamic world was already under pressure in Afghanistan and Iraq. As the *Washington Post* concluded, 'Major and minor powers alike are committed only to stopping killing that harms their national interests. Why take political, financial and military risks when there is no strategic or domestic cost to remaining on the sidelines?'

The Darfur crisis illustrated that there was a clear lack of political will to stop the humanitarian crisis in the Sudan. Equally there had been no concerted attempt to prevent it in the first place. Despite this fundamental shortcoming by the UN there had been a growing recognition in the Security Council that humanitarian crises were also threats to international peace and security.

Overview

The post-Cold War era brought a huge increase in the demand for UN interventions. Many observers argued that the end of Cold War superpower rivalry gave the UN the chance to bring long-standing conflicts across the world to a successful conclusion. The post-Cold War period also brought new challenges for the UN. The range of interventions was much wider and more complex than any previous Cold War interventions. Peacekeeping became significantly more complex. The UN's role extended to nation-building as well as peacekeeping. The humanitarian demands placed on the UN exceeded all previous demands. The notion that the end of the Cold War brought with it a new era of open international cooperation is more than merely misleading, it is clearly inaccurate.

Fig. 5 *Humanitarian work in Pakistan*

Learning outcomes

In this section you have developed a knowledge and understanding of the impact of the ending of the Cold War. You should be in a position to evaluate the shift in the international order that followed the end of the Cold War and the subsequent response of the superpowers, especially the USA.

In addition you should be able to assess the significance of other influences such as eastern European nationalism and the growth of the EU in international relations from 1991. You have also learnt about the role of the UN and how it was affected by the end of the Cold War.

(1) 'Rather than making the role of the United Nations easier, the end of the Cold War simply deepened its problems.' Assess the validity of this view.

It would be useful to have some understanding of the effectiveness of the UN before the end of the Cold War. This question is focused on the effectiveness of the UN as a peacekeeping organisation after a point of significant change. Establish examples of where the UN has had limited success and then consider why that has happened. Was it because of the ending of the Cold War or was it for some other reason?

(2) 'In the years 1945 to 1991 the Soviet Union consistently ensured that the Cold War continued.' Assess the validity of this view.

This type of question is designed to focus on a wide range of issues during the period between 1945 and 2004. In this way it differs from the more specific and slightly narrower questions at the end of previous chapters. The focus of the assessment for this question is on assessing and evaluating the view that the USSR was consistently responsible for the continuance of the Cold War. You need to balance this view against examples of the USSR seeking to shift East–West relations away from a Cold War relationship. There is also the issue of the role of the USA in ensuring the continuance of the Cold War. It is important not to turn this question into a different question. The focus lies with assessing the USSR's responsibility for the continuance of the Cold War rather than the USA's responsibility. Reference to the USA is important in establishing why the Cold War lasted so long but it should only be considered in terms of its contribution to the overall balance of the USSR's responsibility.

You may suggest that the Cold War was started by the USSR. This would show support for the orthodox historiography. There were significiant events which underlined the unwillingness of the USSR to bring the Cold War to an end. You could consider the development of the nuclear arms race up to 1962, the Cuban Missile Crisis, the problems over Berlin between 1958 and the construction of the Berlin Wall in 1961. In 1979 the era of détente came to an abrupt end when the USSR invaded Afghanistan. You may also consider the problems over SALT, particularly SALT II and link these to the attitude of the USSR.

This evidence could be balanced against the revisionist view of the origins of the Cold War. You could consider the efforts of Khrushchev to develop peaceful coexistence and the subsequent willingness of the USSR to participate in, and preserve, détente during the 1970s. A key issue may be the role of Gorbachev from 1985 in bringing the Cold War to an end. Overall, there are points when the USSR appeared to be a major barrier to bringing the Cold War to an end and others when it was a major contributor to the ending of the Cold War. To strengthen the analysis you could consider the role of the USA in terms of the revisionist analysis, particularly the idea that the USA wanted the Cold War to continue in order to promote its own global power.

Conclusion

The end of the Second World War heralded the start of a new order of world politics. The dominance of European powers based on economic wealth, imperial power and military might had ended once and for all. The beginnings of this decline may date back to the start of the 20th century but the end point certainly came in 1945. From then a new world order emerged, but even this was not to reach the end of the 20th century. The Eurocentric system which had dominated international relations was replaced by a bipolar system of international relations dominated by the USA and the USSR. Each of these emerged as 'superpowers' and their differing political, military and ideological interests extended around the globe. These differing interests and the nature of international relations that flowed from them are expressed in terms of a 'Cold War'.

The Cold War may be viewed as a fundamental factor in determining international relations between 1945 and 1991. At its most basic level the foundation of the division between East and West appeared to be the ideological split between capitalism and communism. America's belief that communist ideology was spreading across war-torn post-war Europe and would ultimately destroy democracy was undoubtedly a real issue in the emergence of the new order of international relations. The USA had abandoned isolationism and some historians argue that demonising the USSR in the eyes of vulnerable states was one way of fulfilling the USA's quest for global power. Thus the Cold War became a struggle for power rather than a crusade to protect democracy. Others argue that the Truman Doctrine and the Marshall Plan were essentially defensive and not the first steps towards a struggle for power which would inevitably lead to conflict and confrontation with the USSR.

Ultimately, international relations were based on two factors. First, there was the desire for security. Each side was convinced that the other was determined to destroy it. Second, to ensure security each side needed power on a global scale. The Cold War was a struggle for security through power. This struggle led to confrontation rather than cooperation between the two superpowers. Nuclear weapons provided the power and therefore the security that each side sought. From 1949 a nuclear arms race accelerated. The quest for nuclear superiority simply deepened the frosty Cold War relationship the USA and the USSR shared. However, the Cuban Missile Crisis of 1962 acted as a turning point as each side realised that security, although it may still be based on power, was not necessarily achieved through confrontation.

After 1962 both sides continued to develop their nuclear arsenals but there was a mutual recognition that a second nuclear crisis had to be avoided. International relations and the Cold War environment in which they operated were never constrained by one unchanging method. Nations responded to developments, both global and regional. By the end of the 1960s western Europe wanted to develop greater cooperation with the neighbouring east. This process of détente had, to some extent, to be duplicated by the superpowers if they were to retain regional influence. Détente fitted the aims of security and power but offered a more effective route. It meant that international relations would be managed within a framework of negotiation and cooperation but this did not equate to an end to the conflict or an end to the struggle for power. The USA in particular sought to cultivate the newly emerging superpower of China as an ally. This Sino–American relationship during a period of détente underlined the USA's unchanging determination to ensure its power base was stronger than that of the Soviet Union.

Détente was merely a device through which the power and security of the superpowers could be fulfilled. The problem was that each side had a different perception of how détente should work for them. The USA became convinced that the arms controls agreements that emerged from détente were being used by the USSR to gain a military advantage for itself. This became clear for the Americans when they viewed the involvement of the USSR in conflicts in developing countries such as that in Angola. The USA wanted détente to act as a form of control over the Soviet Union. For its part the USSR remained committed to the idea that it had to defend its security and power and this meant being free to support revolutionary movements in developing countries and to promote the security of regimes friendly to the USSR. Détente died because neither side had a common understanding of how it should work but also because it had outlived its usefulness. The Soviet Union's invasion of Afghanistan in 1979 did not end détente, it merely represented the final act in the process of decline that had begun much earlier.

Fig. 1 *Souvenir hunters break up the final remains of the Berlin Wall*

The period between 1979 and 1986 was sometimes referred to as being the years of the Second Cold War. The Reagan administration appeared to conclude that détente had no place in international relations because it served only to strengthen the USSR. The outcome appeared to be a return to the confrontational relationship that had characterised international relations during the early post-war period. However, Reagan's rejection of détente and his support for developments in nuclear technology belied his real objectives. It was clear that the most certain way to ensure the USA's security was through making the existence of nuclear weapons irrelevant to that security. An event of supreme importance took place in 1985 when Mikhail Gorbachev became leader of the Soviet Union.

Gorbachev changed the basis of international relations. He brought 'New Thinking' to Soviet foreign policy. This was profoundly more significant in terms of ending the Cold War basis of international relations than anything achieved by détente. What Gorbachev did was to work towards international security rather than merely the national security of the Soviet Union. This was a shift in emphasis of huge proportion and it enabled the USA to acknowledge that a confrontational relationship was no longer relevant to its own security. The first steps in this process came with a flood of summit talks during the second half of the 1980s. Gorbachev's rule unintentionally brought an end not only to the Soviet Union's control over eastern Europe but also the control of the communist system there. For the USA the ultimate threat to its security since 1945 appeared to have disappeared. With it, the Cold War came to a complete end by 1991.

The end of the Cold War did not mark the end of nuclear weapons. It marked a success in arms control rather that wholesale nuclear disarmament. The issue of nuclear weapons was a constant theme throughout the Cold War and some historians have argued that the USA's possession of such weapons was a fundamental factor in the origins and subsequent development of the Cold War. Some argue that it was the existence of nuclear weapons that perpetuated the Cold War and therefore acted as the principal determinant that drove international relations for over forty years. Others suggest the existence of such weapons played only a marginal role in international relations. It does seem clear that the struggle to establish nuclear arms agreements was central to establishing lasting agreements on coexistence and cooperation between the superpowers. Nuclear weapons were always at the heart of the Cold War because the Cold War was about power and security and that is what those weapons represented to each side. Some argue that nuclear weapons guaranteed an era of unprecedented stability and therefore, for the most part, economic prosperity. The Cold War did create continuity in international relations for nearly fifty years in that it meant a long-term military and political rivalry between the USSR and the USA and ideological conflict between capitalism and communism.

The end of the Cold War has been interpreted in a number of differing ways. One view is that little changed. Those who adopted this view argued that the USA remained powerful and that the foundations upon which international relations had been built since 1945 remained intact. However, this view has little real currency. The once bipolar world had become unipolar. The end of the Cold War heralded the end of a balance which had preserved stability. The end of the Cold War did not create a new era of guaranteed peace and stability. The crisis in Yugoslavia is a classic example of this instability. Some went on to argue that the end of the Cold War necessitated the creation of a new enemy that would enable the USA to preserve its role as the defender of freedom and therefore preserve its global power status. This view is, to some extent, supported by Noam Chomsky. He has argued in his work *The New Military Humanism* (1999) that the USA has ruthlessly sought to ensure its own global power. To this extent there is some continuity linking the Cold War with the post-Cold War environment.

The view of a post-Cold War world in which there is security and stability is further undermined by the failure of the United Nations to emerge as the key player in dealing with international conflict. The United Nation's role has not been enhanced, it has remained static and uncertain. The rise of Europe has been a more significant outcome of the ending of the Cold War than any increased commitment to any international peacekeeping organisation such as the United Nations. Europe has become increasingly more able to function as an integrated regional force. It is likely that the next step for Europe will be the development of a refined security system which is barely dependent upon the USA. The ending of the Cold War certainly facilitated the expansion and rise of European independence from American control.

The real turning point in post-Cold War international relations came in 2001. America found the means by which it could preserve its international status and influence global events. The terrorist attack on America on 11 September 2001 enabled America to declare itself the defender of the free world, not against communism, but against international terrorism. This attack marked the end of the post-Cold War era and the start of a new order of international interaction. America could justify its invasions of Iraq and Afghanistan in those terms. President Bush's declaration of an "axis of evil states" resembled Truman's declaration in 1947, which formed the foundation of America's global role throughout much of the Cold War era. Terrorism appeared to give the USA a blank cheque as far as international intervention was concerned. In many ways this underlines the view that the end of the Cold War did not mark the start of a new era of peace and stability.

Fig. 2 *US soldiers on patrol in Afghanistan, 2003*

Since 2001, there has been a return to confrontational relations and this has been driven by America and its allies, particularly Britain. However, unlike the Cold War with its East-West peaceful confrontation, the new order has been founded upon active militancy and aggression. Once again this has underlined the ineffectiveness of the United Nations. To this extent, there has been a degree of continuity. Unless the superpowers cooperated with the United Nations, because it was in their mutual and individual interests to do so, the United Nations was hard put to function effectively. America's attitude to terrorism was another example of superpower interests overriding any intervention by an international peacekeeping organisation.

Glossary

A

Anti-ballistic missiles: these are missiles that are capable of defending targets against any incoming nuclear missiles. In 1972 the ABM Treaty limited the deployment of such systems.

Atlantic community: this is the idea that there is a link between western Europe and the USA. Only the geography of the Atlantic Ocean separates the mutual interests of these two regions.

B

Balance of nuclear power: this suggests an even distribution of nuclear weapon capability. Any reduction or growth in such weapons should result in the balance remaining equal and therefore neither side becoming significantly more dominant than the other.

Bilateral: this relates to matters affecting two sides, unlike unilateral which are the actions of one side, or multilateral – the actions of more than two sides. It normally concerns joint actions taken by two sides.

Blockade: this is a form of siege which is designed to stop entrance or exit. A blockade may be established by land or sea forces but it is also possible for an air force to strengthen a blockade. In 1962 the US blockade of Cuba was referred to as a quarantine and it was designed to stop nuclear missiles being brought into Cuba.

C

Capitalism: a system of economics that is based on the idea that money (capital) may be used to create profits and, in the process, create employment. It is a concept based on wealth creation.

Client state: a state that receives support from a more powerful ally. This is mutually beneficial to both sides. Normally the support takes the form of economic and military aid.

Coalition: in terms of international relations this describes a group of states who come together to form an alliance of which they are all members.

Communism: a political ideology based on the ideas of Karl Marx. It is founded on the belief that the state should control the means of production and distribution in order to ensure social and economic equality for all citizens. Marx saw this as being applicable to the entire world.

Consensus: general agreement between different groups over an issue. It does not mean total agreement but rather an acceptance of the principles behind a decision.

Coup: more fully referred to as a coup d'état. This is a sudden seizure of power, usually through the use of force.

D

Decentralisation: power is removed from a central body such as the central government and handed down to a non-central organisation.

Détente: literally means a relaxation of tensions. In terms of international relations it came to describe the idea of easing relations between states.

Deterrent: the means by which a state commits itself to retaliate if any aggression is used against it. The deterrent acts as an incentive to external powers not to use, or threaten, aggression. Nuclear weapons were regarded as the ultimate deterrent for much of the Cold War.

Dissident: an individual whom the state regards as a threat. Dissidents are those who challenge a political system that does not accept any challenges.

E

Economic imperialism: the USSR accused the USA of carrying out economic imperialism through the Marshall Plan in 1947. The Plan suggested that a state increases its power and influence globally by making other states economically dependent upon it. Unlike traditional imperialism which usually involves direct control, economic imperialism is indirect but just as potent.

Embargo: a form of economic pressure by banning or reducing trade with another state in order to get that state to comply with a particular outcome the state imposing the embargo wants.

F

Federation: a grouping of independent states into a united organisation. Such states normally cooperate in order to fulfil some common interest.

G

Geo-strategic: a geographic area which is of strategic importance to a state.

Gradualism: a slow and controlled process of change.

I

Imperialism: establishing economic, political and military control by one state over another.

Islamic fundamentalism: a form of Islamic purity based on the belief that Muslims should remove any form of corruption from their actions. In terms of international relations this is translated into regarding the USA and its western allies as a threat to the interests of Islam and Islamic states.

Isolationism: a state will not participate in international affairs beyond those which are essential to its own security. It is almost the direct opposite of globalism.

M

Mandate: the authority to govern or administer another state, usually temporarily. UN peacekeeping forces are given a mandate to carry out specific actions as determined by the UN Security Council.

Marxist: a follower of the ideas of the founder of communism, Karl Marx. Such a person would accept the idea of communism as an international ideology which is applicable to any state.

Missile gap: the disparity between states' nuclear missile stocks.

N

Neutrality: a condition in which a state declares its non-involvement in a conflict and which other states are bound to recognise. Switzerland has been a neutral state since 1815.

Non-aggression pact: a joint agreement between states in which the parties commit themselves to not using aggression against each other. It represents a peaceful alliance.

Nuclear parity: nuclear weapon capability is roughly the same between those states possessing such weapons. The USSR achieved such parity with the USA by the start of the 1970s.

P

Power vacuum: those who formerly held power are removed and no alternative exists. One source of power has not been replaced by another and this raises the possibility of political and economic instability.

Pre-emptive strike: a military attack carried out before a planned attack by an enemy can take place. It involves striking the first blow as a form of defence rather than an act of aggression.

Proliferation: normally associated with the spread of nuclear weapons as more states become nuclear powers. The intention to control this spread is known as non-proliferation.

Propaganda: material which is designed to deliberately persuade people to believe something. It may have some degree of truth but this may be exaggerated or distorted in order to achieve the desired outcome.

Protectionism: an economic tool designed to protect a state's domestic industries from foreign competition. This is normally achieved by imposing high import duties on foreign goods.

Proxy: action carried out on behalf of one state by another. The latter acts as a proxy for the former.

R

Ratify: states form treaties and agreements between themselves. The end stage is when all the terms of the agreements are settled and finalised. This final step means the agreements have been ratified.

Reparation payments: such payments are normally imposed as a form of punishment on a state for damage it has caused in a conflict. The payments are used to repair the damage to people and property.

Rollback: reversing something. In terms of US attitudes towards communism there was a suggestion of not simply containing the spread of communism to the point it had reached but also pushing its frontiers of growth back.

Retaliation capability: the capacity a state has to reply to any direct or indirect threat from another state. Retaliation capability acts as a form of deterrence and may be measured in both conventional and nuclear capability.

S

Satellite states: those states that are under the influence of a more powerful neighbouring state. Such a relationship was established by the Soviet Union over much of eastern Europe after the end of the Second World War.

Subsidies: usually some form of economic or material support by one nation to another. It acts as a form of aid.

Sphere of influence: a territory or region over which a state has direct influence in terms of military, economic and political affairs. Eastern Europe after 1945 was a Soviet sphere of influence managed through the Soviet model of communism being applied to all these states.

Stalemate: this refers to a deadlock. In diplomatic terms it is a situation where the positions taken by each party means that it is impossible to agree.

Status quo: things remain as they have always been. There is no change.

T

Territorial inviolability: an area of territory that cannot be touched or changed in any way. It remains intact as it is.

Trade tariffs: duties imposed on imported goods. These often act as part of a system of protectionism.

Triangular diplomacy: a process involving three states in diplomatic activities with each other. Often this is characterised by one state 'playing off' the other two in order to strengthen its own position. An example of triangular diplomacy came in 1970 and involved the USA, China and the USSR.

W

Western democracy: the version of a capitalist-based society favoured by Europe and the USA. The political system enables free elections and guarantees a range of other freedoms, such as freedom of speech and freedom of religious belief.

World power: a state that has the economic and military power to exercise its influence globally. Such states are often referred to as superpowers.

Bibliography

Aspects of International Relations, 1945–2004

For student use

Bell, P. M. H. (2001) *The World Since 1945: An International History*, Arnold

Dunbabin, J. P. D. (1994) *The Cold War*, Longman

Hobsbawn, E. (1999) *Age of Extremes: The Short Twentieth Century 1914–1991*, Michael Jones

Keylor, W. (1992) *The Twentieth-Century World: An International History*, OUP

Murphy, D., and Morris, T. (2008) *International Relations 1879–2004*, Collins Educational

Vadney, T. E. (1992) *The World Since 1945*, Penguin

Young, J., and Kent, J. (2003) *International Relations Since 1945*, OUP

For teachers and extension

Bennett, C. (1997) *Yugoslavia's Bloody Collapse*, C. Harsh and Co

Calvocoressi, P. (1991) *World Politics Since 1945*, Longman

Cooley, J. (2002) *Unholy Wars*, Pluto

Evans, G., and Newnham, J. (1998) *Dictionary of International Relations*, Penguin

Gaddis, J. L. (1997) *We Now Know: Rethinking Cold War History*, Clarendon Press

Hanhimaki, J. M., and Westad, O. D. (Eds) (2004) *The Cold War*, OUP

Merrill, D., and Paterson, T. (Eds) (2000) *Major Problems in American Foreign Relations: Vol. II*, Houghton Mifflin

Newhouse, J. (1989) *The Nuclear Age*, Michael Joseph

Waxler, M. L. (2004) *The Truman Legacy: American Foreign Policy 1945–2004*, Trafford Publishing

Section 1: The Emergence of the Superpowers, 1945–62

For student use

Edwards, O. (1997) *The USA and the Cold War*, Hodder and Stoughton

Gaddis, J. L. (2007) *The Cold War*, Penguin

McCauley, M. (1995) *The Origins of the Cold War 1941–1949*, Longman

McCauley, M. (2004) *Russia, America and the Cold War, 1945–1991*, Pearson Education

Smith, J. (1989) *The Cold War, 1945–1965*, Blackwell

Williamson, D. (2001) *Europe and the Cold War 1945–1991*, Hodder Murray

For teachers and extension

Crockatt, R. (1996) *The Fifty Years War*, Routledge

Kaplin, L. (1994) *NATO and the United States*, Twayne

Khrushchev, N. (1970) *Khrushchev Remembers*, Little, Brown

Khrushchev, N. (1974) *Khrushchev Remembers: The Last Testament*, Little, Brown

Swain, N., and Swain, G. (1993) *Eastern Europe Since 1945*, Macmillan

Taubman, W. (2003) *Khrushchev: The Man and His Era*, Norton

Westad, O. A. (2000) *Reviewing the Cold War*, Frank Cass

Section 2: From Cold War to Détente, 1962–81

For student use

McCauley, M. (2004) *Russia, America and the Cold War, 1945–1991*, Pearson Education

Munton, D., and Welch, D. A. (2006) *The Cuban Missile Crisis: A Concise History*, OUP

Phillips. S. (2001) *The Cold War*, Heinemann

Sewell, M. (2002) *The Cold War*, CUP

For teachers and extension

Beschloss, M. R. (1991) *Kennedy v Khrushchev: The Crisis Years 1960–1963*, Faber and Faber

Cohen, W. I. (1993) *America in the Age of Soviet Power, 1945–1991*, CUP

Crockatt, R. (1996) *The Fifty Years War*, Routledge

Gaddis, J. L. (1990) *Russia, the Soviet Union and the United States*, McGraw-Hill

Garthoff, R. (1994) *Détente and Confrontation*, The Brookings Institution

Young, J. W. (1991) *Cold War Europe 1945–1989*, Edward Arnold

Section 3: The Final Years of the Cold War, 1981–91

For student use

Halliday, F. (1986) *The Making of the Second Cold War*, Verso

Marples, D. R. (2004) *The Collapse of the Soviet Union*, Pearson Education

For teachers and extension

Bowker, M. (1997) *Russian Foreign Policy and the End of the Cold War*, Dartmouth

Brown, A. (1997) *The Gorbachev Factor*, Oxford Paperbacks

Fischer, B. (1997) *The Reagan Reversal: Foreign Policy and the End of the Cold War*, University of Missouri Press

Goldman, M. (1992) *What Went Wrong with Perestroika*, Norton

Gorbachev, M. (1996) *Memoirs*, Doubleday

Hogan, M. J. (Ed) (1992) *The End of the Cold War*, CUP

Hutchings, R. (1997) *American Diplomacy at the End of the Cold War*, John Hopkins University Press

Lebow, R. N., and Stein, J. G. (1994) *We All Lost the Cold War*, Princeton University Press

Stokes, G. (1993) *The Walls Come Tumbling Down: The Collapse of Communism in Eastern Europe*, OUP

Wapshott, N. (2007) *Ronald Reagan and Margaret Thatcher*, Sentinel

White, M. J. (1997) *Missiles in Cuba*, Ivan R. Dee

Section 4: Post-Cold War Relations, 1991–2004

For student use

Berdal, M., and Economides, S. (2007) *United Nations Interventionism, 1991–2004*, CUP

Finlan, A. (2003) *The Gulf War 1991*, Osprey

Finlan, A. (2004) *The Collapse of Yugoslavia*, Osprey

For teachers and extension

Avery, G., and Cameron, F. (1998) *The Enlargement of the European Union*, Sheffield Academic Press

Booth, K. (Ed) (1998) *Statecraft and Security: The Cold War and Beyond*, CUP

Brimmer, E., and Frohlich, S. (2005) *The Strategic Implications of European Union Enlargement*, John Hopkins University

Israeli, R. (2004) *The Iraq War*, Sussex Academic Press

Lansford, T. (2003) *A Bitter Harvest: US Foreign Policy and Afghanistan*, Ashgate

Mayall, J. (Ed) (1996) *The New Interventionism, 1991–1994*, CUP

Mingst, K. A., and Karns, M. P. (2007) *The United Nations in the 21st Century*, Westview

Nugent, N. (2004) *European Union Enlargement*, Palgrave Macmillan

Pavkovic, A. (2000) *The Fragmentation of Yugoslavia*, St Martin's Press

Pillar, P. R. (2001) *Terrorism and U.S. Foreign Policy*, The Brookings Institution

Rai, M. (2002) *War Plan Iraq*, Verso

Spurling, J. (Ed) (1999) *Europe in Change*, Manchester University Press

Weymouth, T., and Henig, S. (2001) *The Kosovo Crisis*, Reuters

Films

Thirteen Days

The Missiles of October

Websites

www.foreignaffairs.org

www.besthistorysites.net/index.shtml

www.archives.gov

http://csis.org

There are extensive lists of website details available via Google. Add the appropriate element from the specification into the search box. There are some detailed contributions via Wikipedia, e.g. en.wikipedia.org/wiki/Yalta_Conference.

Index